Walking Through Fire

Walking Through Fire
Iraqis' Struggle for Justice and Reconciliation

Peggy Faw Gish

With a foreword by Jonathan Wilson-Hartgrove

CASCADE Books • Eugene, Oregon

WALKING THROUGH FIRE
Iraqis' Struggle for Justice and Reconciliation

Copyright © 2013 Peggy Faw Gish. All rights reserved. Except for brief quotations in critical publications or reviews, no part of this book may be reproduced in any manner without prior written permission from the publisher. Write: Permissions, Wipf and Stock Publishers, 199 W. 8th Ave., Suite 3, Eugene, OR 97401.

Cascade Books
An Imprint of Wipf and Stock Publishers
199 W. 8th Ave., Suite 3
Eugene, OR 97401

www.wipfandstock.com

ISBN 13: 978-1-62032-852-1

Cataloguing-in-Publication data:

Gish, Peggy Faw.

    Walking Through Fire : Iraqis' Struggle for Justice and Reconciliation / Peggy Faw Gish ; with a foreword by Jonathan Wilson-Hartgrove.

    xvi + 238 pp. ; 23 cm. Includes bibliographical references.

    ISBN 13: 978-1-62032-852-1

    1. Iraq War, 2003- —Influence. 2. Peace—Religious Aspects. I. Title.

DS79.76 G5755 2013

Manufactured in the U.S.A.

Biblical quotations are from the *New International Version of the Holy Bible (NIV)*, © 1990. Used by permission of Zondervan, www.Zondervan.com.

Book Cover Photo: The Wall of Peace stood between the security forces and the crowd to prevent violence, Suleimaniya, Feb. 22, 2011 (photographed by the CPT Iraqi Kurdistan team). Used with permission from Christian Peacemaker Teams.

*This book is dedicated to Art Gish, my beloved husband,
who lived his life learning from and walking
with the oppressed people of the world,
who did not let religious or ethnic pride
block him from opening his heart
in love to our brothers and sisters of other faiths,
who in turn enriched his life.*

When you pass through the waters, I will be with you;
And when you pass through the rivers, they will not sweep over you.
When you walk through the fire, you will not be burned.

—Isaiah 43:2 (NIV)

Contents

List of Illustrations ix
Foreword by Jonathan Wilson-Hartgrove xi
Introduction and Acknowledgments xiii

Prologue 1

Part One: Summer 2004–Spring 2006

1. Changes 9
2. "It's Hard to Appreciate Even the Positive Things" 18
3. Realities of Danger 28
4. Nonviolent Responses 37
5. In the Heat of the Summer 46
6. Fallujah Explodes 54
7. Karbela 61
8. Finding Friends in the Midst of Rubble 70
9. Continuing the Legacy of Torture and Abuse 82
10. The CPT-4 92
11. Seeing the Broken and the Beautiful 101
12. Tragedy and Keeping Hope 110

Part Two: Summer 2006–Fall 2011

13. We Are Kurds First 121
14. They See Saddam 130
15. A New Crisis 140
16. Voices of Change 150

Contents

17 Anfal and Halubja Testimonies   157
18 "Bombing Hurts, Please Stop"   165
19 Choosing Paths of Healing   175
20 "Kurds and Turks Are Brothers"   184
21 "We Do This Work Because We Must"   193
22 What Does One Say to the Parents of a Fourteen-Year-Old Girl Who Was Killed?   202
23 Kurdish Spring   209
24 Returning to Rutba   221

Afterword—Walking Through Fire   229

Glossary   231
Bibliography   237

Illustrations

Maps

1. Map of Iraq   5
2. Map of Northeastern Iraq   6

Figures

Cover: The Wall of Peace stood between the security forces and the crowd to prevent violence, Suleimaniya, February 22, 2011.

1. Guard shows Maxine Nash and Doug Pritchard damage of college buildings in Baqubah by MNF-I in June 2004   26
2. Caravan of Iraqis moving toward Najaf on August 26, 2004 for vigil called for by Grand Ayatollah Ali as-Sistani   44
3. MPT nonviolence training participants role play a street conflict, Karbela, January 25, 2005   62
4. Men voting in Karbela on January 30, 2005   66
5. Pushing wheelchairs over bridge in Fallujah, March 14, 2005   76
6. Tents in the midst of the rubble in the Gebeil area of Fallujah, March 14, 2005   77
7. Visiting family inside tent in Gebeil area of Fallujah, March 14, 2005   78
8. Banner in Suleimaniya calling for severe punishment for Saddam, September 9, 2009   138

Illustrations

9   Prde Hazwa IDPs and CPTers hold up "Bombing Hurts! Please Stop" banner, August 9, 2008   165

10 IDP camp child's drawing of bombing of his village home   171

11 Aram Jamal (center) and other Kurdish human rights workers vigil, with tape over their mouths, symbolizing the silencing of women   178

12 Turkish base on hill, school below, in village of Grebye, January 1, 2009   187

13 Women and children eating in tent at Basteson IDP Camp on "Dolma Day," July 23, 2010   205

14 Wall of Peace standing between crowd and security forces in Azadi Square, Suleimaniya, February 22, 2011   210

15 Soldiers with flowers in their gun barrels, in Azadi Square, Suleimaniya, February 22, 2011   211

Foreword

PEOPLE OF THE BOOK know the story of Shadrach, Meshach, and Abed-nego—the three friends who, while exiles in a strange land, refused to bow to the imperial gods because they had pledged their allegiance to YHWH. For their divine obedience, they were sentenced to death by fiery furnace. No cross, no firing squad, no lethal injection. This was execution Babylon style.

But, as Daniel records the story, the crowd noticed a fourth person walking with the three friends in the flames. And when they came out, there wasn't even a hint of smoke on their clothes. This is Pharaoh's-army-got-drowned, Jesus-didn't-stay-dead sort of humor. The Bible loves to stick it to the powers with little details like this. I know Christian preachers love to suggest that Jesus was there with them, and I believe he was. But I've always wondered if the author of Daniel, rascal that he was, didn't mean for his reader to think that maybe, just maybe, Daniel jumped in there with his buddies and lived to tell the story.

In the spring of 2003, when the military industrial complex of the U.S.A. transformed Baghdad into a fiery furnace, Peggy Gish was there. She was there spending time with children in a Sisters of Charity orphanage and with families on the streets. She was there and she told her government that she had no plans to leave, no matter what they decided to do.

She was there, I think, as an act of divine obedience, not unlike her predecessors in the great cloud of witnesses. She knew she was not the first, that she probably wouldn't be the last. But this is what God's people do when forced to choose between unfaithfulness and the fire. You step into the fire, presenting your body as a living sacrifice—a reasonable act of worship. What happens after that is up to God.

God can make a way out of no way.

One of the great gifts of my life is that, when I faced the same choice that God's people have had to face since the days of Babylon, I was given the grace to step into the fire. My wife Leah and I drove into Baghdad with a Christian Peacemaker Team delegation five days after the "shock and awe" bombing had begun. When we arrived at a little hotel in that great city that sits on the Tigris and the Euphrates, the city was literally burning. Smoke was everywhere. Oil wells had been lighted, creating ten-foot flames.

But there in the midst of the furnace was Peggy. She greeted us with open arms. She welcomed us into the Movement of those who know the God who can make a way out of no way.

The great gift of this book is that it is an invitation for you to join that Movement, too. Peggy has stories to tell that feel like they came right off the pages of the Bible. And in a sense, they did. Because the same God who raised Israel of out Egypt raised Jesus from the dead. And we who live life with that God know that, by faith, the waters are still parting and the dead are still getting up from their graves.

Some are even walking through flames—and writing to tell us about it.

Jonathan Wilson-Hartgrove
Pentecost, 2013

Introduction and Acknowledgments

IN THE AFTERMATH OF the 2003 war, U.S. government officials described the Iraqi people as liberated and claimed that new possibilities for the Iraqi society were worth the deaths and destruction. We who lived for awhile in Iraq saw from on the ground a different, more accurate reality—one of a broken society that would be difficult to heal.

This book is the story of the Iraqi people. Through their eyes—through their stories—this book "tells the truth" about what war and our government's anti-terrorism policies have really meant for them. Prisoners in the U.S. detention system, and their families, tell about the abuses they experienced in that system. Iraqis from various social and ethnic backgrounds tell about the excessive violence of the U.S.-led occupying forces. But, these stories also describe the efforts of many courageous and creative Iraqis as they speak out against injustices and build movements toward nonviolence and reconciliation.

My personal acquaintance with the Iraqi people began in October 2002, five months before the March 2003 U.S. invasion, when I started working there with the Chicago and Toronto-based organization, Christian Peacemaker Teams (CPT), and the Chicago based Voices in the Wilderness (now called Voices for Creative Nonviolence). After staying on into the war, I continued to come and go over the next nine years as part of a team of trained CPT peace-workers. My most recent time there was from March to the end of June 2011. Throughout that time, I lived among the Iraqi people, and so was a firsthand witness of the suffering caused them by Saddam Hussein's Ba'ath Regime, the international economic sanctions from 1991–2003, and then the 2003 U.S.-led war and occupation of Iraq. Our team accompanied Iraqis to get help or to escape violent situations and worked alongside Iraqis as they sought peaceful alternatives to the

Introduction and Acknowledgments

escalating violence. Having had amazing experiences and the unique perspective of one being on the ground over this nine-year period, I feel compelled to share this experience with others.

This manuscript continues the story told in my first book, *Iraq: A Journey of Hope and Peace*, published by Herald Press in September 2004, which deals with our team's presence in Iraq from October 2002 to June 2004. The first half of *Walking Through Fire: Iraqi's Struggle for Justice and Reconciliation* covers events from summer 2004 to spring 2006, when our team lived in Baghdad and worked mostly in central and southern Iraq. It includes our work with the Muslim Peacemaker Team and the time of CPT's Baghdad kidnapping. In the second half of the time recounted in this book, summer 2006 to summer 2011, we were living and working mostly in Kurdish areas of northern Iraq. This part of the book includes an account of the shorter kidnapping I experienced.

This on-the-ground view of many of the social and political events in Iraq between 2004 and 2011 counters the myths about the superiority of violent force to root out evil in places such as Iraq. Woven through the stories of Iraqis are the experiences of our peace team. These stories demonstrate that the power of nonviolent suffering love (the way of Jesus) is stronger than the power of violence and force, and can break down barriers and be transformative in violent or threatening situations.

I weave in bits of my own struggles of fear or pain while working in a war situation and in the context of U.S. global intervention and oppression, hoping this will help the reader identify with the struggle and pain of Iraqis and know them as real people. I also share personally to assure the reader that peace-workers do not do this work in a vacuum or out of a unique fearlessness or superhuman qualities, but deal with the same human struggles and weaknesses of most people.

Since its founding in 1986, Christian Peacemaker Teams has sent teams into global areas of conflict. As appropriate to the local situation, members of CPT act as international observers and engage in nonviolent direct action, working in partnership with local people to transform violence and oppression. More information about CPT can be found at www.cpt.org.

In securing information and opinions of other people (sometimes quoted, sometimes summarized) used in this text, I took extensive notes, asked clarifying questions, and checked with other sources or with other team members or our interpreters who were present during the interviews. When it was not possible to write down the conversations word for word I

Introduction and Acknowledgments

re-created parts or summarized the conversations afterward, as accurately as I could. I ask forgiveness from anyone that I may have inadvertently misrepresented.

I have changed the names and demographics of many individuals, because identifying them may put them in danger. Names given of my teammates are accurate, but after first naming them, I only give their first names. Many more team members and Iraqis who have done good work have not been named. When describing the work of Iraqi organizations, I give some additional information in the glossary. Anyone wanting more information should look at the organization's website on the Internet. There is often more than one spelling for names of persons, cities, or institutions when translating from Arabic or Kurdish. I picked the spellings most authentic to or used by the local people in that location or more commonly used internationally. In many stories, there is a lot more that could be shared about what Iraqis or other teammates experienced that I omitted because of space constraints or because it seems that those are their stories to tell. There are many historical events in Iraq during this period that I do not mention. Instead, I chose to focus on events that illustrated the points made in this book or which I felt needed be added to the public accounting of these events. At times I give more of the Iraqis' points of view than the views of the U.S. military or officials, judging that this balances what we normally hear, which is weighted more heavily with the Western viewpoint.

I am grateful for the love and prayers of my family and friends who have supported me during these years of work in Iraq, especially my late husband, Art, who had a similar vision of peacemaking and encouraged me each step of the way.

I am grateful for the following who critiqued this manuscript or advised me: Chabele Graziani, John Thorndike, Ivars Balkits, Cliff Kindy, Leah Vincent, Ellyn Burnes, and several members of the CPT team in Iraq. I am also grateful to our team's Kurdish partners, who read portions of the manuscript, and to Lisa King for designing the maps. And thanks to Tim Kraus, who helped with the final editing and formatting. A special thanks to the countless Iraqi people who have, often with risk, helped our team in our work and opened their homes and lives to us in love—many of us being strangers coming from countries waging war on and occupying their country.

Peggy Faw Gish
Athens, Ohio
July, 2013

Prologue

TREMBLING, ALLIA HELD HER six-month-old child tightly on her lap in her living room in Baghdad, as though she feared he, too, might be taken from her. She looked up with her tear-filled puffy eyes as she thanked us for coming. Her mother and other relatives cared for her older four children as they wandered in and out of the room. A strong woman, Allia now looked weaker and paler since we had last seen her two weeks ago.

In mid-February 2006, she and several neighbors had come to our team's apartment, asking for help. Her husband and six other men from the Baladiyatt neighborhood had been detained during house raids by Iraqi Special Police forces. We began visiting detention facilities and U.S. offices with members of her family to find out where her husband and the other men were being held and what they were charged with, but found no clue. This meant sleepless nights for their families, crying together, jumping every time the phone rang. A week later, we heard that the body of Allia's husband was found mutilated and buried in a sewer in Najaf.

"My husband's done nothing! What will become of us? Where can I go, so my children can grow up in peace?" This was not a time for *our* questions, and we did not have answers to hers. We could only be present with her and cry with her as she poured out her pain and fear.

Unfortunately, such circumstances were not new. I had been working in Iraq since October 2002, five months before the March 2003 U.S. invasion. After staying on into the war, I continued to come and go over the next nine years as part of a team of people from the Chicago and Toronto-based organization, Christian Peacemaker Teams (CPT). Living among the people, we saw their suffering and what the war and occupation meant for their lives. We accompanied them to get help or to escape violent situations. We worked alongside Iraqis as they spoke out against injustices and built movements of nonviolence and reconciliation.[1]

---

1. For the story of those early years, October 2002 to the summer of 2004, see Gish, *Iraq*.

Four and a half years later, in 2010, the image of Allia's pain came back to me in a more personal way. Over these years, I had experienced terrifying things. I had seen bodies torn by bombs and felt the terror of the people around us. Militants had come into our own apartment and threatened our lives. When we met Allia, we were trying to free four of our own kidnapped team members. After that ordeal was resolved, we moved to the Kurdish area of northeastern Iraq. A year later, in January 2007, I was kidnapped in northwestern Iraq, and so like Allia, was a victim of perpetrated violence. *But today a new tragedy shook my life. This time it was my loss.*

This day, July 28, 2010, in Suleimaniya in northern Iraq, started out in a normal sort of way—hot, even in the early morning. After our team's morning meetings, my teammate, Marius van Hoogstraten, went to interview two Kurdish Iraqis about how they saw the "drawdown" of U.S. troops affecting Iraqi society. Garland Robertson, Chihchun Yuan, and David Hovde went to the downtown Suleimaniya market. I decided to stay home and write.

By mid-afternoon, my article about an event that brought urban Kurds together with displaced families living in the Zharawa tent camp still needed some work. The team cell phone that I carried rang. No name registered on the phone.

My oldest son's voice sounded strained. "Hi Mom. It's Dale." My heart jumped a beat with excitement. But then he added, "I have bad news." My stomach tightened as I unconsciously braced myself. "Dad just died . . . in a tractor accident . . . about an hour ago." It took awhile for his words to sink in, but they still seemed unreal. Then my heart hollowed out in anguish. Dale relayed all he had heard about the accident that had killed his father and my husband, Art. That was not a lot, since Dale was in San Francisco and the accident happened in Ohio. I questioned Dale, desperate to learn as much as I could. "Of course, I'll come home as soon as possible," I managed to say.

While other members of the team did what they could to support and help me, our team's support staff in Toronto arranged for flights home. Holding myself together, I packed and organized information to leave on the computer. I told my teammates that my life had just been torn apart. Neighbors dropped in to share their sadness, cry with me, and say goodbye. I drifted back and forth between numbness and intense pain.

Is this even a fraction of what Allia felt when her husband was killed? She had the added horror of his being the victim of brutal murder. Her grief-stricken face still haunts me. Is this what drives Iraqi fathers, mothers, and brothers to come and plead for us to help find their family members who have disappeared, or are imprisoned? Is this kind of pain the seed of the growing anger and disillusionment of Iraqis, who managed to survive the invasion and then had hope that things would be better with Saddam gone, but who now wanted the U.S. to leave?

Navigating through the checkout counter in the Amman, Jordan airport the next day, I walked frozen, as in a dream, still finding it hard to believe it was real. *Here I was, halfway around the world, working with others as they struggle for justice, but I wasn't there for Art in his last moments of life!* The world around me had caved in and a dark pain tightened its grip. Waiting at the gate and sitting on the plane I read a historical novel to keep my mind and emotions at bay until reaching home.

Every one who knew my husband expected he might die or be injured by a violent act in the West Bank, where he worked with CPT each winter for the past fourteen years. Instead, the accident happened on our farm in southeastern Ohio, where we earned our living selling organic vegetables at our local farmer's market. We had moved there years earlier with a group of families that formed a Christian communal farm. Here our three boys, Dale, Daniel, and Joel, grew up roaming the woods, working alongside us in our gardens, and being taught at home until high school.

Art and I had long felt outrage and grief for people around the world living under oppression and war, and had been working in the U.S. in various movements for justice and peace since we were in college in the mid-1960s. We had known people whose relatives had been horribly murdered in concentration camps under Hitler, after our country had refused the immigration of thousands of Jews in World War II. We knew our country was founded on genocide against the native peoples on this continent. It was also built upon the mass killing, rape, and oppression of enslaved Africans and their descendants. It had trained and supported death-squad fighters in Central and South America. We saw how people in our country have looked the other way or justified violence perpetrated against women and people of various gender orientations, and many other here unmentioned groups of people.

But this was new territory. *This tragedy was happening to me. There was no way to change it.* I thought, *I must find a way to walk ahead . . . find my way to the other side of this vast stormy sea . . . care for the empty hole inside me. I have no other choice. It is horrible and hard.*

Once I was home, loving family and friends surrounded me and walked with me as I struggled through my grief and found healing as I soaked in the beauty of the woods, worked in our garden, sold vegetables at our farmers market, and took part in local justice and peacemaking activities. Eight months later, feeling stronger, I was able to return to Iraq with a deeper, more personal understanding of the pain of the Iraqi people and a realization that *more* of *their* story must be told. This account of the story starts six years earlier than my husband's death, in the summer of 2004, where my book *Iraq: A Journey of Hope and Peace* left off.

It's the story of a beautiful people with a beautiful land and culture that has been besieged and wounded, but not totally broken. As I lived among them, their struggle has also become my struggle. It's the struggle of thousands of people around the world who resist forces of injustice and oppression through nonviolent means and discover peaceful alternatives to the ways of grasping power and institutional violence or brutal force.

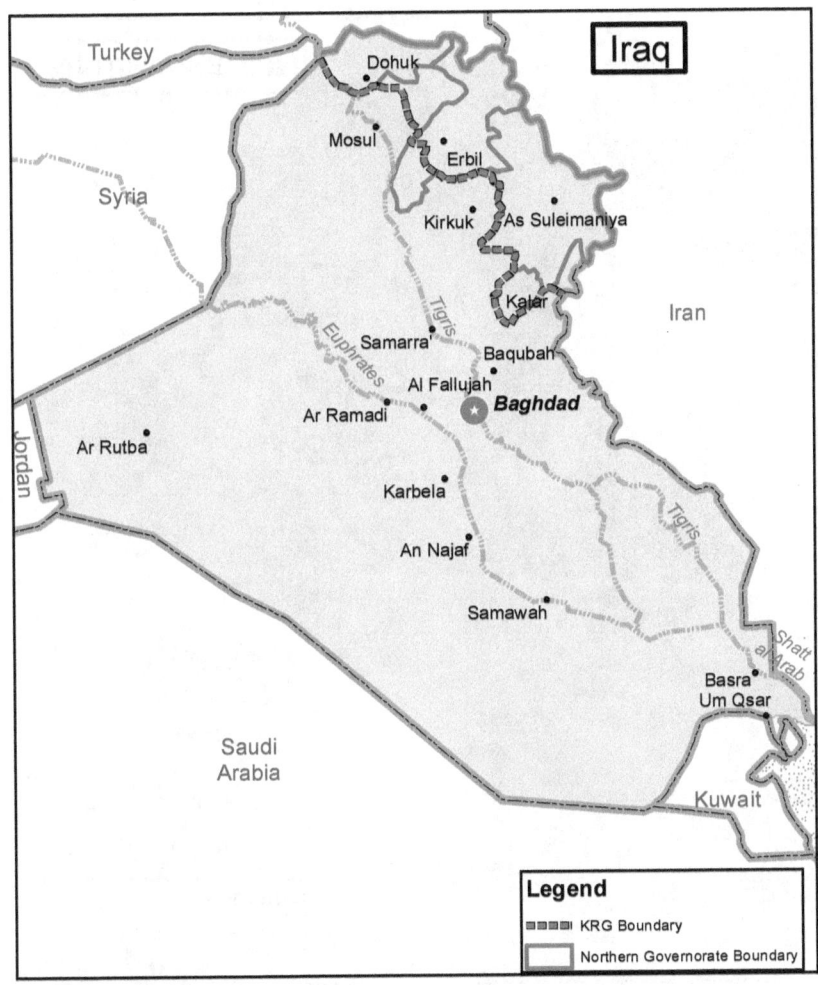

(Courtesy of Lisa King)

Map 1: Map of Iraq

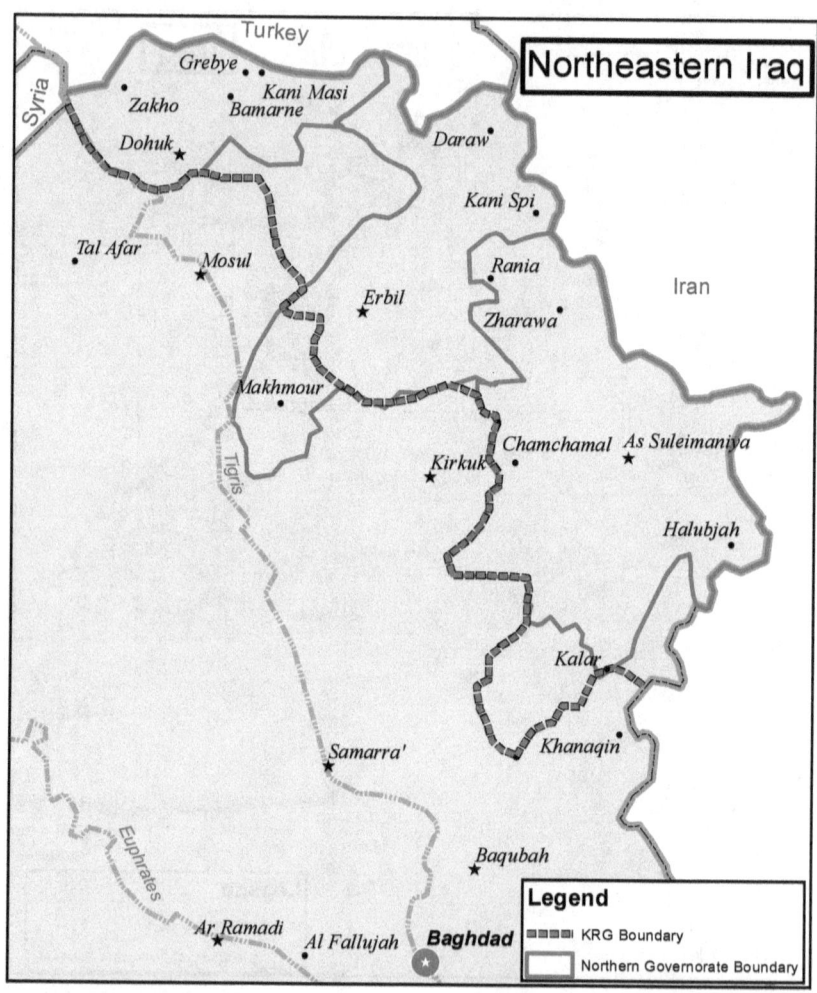

(Courtesy of Lisa King)

Map 2: Map of Northeastern Iraq

Part One

Summer 2004—Spring 2006

1

Changes

"M*IRIAM! SALAAM ALLE'KUM.* So good to see you! How's your family?"

"*Zeeniin!*" ("Good!"), she answered. After initial greetings on this July 2004 day, we each asked myriads of questions, using my broken Iraqi Arabic and Miriam's limited English. We sipped tea in her sparsely furnished sitting room, dimly lit because the electricity was out.

First she poured out the good news. "We can now use the park along the [Tigris] river. Ma'a just started school, and Marwan just turned twelve ..." Then a worried look flashed over her face. "But Salah still has no work. Things are not good here in Baghdad. Last month a bomb exploded near the Sadeer Hotel and also broke the windows of our house. We live in constant fear. Our neighbor, Thamer, has been kidnapped."

I couldn't count my visits at Miriam and Salah's house since October 2002. Especially enjoyable were the times we sat around a tablecloth on the floor with heaped up dishes of rice with chicken, or of dolma— vegetables stuffed with a rice and meat mixture—my favorite Iraqi food. One memorable day in late March 2003, during the bombing of Baghdad, Miriam and I heard a bomb blast in the distance while we were talking. We hugged each other and cried.

Now, in 2004, I just returned to Baghdad after a three-month break. Hours ago I was on a plane as it did its usual steep spiral descent into the Baghdad Airport. The airport bus took me to the checkpoint where one of my teammates, Maxine Nash, and our driver were waiting. Our driver drove amid a cluster of other cars, slowing down when we caught up with two U.S. Military vehicles ahead of us, and staying a safe distance behind.

Part One: Summer 2004—Spring 2006

When they stopped before an overpass, all the cars behind stopped too. The road from the airport into the city was still targeted periodically by resistance fighters and considered one of the more dangerous roads in Baghdad. Fortunately there was no problem today.

My thoughts drifted back to those I left two days ago in the U.S. It was always hard to say goodbye to my three adult sons and my husband, Art. Even my sense of calling and excitement about returning didn't remove the pain of leaving those I love and the lingering doubts about seeing them again. I clung to and treasured the good times we've had together.

This pain of leaving was doubled by my middle son Dan's negativity about my working in Iraq. He lived in Cincinnati, three hours away from Art's and my home near Athens, Ohio. On the phone, before leaving for my third trip to Iraq in December 2003, I had listened to him for about an hour as he heatedly gave political and practical reasons why I shouldn't go back. "It's stupid for you to go! . . . There's so much violence there. What good can you do? . . . How do you know you won't just be used by the militants to accomplish their agenda?" But before our conversation stopped, his tone changed and we talked more personally. He acknowledged that behind all his arguments was his fear of something happening to me. Our talk ended tenderly as we each said "I love you."

But after that phone conversation, he withdrew from me and the rest of our family and would not return our calls, letters, or e-mail messages. I was thankful for the support I received from my other two sons, Dale and Joel, even though their lives took them in different directions. I carried a well of pain about Dan, even though deep down inside, I knew he loved me. I believed this was his way of trying to protect himself from having to go through the emotional pain of consciously worrying about me. I struggled with whether or not I should give up this work because it was so difficult for him. I didn't want to cause him grief, but I also felt something would *die* in *me* if I gave up the deep calling I felt to continue to work in Iraq.

Back in early October 2002, I was standing in front of a crowd of about two hundred outside the Athens, Ohio County courthouse, speaking against war in Iraq. "In two weeks I'm joining a delegation to Iraq," I said. "Could hundreds of Americans going there now, possibly help prevent a war? We don't know. But we must try. If we are not ready to give ourselves for peace, who will? We want to be present with and understand what the conditions are for the people there, who are now under threat of attack. The Iraqi people should not have to bear the tragedy of another war. I love my three children and my grandchildren, and I want them to grow up to live free and healthy lives. But Iraqis want the same for *their* families. And *their* lives are just as important as the lives of North Americans."

Then, after living and working in Iraq, my love for the Iraqi people deepened. They became part of my family—it just kept expanding. Yet, Dan's challenges stayed with me. What could we do in a place of such pervasive and complex violence? Were we taking unworthy risks? Could we really make a difference there?

Filled with such questions, here I was, back in Iraq. Once our car left the Airport Road, we drove into the Karrada Dakhil neighborhood, past familiar shops, to our apartment on Abu Nawass Street. It felt like coming home.

As usual, I looked for what had changed, and over the next days and weeks Iraqis were quick to fill me in. One man told me, "Now we have a different kind of freedom, freedom with misery." A teenage neighbor said, "After the invasion we got mobile phones, the Internet, and satellite TV. We lost gasoline, electricity, and cooking gas."

Several people in Tahrir Square in central Baghdad expressed their concerns about the economic problems in Iraq. "I've been out of work for many months," one man said with tears in his eyes. "I had to sell many possessions to survive." With the end of the UN sanctions on Iraq, and the new unregulated import policy, there were more manufactured goods in the markets of Iraq's cities, yet poverty was severe, with 40 to 60 percent unemployment and increasing malnutrition. Foreign goods flooding into Iraq and the U.S. takeover of many of Iraq's businesses were eroding the economy. Meanwhile, most Iraqis tried to go on with life as normally as possible.

Resources like gasoline were harder to get. It was common to see lines of cars up to a mile long outside the gas stations. One time that summer, the entire city was without running water for five days. We sparingly used water from the reserve tank our landlord kept on the roof.

And the heat! It was like an oven. Before I adjusted to it, the heat consumed much of my energy. With only three hours a day of grid electricity in this large city during the extreme summer heat, resentment against the U.S. thrived. We were fortunate that our landlord gave us a few hours each day of backup generated electricity. After a local church service, a member commented that since Americans didn't seem to know how to restore Iraq's electrical system, damaged in the invasion and with any repairs now under American control, maybe Iraqis should go to the U.S. and teach people electrical repair.

PART ONE: Summer 2004—Spring 2006

Iraqi soldiers were now on training exercises alongside the U.S. troops. Iraqi Police (IP) organized raids searching for criminals throughout the city, and traffic police directed intersections choked with cars.

And yes, it was good to find a few positive changes. A ten-block stretch of Abu Nawass Street along the Tigris River, previously known for its fine fish restaurants, was still closed to cars by huge concrete-slab walls around some of its larger hotels that housed internationals, but we saw some progress being made in cleaning up the rubble and trash. An organized city trash collection now gave jobs to many. Men in orange jumpsuits now worked to level the ground, lay bricks for sidewalks, and mix up cement for short brick walls.

In the park along that stretch of the river, and across the street from our apartment building, mothers pushed their children in new brightly colored swings and watched them glide down sliding-boards. They welcomed me warmly and posed happily for pictures. At the same time boys and men were playing rousing games of soccer. It was refreshing to see them, hear their happy banter, and know that at least for these short periods they could forget and release their worry and frustration.

In a bomb-damaged building around the corner from our apartment a homeless father and his children lived amidst the rubble. Neighbors regularly took them food or gave them money. The children often came to our door for first aid or for playful attention.

On June 28, 2004, there was an official "transfer of government" to Iraqis. The Iraqi Governing Council (IGC) had been formed July 13, 2003. Then L. Paul Bremer, head of the Coalition Provisional Authority (CPA), the post-invasion international civilian administration in Iraq, handpicked the council members and loaded the IGC with wealthy Iraqis who supported U.S. presence and didn't represent the common people. Some of them had committed human rights violations when they worked with Saddam Hussein, before leaving and living out of the country and then while working with the CIA to attempt to overthrow Saddam. Many Iraqis called the IGC a puppet government of the U.S. Now, in June 2004, the IGC became the Interim Government of Iraq (IGI). The U.S. military, however, was still in charge of general security.

When Bremer took charge of the CPA on May 2, 2003, he tried to rebuild Iraq's economy by enacting laws to privatize and sell off state-owned companies, remove or reduce tariffs, inspections, and taxes, and allow foreign companies to own Iraqi assets in non-natural resource sectors and take all of the proceeds out of the country. He also lowered Iraq's corporate rate, making it very lucrative for Western investors. He fired 500,000 state workers, the majority of which were soldiers and police.[1]

It was illegal, however, under the Geneva Conventions of 1949 and The Hague Regulations of 1907 International Conventions, for the CPA to sell off state assets. The May 2003 UN Security Council Resolution 1483, that authorized the CPA to occupy Iraq, obligated the U.S. and UK to follow these conventions. So in the spring of 2004, Bremer attempted to push the IGC to pass an "interim constitution" stating that "the laws, regulations, orders and directives issued by the Coalition Provisional Authority ... shall remain in force" and couldn't be changed until after the general elections seven months later. So during this period, the new Iraqi government could do the work of selling Iraqi assets and enacting the new economic measures. Foreign investors would come and sign long-term contracts and get established before policies could be changed.[2] Many Iraqis told us, "We don't like it, but what can we do?" Others held on to hope that even if this document were ratified now, it would eventually lead to more autonomy and improvements.

A prominent Shia cleric, Grand Ayatollah Ali as-Sistani, called for earlier elections and tried to block Bremer's economic laws and the passing of this interim constitution. Then in early March, five bombs exploded in front of Shia mosques, killing 200 worshipers, and talk began of civil war. Sistani backed down and gave the OK for Shia members of the IGC to sign these measures. Meanwhile the young radical cleric Muqtada as-Sadr and his followers, called "Sadrists," also voiced opposition in interviews, fiery sermons, articles in their newspaper, and in public protests, calling the constitution an unjust and terrorist document. The CPA appealed to the UN Security Council to pass a resolution endorsing the interim constitution and other plans for handing the government over to the Iraqi governing body. But on June 8, the UN resolution (1546) only ratified the hand-over plan and not the interim constitution.

Advisors Bremer appointed, from countries in the coalition forces, for each of the new twenty-six Iraqi ministries, had veto power over decisions the ministries made. Before leaving Iraq on June 29, Bremer signed an order giving immunity from Iraqi law to Western defense contractors.

U.S. officials had also instituted a system that gave the money and decisions about rebuilding the infrastructure to the international corporations, rather than to the Iraqi skilled and professional working force. The

---

1. For more information on the U.S. administration's economic plans for Iraq, see Klein, "Baghdad Year Zero."
2. Ibid., 47.

Part One: Summer 2004—Spring 2006

corporations delayed the rebuilding as they allowed multiple subcontracting. Iraqis saw that caring for their physical needs and rebuilding Iraq's social, educational, and health care structures were not high priorities for U.S. officials.

The ways that U.S. civilian and military leaders in Iraq operated actually did more to hinder than foster democracy and self-determination in Iraq. Had building democracy and addressing the needs of the people been real goals of American officials, they would have brought together the different political factions to build coalitions and work on collaborative government building early in the government forming process, before tensions erupted into violence. Instead, U.S. leaders did little to encourage real dialogue among divergent Iraqi voices.

The leader of a woman's organization who openly opposed U.S. occupation had been excluded from U.S. sponsored policy-making conferences and the resources given to other organizations. U.S. leaders did not support grassroots democratic movements or take seriously the concerns they voiced. Instead of empowering experienced and qualified Iraqi lawyers and human rights workers to develop the new justice system, American officials imposed a U.S.-controlled system that was brutal and lacked a due process of law. It was not hard to see that these actions and policies nourished the soil for seeds of anger and resentment toward American presence to grow and the resistance movement's desire to sabotage the occupation to flourish.

I thought more about changes when I was with the children at the "Dar al Muhabha," an orphanage, two blocks from our apartment, run by the Sisters of Charity of Mother Teresa. Volunteering there since October 2002 became a regular part of my routine. Along with Iraqi volunteers, I played with and helped feed the twenty to twenty-five handicapped children. Sitting with them on the mat-covered floor of the playroom, we would sing or play finger games. These children had given me much love and joy in the midst of the stresses of our work.

It lifted my spirits to see progress with the children. Yasser was walking with a wheeled walker. Two-year-old Nura, with stubs for arms and legs, was learning to talk. She could sit up, turn over, and scoot around on the floor and now showed me her new trick. Using her tiny half-foot with three toes, she triumphantly picked up a ringed toy with beads hanging down and shook it in play.

One day at the orphanage, I talked with a couple of soldiers from a U.S. military unit, who had just started coming occasionally to play with and feed the children. They brought a shipment of goods for the orphanage and for the sisters to give out to people in the neighborhood. It wasn't difficult to understand their wanting to come here, in the midst of the turmoil, and also be graced by the love and exuberance of these children.

A new girl, Ghassran, was upset and disoriented, crying much of the time after being brought to the orphanage. Change for her has been painful, just as change has been for the general population, who also had little control over what was happening around them.

Huge boxes of new equipment were piled around the courtyard, and extensive remodeling was taking place at the Nuclear and Radiation Hospital in Baghdad. The director described their current situation. "We hope to have the remodeling done and equipment installed in six months. Slowing down the work is the lack of security. Several other hospitals offer chemotherapy, but this is the only one in Iraq that offers radiation treatment." We knew that after the 1991 war with Iraq, cases of cancers and leukemia had risen dramatically, yet the entire country had only three radiation machines, all manufactured in 1982. Also, much of the other cancer-treating equipment donated by other countries was defective or outdated.

"The Ministry of Health has now allocated enough money for us to buy modern equipment and send staff out of the country to be trained to use it," the director continued. "It hopes to build new radiation hospitals in other regions of Iraq. Last year they treated 12,000 patients. This year it was more, since there was already an increase in cancer, leukemia, and birth defects from the depleted uranium (DU) fallout during this invasion."[3] Most hospitals in Iraq don't have enough medicines, and it's difficult finding truckers willing to risk the danger of driving them in. Another obstacle in offering medical care is the lack of adequate and clean water. In spite of these momentous problems, the director seemed hopeful about more progress.

---

3. Uranium 238, a highly radioactive and toxic byproduct of enriching uranium, with a half-life of 4.5 billion years, was used by the U.S. in the 1991 and 2003 wars in Iraq, in bullets and bombs and in the lining of military tanks.

Part One: Summer 2004—Spring 2006

An oncologist in Basra we visited several months later was not as hopeful. He was connected with the Basra Teaching Hospital and internationally known for his research on DU. He reported an increase of cancer of all kinds since the 2003 invasion, especially acute leukemia. Breast cancers increased 30 percent, but the basic therapies to treat them were not available. Medical treatment for Iraqis was free, but the quality of medical care had deteriorated during the last ten years of sanctions and had continued to get worse since the U.S.-led invasion.

The oncologist's small clinic was in a dilapidated building in the midst of crowded markets. To get there, one had to step over garbage and around pools of sewage. In addition to these difficult physical conditions, the oncologist lived in constant fear of being killed or his clinic being looted. He knew of twelve health care providers who had been killed in the last several months. Many other doctors, working under similar conditions, had left the country. He was one of many physicians who continued to take incredible risks to serve the needs of his patients.

At the entrance of the Al Wathba water treatment plant, Abdul, who had been a guard there during the March 2003 bombing of Baghdad, welcomed us excitedly. Our team, then called the "Iraq Peace Team," made up of internationals representing CPT and the Chicago-based organization Voices in the Wilderness, had slept here in tents during that time. We did this to be present with the people of that neighborhood and to make the statement that Iraqis in their homes were in no less danger than we were in tents. Abdul, who now, in the summer of 2004, worked here as an Iraqi policeman, took us to see Hala, the head water-treatment engineer.

Hala was proud to show us improvements in the treatment system. A UN agency had provided alum, used to separate large particulates out of water. A new U.S.-supplied generator gave them backup electricity. Al Wathba was one of four "water projects" servicing the neighborhoods on the east side of the Tigris River. It provided water to a large complex of hospitals, Hala explained. But most of Iraq's water systems was not repaired or refurbished. The Adhamiyah system still had pipes plagued with cracks and breaks, some dating back to 1935.

The small date-palm tree planted at the water plant in March 2003 by a CPT delegation and labeled the "Tree of Life," was still alive and freshly watered. During that pre-war time, it had been a symbol of hope for the peace and new life the Iraqi people desperately needed. Now, just like the tree, progress toward peace in Iraq was still very small and fragile. To flourish, it needed the kind of dedication shown by Hala, who worked long hours to keep the treatment plant running during the bombing, and by Iraqis who spoke out against further oppression of their people. It needed the fresh leadership of a new generation. But with the fracturing of the underpinnings of the society and unleashed forces of anger and grasping for power, the work of rebuilding would need more. It would require occupying countries to put the well-being of the Iraqi people over their own goals of economic or power gains. It would take skillful leadership in bringing together opposing factions as well as coalition forces to authentically turn over the leadership and the rebuilding of their society to Iraqis. The opportunity for coalition forces to leave Iraq and turn over security and leadership to a transitional UN presence was still possible at that time, but U.S. leaders held on to power.

And what about the people detained by American troops?

2

"It's Hard to Appreciate Even the Positive Things"

WE SAT IN A modest home on a fruit farm just south of Baghdad while Nassim, a sturdy, medium-built man of about thirty-five, with scars on his wrists from cuts made by handcuffs, recounted what had happened to his family. Because an explosion along the road near his farm killed a U.S. soldier traveling in a convoy, American forces conducted nighttime raids in all the homes in that area. Soldiers entered Nassim's family's house and took him, along with his father and two brothers, to the Al Dora Refinery Plant. For twenty-four hours they were handcuffed with their heads covered. Soldiers periodically kicked them and beat them with rifle butts. Then they were moved to the Scania U.S. Military Base and kept in tiny solitary confinement cells for nine days.

Interrogators accused Nassim of setting bombs and threatened to force him to do sexual acts with a man and send pictures to his wife if he didn't confess to the crime. Three and a half months later, he and his brothers were released, but not their seventy-four-year-old father with multiple health problems. It seemed a common practice to detain many from a family, and then release all but one to insure that the other members didn't cause problems when they get out.

We had seen the strip along both sides of the road where soldiers burned bushes and trees to take away hiding places for resistance fighters. We saw the two-feet-deep, fifteen-feet-diameter crater from the explosion that had ended the soldier's life.

"It's Hard to Appreciate Even the Positive Things"

Next to Nassim was his nephew, Ziad, a twenty-four-year-old physician's assistant with large scars on his face. His nose was crooked from being broken eight months earlier in one of the three raids on his uncle's home, where he was staying to keep the trees watered and protect the women and children of the household while the older men were imprisoned. "About 4:00 in the morning," he said, "I was asleep on the floor with other family members when American soldiers forced their way in. Before I could get up, one of the soldiers started beating me in the face with the barrel of his gun and broke my nose. It was bleeding and I had to breathe through my mouth. They cuffed me and put me roughly in the back of a truck. They laid me down on the end of the truck bed so that soldiers stepped on me when they climbed in and out."

As he spoke, I thought of my youngest son, Joel, who was a physician's assistant living in relative safety.

Ziad continued, "When we got to the base, they grabbed me and threw me down on the ground with my hands still tied behind my back. I understood some of what the soldiers were saying—they called us 'animals.' At night [in January] soldiers poured ice cold water on us and wouldn't let us sleep. When a doctor was treating my broken nose, another soldier came in the room and hit me. The doctor told him, 'Don't you see I am trying to heal him, so don't beat him. Treat him like a human being.' The soldier snapped back, 'A friend of mine *died*.'"

Tears came to Ziad's eyes and he now stopped talking to us, seemingly to rein in his feelings. Farhad, another uncle, a slightly balding man of about fifty also in the room, interjected quietly, saying, "When Ziad was released, we couldn't see his eyes, his face was so swollen up."

I looked at Nassim's mother, Sarah, and his wife, Eman, who had served us tea and sat quietly the whole time the men were talking. I took the opportunity of that pause to ask the women what they had experienced during the house raids. I had to be persistent, because Nassim interrupted his mother several times. When he finally let her talk, she said, trembling, "For four or five months after the raids, I had trouble sleeping. I would stand by the door, afraid."

Eman took us to another room and showed us where soldiers smashed in the door that wasn't locked and broke glass shelves and the door of a cabinet. There, she said, they grabbed her and threw her on the floor. She pulled up her sleeve and showed us a still slightly swollen and bruised place on her arm. She said her mother-in-law and her one-year-old

Part One: Summer 2004—Spring 2006

daughter suffered psychologically. The baby seemed anxious and lethargic so they took her baby to a doctor.

As they appeared finished, Farhad vented feelings that seemed to have been building up in him. "If my brother was killed by U.S. forces, I wouldn't go out and kill all Americans. If you gave me a million dollars, I wouldn't shoot another human being. I have no *right* to."

Farhad grimaced as he continued. "I hate Saddam, but he never treated us like *this*, driving tanks in our streets, shooting at people. I understand U.S. soldiers have to protect themselves, but things are getting worse. If soldiers have to go into homes, they could treat the people with respect and not kick in the door and beat people. Instead, they're very aggressive and have no manners, no human sense. They said they were coming to bring freedom. It's almost two years—they must leave now. My father, who's still not home, is a respected man. This farm has been in our family for generations. Besides, if I were going to set a bomb against Americans, *I certainly wouldn't put it out near my own property!*"

It was back in June 2003 that our team first tried to visit the U.S. detention center at the Baghdad International Airport Prison (BIAP). We weren't allowed in, but we met Iraqis who were looking for family members arrested by American forces. Iraqi families started coming to us, asking for help. We went with them to U.S. military bases, offices, or prisons—places they had difficulty accessing—to track down where a prisoner was being held and what he was charged with, and hopefully to arrange visits.

At first, the CPA had no central database for prisoner information. Later that fall, they opened the Iraqi Assistance Center (IAC), an agency that acted as the CPA's liaison to Iraqis. The IAC developed a prisoner database, but more often than not, names and information about the prisoners would not be on these lists. Iraqis were supposed to have access to this office, but often weren't allowed in.

We were hardly prepared for what these people told us—accounts of violent house raids made in the middle of the night, the destructive ransacking of homes, the stealing of money and valuables, and finally the brutal and often tortuous treatment during arrest, interrogations, and imprisonment, sometimes resulting in permanent injuries or death for prisoners. Mid-level U.S. military officers acknowledged that it was standard practice to enter a home violently with thirty or forty seconds of "absolute

"It's Hard to Appreciate Even the Positive Things"

fury," during which they would try to subdue the men of the household however they could, usually knocking or kicking them to the floor.

It was common for Iraqis to be held for months without charges or a hearing. We found on the lists charges such as "bad father" or "suspicious." Several men we interviewed said interrogators forced them to sign statements waiving any rights to legally contest their treatment and detention status, or seek compensation for any harm done to them or their property. There was no system in place for investigating their cases or granting them fair trials. It became clear to us that the abuse and mistreatment were not limited to Abu Ghraib, but extended to all of the American-run security prisons (Camp Bucca in Um Qasr and BIOP, the prison at the Baghdad International Airport), as well as the many intake facilities for prisoners at local Multinational Forces (MNF) bases.

Like other international or Iraqi organizations working on prison issues, we estimated that 80–90 percent of the security detainees had no involvement in acts of violence, but happened to be nearby or were rounded up in indiscriminate neighborhood sweeps after an act of violence occurred.

> I remember two brothers telling us about their seventy-year-old father being knocked down on the floor of their kitchen, taken away by U.S. soldiers in a military vehicle with his hands tied behind his back and a plastic hood put over his face. Every time he complained about not being able to breathe, U.S. soldiers cursed or hit him with their rifles. Soon he was quiet—he had suffocated. The pain I saw in the two sons' eyes, as they told me this story, still haunts me.

We felt compelled to help families of prisoners find the information and help they needed, but also to tell the truth about the appalling physical and psychological abuses and the injustices of the whole detainee process. We worked alongside local Iraqi human rights groups, such as the Human rights Organization in Iraq, the National Association of Defense of Human Rights in Iraq, Organization for Women's Freedom in Iraq, and the Society for Human Rights in Iraq. Together we took part in local vigils and public forums, and met with public officials. Whether these detainees were guilty or innocent, we believed they should be treated humanely and given a fair legal process for resolving their cases.

In our team's report on seventy-two prisoners in the U.S. detention system in Iraq, completed in December 2003, we outlined violations of

PART ONE: Summer 2004—Spring 2006

human rights of prisoners and their families and made suggestions for change. In early January 2004, we sent it to government officials in the U.S. and spoke about our findings to top assistants in the offices of Paul Bremer and top U.S. military official in Iraq, Lieutenant General Ricardo Sanchez. We sent testimonies and information to people in our home countries, urging them to call on our governments to change their policies and practices. It became clearer later that these policies came from higher government officials, not from a few disturbed soldiers. This campaign drew a significant amount of media attention.[1]

Along with recording new testimonies this summer, we followed up on the earlier seventy-two cases, meeting with detainees and their families once they were released. One new testimony was from a fifty-nine-year-old, frail looking man named Najib, with a history of heart problems. As he told his story he did not sound bitter, but he often tensed up with pain or his voice wavered. He had worked for the governor of Karbela, who sent him on a business trip on May 15, 2003. When he returned, U.S. intelligence officers arrested him and took him to a military base where soldiers beat and sexually abused him. For nine agonizing months he was in and out of different prison camps, hospitals, and military bases, physically mistreated and humiliated.

During that time Najib suffered a heart attack and spent forty days under guard in a public hospital. His son came one day and begged the staff, "Please release my father. He's sick." He wasn't released, but sent to a military hospital in Baghdad. From there he was taken to the detention center at the airport where he suffered beatings and verbal abuse, and then finally to Abu Ghraib prison. One morning, he had a stroke and temporarily lost the use of the left side of his body. Another heart attack followed.

Fortunately an American doctor tried to help him. Human rights organizations and CBS News learned of Najib's story and pressured Coalition authorities to release him. Interrogators at Abu Ghraib admitted that they had no incriminating evidence. Finally he was released, but he never knew why the Iraqi governor in Karbela wanted to get rid of him. Perhaps it was because he had criticized local corruption.

---

1. See Gish, *Iraq*, chapters 15–18, for more description and stories about this campaign.

"It's Hard to Appreciate Even the Positive Things"

In July, a young man, Sa'ad, came to our apartment requesting help for his uncle, Ehab, who had been held without charge at the Al Dora Police Station for four months. He believed his uncle was innocent, but someone gave false information about him. When teammate Greg Rollins and I went to the station he seemed depressed. The police chief said that a U.S. military officer brought Ehab there without any official papers or charges and ordered him, "Just keep him."

Another teammate, David Milne, and I went with Sa'ad to the Scania U.S. Military base on the edge of Baghdad to talk to the commander of the unit that had arrested Ehab. After navigating two checkpoint searches by Iraqi guards and past three concrete walls, we entered the base, a fortified island of U.S. troops. In a reception room, U.S. soldiers joked around with Iraqi workers and responded politely to people who had come for information or to register a complaint.

About two hours later, a soldier escorted us through the base, past buildings that were headquarters for different military units and through groups of soldiers in uniform or in casual dress. "Where'ya from?" several soldiers asked. One came up to us with a big grin saying, "Hey, real Americans here!" Feeling cut off from their families and "real" lives, they welcomed some diversion or reminders of home. Many seemed shocked that we were in Iraq and traveled around the way we did.

We were taken to a drab meeting room where the colonel's executive officer started out in a gruff manner and seemed irritated with our concerns. He showed us pictures of men standing in a crater and brought in a soldier who had scars on his neck from shrapnel wounds. "This man came out alive, but we have reason to believe that Ehab made the IED's [improvised explosive devices] that led to the first death in our battalion," he said.

At first, Ehab had been detained as a security prisoner at BIAP, but U.S. military personnel in charge released him, saying that they didn't have enough evidence against him. Before he could be released, however, the arresting unit took him to the Al Dora Police Station, claiming to have such evidence. Now, the officer said they would keep him there as long as it took to prepare his case.

I told the soldiers we were sorry about the injuries and pain the attacks caused them, but we were also concerned that this man be treated fairly. We had no way of knowing if Ehab was guilty or innocent, but asked that they either formally charge him, so he could be legally processed, or release him. The officer told Sa'ad to check with the GIC (General Information Center) or the IAC (Iraqi Assistance Center) in two weeks, when they hoped to have this resolved. I said we would continue to watch this case.

Two weeks later, Sa'ad came back to our apartment, since nothing had happened with his uncle's case. We voiced the dilemma we felt about returning to the base with him to talk to the colonel. We didn't want to make matters worse for Ehab, since it was better for him to be held in the jail than in Abu Ghraib. Sa'ad could see that going back to Scania might be useless, but wanted to do *something* to help his uncle. We eventually got an appointment with the head commander over at the Rasheed district.

The commander claimed that they had sent a file to the Al Dora Police Station, but someone must have taken it or not delivered it. They intended to keep Ehab at the station until the Iraqi Police could charge him and prepare his case for the Iraqi court system. "You have to realize that violent attacks against my men have increased," he said.

Then he spoke glowingly about how the military was working with the local leaders to establish security and help the people in that region. "We've spent $16 million in the last six months, fixed water, power, and sewage systems, cleaned a garbage dump, and employed 2,000 Iraqis," his assistant told us. "When school starts, we're going to give the children backpacks."

"Iraqis don't know much about democracy," the commander said. "We really have to teach them." At this, I couldn't hold back, and responded, "This is not what we've observed. Iraqis seem to have an innate understanding of and desire for democracy. We have met many who are taking risks to work peacefully for it." As he spoke about how difficult it is to work with and trust Iraqi people, we felt he voiced common but groundless stereotypes and little understanding of the roots of the anger Iraqis were expressing.

I suspect that both the military officers and our peace team walked away perplexed, seeing the other as lacking some reality about the situation in Iraq. They may have thought that we were not realistic about the need for military solutions to security issues and a bit crazy for traveling around Iraq unarmed. We saw them as being isolated and not focusing on what most Iraqis needed to feel secure and respected.

Iraqis had told us that the bits of improvements the U.S. *had* provided in almost a year and half of occupation, mostly with money from Iraqi oil sales, were like a drop in the bucket of the country's huge need. As one man said, "Those of us who've had our homes bombed, raided and ransacked, or have been imprisoned by U.S. forces, have a hard time appreciating even the *positive* things American soldiers have done." Often improvements or services to communities were contingent on the local people providing security for U.S. troops. Many viewed receiving help from the U.S. military or cooperating with the Interim Government as buying into the long-range goals of the U.S. here, and that put them in more danger from Iraqi individuals or groups violently resisting U.S. presence.

We met some good-hearted soldiers at the base, but many seemed to buy into what the U.S. administration told them about the Iraqi people needing help to build democracy, or that anyone who resisted occupying powers hated freedom. We saw them defending a system of occupation that did not build trusting or empowering relationships with the local people, but focused on maintaining their own safety and control and achieving the U.S.'s economic and political goals. We saw a circular relationship with the military approach and continued violence in Iraq.

Some Iraqis sought compensation for damage or injury caused by U.S. soldiers in raids or other military actions. In Baqubah, forty miles northeast of Baghdad, Dr. Hassan, a medical doctor and director of a private college offering degrees in dentistry, pharmacy, architectural engineering, and law, told us the following story:

On June 24, 2004, a small group of resistance fighters forced their way into the college buildings to flee a battle in the streets. According to witnesses, the fighters fled the buildings and the area as soon as they heard airplanes coming. The coalition forces (now called "Multinational Forces-Iraq," or MNF-I) responded with air strikes, destroying buildings and equipment. Then ground troops invaded, refusing the offer of keys, and broke down the doors of all classrooms left standing. The whole operation took about an hour.

A few weeks later, our team saw the damage from these attacks. The central building, where newly equipped chemical and pharmaceutical labs had just been furnished, was in rubble, and the surrounding buildings severely damaged and unusable. It was sickening to see. Classes were to resume in September. "It took ten years to build up the college, but only one hour to destroy it," commented Dr. Hassan.

PART ONE: Summer 2004—Spring 2006

Figure 1: Guard shows Maxine Nash and Doug Pritchard damage of college buildings in Baqubah by MNF-I in June 2004

My teammate, Anne Montgomery, drew an analogy between what happened here and what might have happened in the U.S. when she wrote: "Imagine a scene in New York City at the smallest city college. A drug gang has a gunfight in the street, runs into the student center and then escapes through back entrances. Police helicopters, emergency forces, and college administrators arrive. How do the police handle the situation? By bombing around the college? By immediately invading and breaking down doors? Or do they surround the building, consult with college officials, send for a negotiator, and patrol neighboring streets to find the perpetrators and interview witnesses?"

We went with Dr. Hassan to the local Civilian Military Operations Center (CMOC), a coalition military office where Iraqis could register complaints or ask for information, and where he had already applied for compensation. The officer in charge didn't deny that U.S. forces had caused the damage, but said the destruction was considered "combat related," so they wouldn't take responsibility for the damages. This countered every sense of fairness bred in me.

"It's Hard to Appreciate Even the Positive Things"

Among other things, we mentioned that it would be better to have 1300 students in school than not have something productive to do. The officer said he would send an appeal to a higher office and also explore possibilities of private funding for the rebuilding. The following summer, he was granted a portion of the compensation money toward rebuilding the college, but not enough to pay off the bank loans he had taken on for that purpose.

The situation of thirty-nine-year-old Sa'id, the father of four, was tragic. He was now confined to his bed. In his his upper left arm and his lower right leg he had rods attached with pins and clamps. Bullets had shattered both bones.

In January 2005, Sa'id and his friend were driving past university buildings that U.S. forces had taken over for a base, when fifty-two bullets hit his car. Eight bullets hit him, and five, his companion. Apparently shots had been fired at the buildings from across the road and the convoy returned fire, but aimed at the passing vehicles of innocent people. Sa'id's car had been the last of four hit. Five people died, and fifteen injured in the other cars. "The soldiers didn't stop to help," he explained, "but people nearby took me to the hospital."

Before this happened, Sa'id and his brothers manufactured metal frames for windows and doors. He can no longer do that work because he can't move the fingers in his left hand. His brother asked a U.S. Army officer, "Why do you shoot civilians?" The officer responded, "Unfortunately we have too many soldiers acting irrationally." We heard many stories of troops over-reacting and shooting uncontrollably at checkpoints or from convoys. The tragedy was very real for the victims.

*Meanwhile we were aware of
the increasing violence around us.*

3

Realities of Danger

"About a month ago, two bombs exploded outside this building," Zaleka, a twenty-eight-year-old woman, dressed in conservative Muslim dress, told us with wide eyes. We had come to have a report printed at her second floor shop. "The blast destroyed a restaurant on the ground floor. I hadn't come to work yet, or I could have been killed." She broke down, saying, "I can no longer bear this. I have so many plans for my life. I want to go to graduate school. But I don't know if I'll be blown up, kidnapped, robbed, or lose my legs or life in an explosion." Everywhere, Iraqis struggled with the violence around them.

"Yesterday, bullets from a gun battle out on the street flew into my room and hit the wall a few meters from my head," said Ali, one of our drivers. "We don't ever feel safe."

At her Baghdad University office, a professor told us, "I know of 280 university professors in Iraq who've been killed, some because they publicized their studies about the effects of DU. But the CIA causes some of this violence so we will 'need' Americans here. Who created Osama bin-Laden? The CIA. Saddam is not *our* Saddam, but *America's* Saddam. Bush should apologize to the people of Iraq and the U.S. At first we thought America would help with humanitarian problems. We have only seen its claws and fangs."

Then she paused and with a tremor in her voice and her eyes tearing, said, "It's *so* hard, *but we have to keep going*. When I leave my home, I'm afraid I'll be killed. When I'm giving lectures I wonder if my husband and children will be there when I come home. It's hard to concentrate on my work."

Another woman told us, "Women are suffering more than men. Since the occupation, we need the protection of our men and so are more dependent on them. We're going backward." Later, a female university student complained, "My family won't let me go anywhere now without my father or my brother going with me."

A young Iraqi man who had worked with the U.S. military, but had left his job, visited our team. "I no longer fit into Iraqi society," he said sadly. "My former friends don't trust me, and I've received death threats."

The son of our neighbors was driving with his mother and sister when a car started following them. It drove in front of their car and blocked their way. When the son managed to quickly turn around, men got out of the other car and shot at theirs. Even though a tire went flat, the son kept driving, weaving through traffic and side streets until they got away. The relative of another neighbor was kidnapped and released after the family paid a $20,000 ransom.

Hearing explosions in the background was a common occurrence. We assumed that most of it was part of the widespread resistance movement against U.S. occupation. When there was a series of blasts coming from the direction of the Green Zone,[1] it was usually a controlled blowing up of unexploded ordnances. If we heard an accompanying air raid siren, however, we knew it was mortars hitting the Green Zone. On the evening of August 12, when we heard lots of gunshots, we imagined gun battles around our neighborhood. Neighbors told us the next day it was just celebrations from the Iraqi soccer team beating Portugal in the Olympic games!

Security was an issue that wove through our thoughts and decisions, but we knew that problems of security were even greater for Iraqis. *We* had the choice to leave and get respite from it in more stable places. There were guns everywhere, and usually high-powered, automatic ones. At the door of any office or business, there was usually an armed guard. Our neighbor offered us the use of his Kalashnikov. We refused it and explained that we would not use violence to protect ourselves. "I hate this gun," he said. "But how else can I protect my family?" Guns had become a normal part of life here, but they didn't seem to make people feel safer.

When we met American soldiers at their bases or while walking around the city, we often stopped and talked. "What are *you* doing here, walking around the streets of Baghdad?" many asked, amazed. "You don't

---

1. The heavily fortified area in central Baghdad that was the headquarters for the CPA and the U.S., UK, and Canadian embassies.

PART ONE: Summer 2004—Spring 2006

have a gun, or armed guards! Don't you know how *dangerous* it is?" "We're safer than you are, carrying your guns," I answered. "And without weapons, we can go places you can't go, and meet people you can't, because we're not seen as threatening to them."

To others concerned about our safety, I said more. "If we carry guns out of suspicion that someone might hurt us, we instead become more suspicious to *them* and are more likely to be a target of violence." We knew that without guns we would be forced to use other strengths we have, such as our creative thinking, our ability to talk to someone threatening us, transform a tense confrontation, or prevent others or ourselves from being hurt or killed. And in most threatening situations, having weapons would not make us less vulnerable.

> Back in February, two men entered our apartment and threatened us with a knife and gun and then announced that in twenty minutes, explosives around the waist of one would blow up the building. (See more of this story on pages 224–27 Gish, *Iraq*.) In spite of our fear, we managed to act calmly and engage the men in conversation and express our concern for them. After about an hour they left, with no one hurt, but taking computers and some of our money.

Most internationals living in Iraq surrounded themselves with blast walls, checkpoints, and razor wire. By doing this, however, they put themselves in a kind of prison and cut themselves off from ordinary Iraqis. "How can you live in the Red Zone?" some asked members of our team with a sense of dread. *We*, however, felt it was a gift to live among and get to know the Iraqi people more personally and understand what they were thinking.

There was never any question that it was dangerous, but CPT differed from other organizations concerning the amount of risk we were willing to accept to do our work. We joined the team, willing to take the same risks as soldiers, to work for peace. We knew it was possible for any of us to be a victim of violence, but, for us, the importance of working alongside Iraqis for justice and peace outweighed the dangers.

Taking precautions, as in acting in ways to minimize the dangers and not acting foolishly or carelessly, is wise. But as a team we didn't want security to be the primary factor in our decision-making, and hold us back from doing the work we judged important. We sought to support Iraqis who wanted to "take back the streets," as well as take back the legitimate resistance to the occupation from those who would use violence, and to find as an alternative more powerful, transformative nonviolent ways. We believed such risk-taking actions would in the long run result in fewer people being killed.

We wanted to act out of a "non-mushy" love that compelled us to work in situations where people were under threat. Most people wouldn't think twice about giving their lives for a family member or risking our lives to pull a child out of a burning house or a river. Could we see all persons as part of our family and their lives as equally precious? Our organization has used the slogan "getting in the way" to refer to Jesus's way of nonviolent suffering love, as well as standing in the way of those who would cause harm. When we were willing to put our lives on the line to witness for truth, justice, and peace, God could empower us, work through us, and transform threatening situations.

We refused to see people as our enemies or label people as "terrorists," so evil that we can't talk with them. Carrying guns, using armor, or beginning with a show of force generated mistrust and could provoke a violent response. How we responded on an interpersonal or international level could make the difference between violence and transformative breakthrough. Working out of trust here was not only a gift, it was a necessity. It was encouraging to us when Iraqis, who took risks to work for justice, related to *us* in openness and trust.

> When Art (who had dealt with threatening situations, working with CPT in the West Bank) and I spoke back home, we were often asked about how we dealt with fear. "It's something we have to face over and over," we answered. "The main thing that helps us deal with fear is the love God keeps giving us for the people around us, so we've learned to continually pray for love rather than for courage. We are not any *braver than you are.* We are *weak cowards.* We don't have the strength to do this work, but need to ask for the love that gives us the strength to do it. What has made it possible to sustain this work is learning how to tap into such resources of faith."

As a team, we constantly faced decisions about where to travel, how many would go, and what ways to operate to minimize the dangers. There was never one right answer. We had our own drivers and wore traditional Iraqi clothing on the streets. We took our Iraqi partners' advice seriously when they advised us not to go into certain areas. We felt free to walk alone within a several block radius of our home to shop, take care of business,

Part One: Summer 2004—Spring 2006

or visit families, churches, or mosques. Otherwise we went in pairs, not in large groupings. Where people knew us and understood something about our work, we felt a greater degree of safety because of those relationships. It felt like we were being watched out for here—by neighbors, groups we work with, but also by a higher power.

Did I struggle with fear? Of course. When at home, preparing to return to Iraq from a break, fear would creep into my consciousness the last week or two before leaving. Walks in our wooded hills became a place where I dealt with the feelings. In that process, I would come back to the strong sense that I am to walk with, serve, and care for those living under threat of war or violence—that this is something I must do. I realized that I could do nothing to preserve my life wherever I am. Not all my fear or uneasiness dissipated, but I would be given the sense that whatever happened, God was with me and would help me walk through it. This was something I couldn't completely explain and came to me as a gift.

> Before working in Iraq I had talked about, and thought I really knew, what trusting God meant. But facing the very real possibility of death or torture myself stripped away simplistic beliefs. I had to rediscover what gives me hope and strength in life and death situations. In the midst of dangerous situations I felt my weakness and lack control, and didn't know what else to do but cry out for help. Somehow I've been given strength beyond my own and the ability to walk forward in spite of my fear.

Once back in Iraq, fear was less of a struggle. I'd be thrust into the midst of a beautiful people who welcomed us to stand with them in their pain, and work alongside them to prevent and reduce violence. I sought a wise balance between caution and not letting fear dominate. I didn't want to allow fear to block my love for the Iraqi people and the joy of being with them.

While in the U.S., I heard warnings from internationals in Iraq, usually picturing it as more impossible to live in and travel around than I would find once I had returned to Iraq. It still took me a few weeks to regain my own inner sense of the situation. Was the stern, pained, or anxious look on the faces of men on the street hostility toward us as foreigners, or just a reflection of their fear and anguish? The longer I'd be here, the more friendliness I'd feel from Iraqi people. It seemed clear that my feelings played a significant role in how others responded and how I saw the degree of safety on the streets. Most Iraqis respond from the heart.

Realities of Danger

At times I wrestled with what I might do if a team member, interpretor, or neighbor got injured? Would I know what to do to save her or his life? Would I be able to act quickly and wisely? I didn't know for sure. The question was, "Does not having greater certainty about these things mean we shouldn't move ahead, or do we risk walking ahead, knowing it could end in either failure or in unimaginable breakthrough?" I chose to walk ahead.

One time, after I spoke in the U.S. about working in Iraq, an ex-military person challenged me, saying, "Just wait until you face the terrorists yourself. Then we'll see how far your nonviolence goes and whether you'll still go trotting around the world talking about peace!" He was right that there was no way to know, but I hoped such an incident wouldn't change my commitment to peacemaking and nonviolence. I didn't know then just how I would feel three years later, after being abducted *myself*.

One morning in Baghdad, knowing there had been gun battles and fighting near his home, I asked Sattar, our main interpreter, "How is it in your neighborhood now?" He responded, "It's more peaceful today." A tall lanky, friendly man of about forty, he had graduated from Baghdad University, and spoke French and English, as well as his native Arabic. He provided an income for his family since his father was disabled from fighting in the Iran-Iraq war and one of his brothers was handicapped. My next question was one we asked our employees periodically. "We know that it's risky to associate and work for us [as internationals] and appreciate your willingness to do it so far, but how is it for you now?"

Our conversation was real, and he soberly acknowledged the possible dangers he faced. This weighed heavily on us. We didn't want our presence to increase the danger for him and other Iraqis working with us, yet it was one of the realities of working here. Members of our team studied Arabic, but most were not fluent enough to conduct deeper interviews without an interpreter. We had to balance our belief that it was important to work here with the possible negative consequences. We tried to develop relationships of trust with those we worked with, allowing them to be open and honest with us about their choice to take or not take that risk.

"The work your team is doing is important," Sattar answered. "Working with you is one way I can help my people. I'm willing to take the risks." Then, he added, "We shouldn't be careless, but we can take risks because we trust God." I appreciated his spirit of operating out of trust and faith, rather than fear. It was important to keep asking him that question, however, and not assume that the answer stayed the same.

Miriam and her husband invited us to come to their home after dark. Some of their neighbors had questioned them about their associating with Americans. They told the neighbors that we were not connected with the military or with President Bush, but were "people who help Iraq." We said we didn't want to be a source of danger for them and to let us know if this became the case. We came to realize that conditions of safety were fluid, and changed.

Danger for everyone increased during the times American forces conducted a siege on a city or when battles with resistance fighters were at their peak and there was a ripple effect of heightened anger toward the U.S. This happened after a critical event in March and April 2004, concerning Fallujah and Muqtada al-Sadr. Hostility between al-Sadr and U.S. authorities in Iraq began early in the occupation. While many other Shia Iraqi leaders and parties opposed the occupation, Sadr was one of the few that openly denounced its methods and policies. Media articles often referred to him as the "firebrand cleric."

In November 2003, Paul Bremer issued a warrant for Sadr's arrest, accusing him of being instrumental in the death of Sayyed Majid al-Khoei, a Shia leader seen as a rival of Sadr. Then on March 28, 2004, Bremer closed the Baghdad office of the Sadrist newspaper, the *al-Hawza*. Articles in the *al-Hawza* had voiced opposition to Bremer's interim constitution and economic policies. One article in the *al-Hawza* stated, "The United States did not only come to overthrow Saddam or take our oil. It came with the intention of destroying the whole cultural, moral, humanitarian structures of Iraqi civilization …" Another article claimed that Bremer was "pursuing a policy of starving the Iraqi people to make them preoccupied with procuring their daily bread so they do not have the chance to demand their political and individual freedoms."

Then in a seemingly unrelated incident on March 31, insurgents in Fallujah ambushed a convoy of Blackwater security guards, a horrific act that seemed part of the ongoing attempt to sabotage Bremer's policies and make it undesirable for Western corporations to work in Iraq. After killing the guards, the assassins ran off, but a mob on the street gruesomely desecrated their bodies. U.S. forces responded with massive attacks on Fallujah. About that same time, April 3, Bremer arrested Sadr's senior aide. The Sadrists responded with demonstrations in Sadr City and militarily seized control of several large cities in southern Iraq. A week later they retreated from these areas into a mosque in Kufa and the Imam Ali Shrine in Najaf.

Realities of Danger

Battles around the shrine continued until the strength of Sadr's militia, the Mahdi Army, waned, and Sadr agreed to a settlement with the CPA, arranged by Grand Ayatollah Ali-al-Sistani. Sadr agreed to a cease-fire and agreed to leave the shrine and Najaf. The CPA also retreated and refrained from arresting Sadr, yet insisted the Mahdi Army disband.

Meanwhile, U.S. forces were met with fierce resistance as they bombed and destroyed Fallujah's main hospital and took over a second hospital for a military base. We heard through non-American international peace workers inside Fallujah that the hospital's medical staff opened a makeshift clinic in a garage without sanitary facilities and with few medical supplies. They said that U.S. Marine snipers fired on ambulance crews and on "anyone who moves."

Four days into the siege, hospital workers reported 600 Iraqis killed by U.S. soldiers and more than 1,200 people wounded, two-thirds women and children. We understood that under international human rights laws, occupying forces were obligated to protect women, children, elderly, and the wounded and were forbidden to take over hospitals for military purposes. U.S. troops, however, said they weren't bound by international laws because this was a situation of war. As horrible as the killing and dismembering of four U.S. security guards was, the search for the perpetrators did not justify the collective punishment deaths of over 600 Iraqis.

In response to what was happening in Fallujah, resistance groups in Baghdad, Kufa, Samarra, and other cities increased their attacks on American forces. In Najaf, U.S. soldiers also took over the hospital. Fighting broke out in the Adhamiyah and Khadhumiyah neighborhoods of Baghdad. An Iraqi friend of the team was an eyewitness to U.S. helicopters spraying bullets into heavily populated streets in the Sadr City neighborhood in Baghdad. Several neighbors reported that their school or their work was canceled because various resistance groups called for a strike, leaving them without drivers, teachers, managers, and other personnel.

From talking with teachers and other professionals in Fallujah, we had known of past events there that had contributed to their hostility toward the U.S. military, such as the time in April 2003 when American soldiers shot into a crowd of citizens who were demanding the military return a school they had taken over, killing eighteen and injuring seventy-five. After that, violence in Fallujah escalated with revenge attacks. Resistance groups there also grew after Bremer disbanded the security forces of Saddam's regime on May 23 of that year.

Now, in the retaliatory violence that followed the April 2004 siege of Fallujah, militant groups around the country took hostage over thirty internationals and executed several. Independent contractors and humanitarian workers started leaving the country. Iraqis urged us to limit traveling and not to travel the road to Amman, Jordan, where they heard that gangs were stopping cars and looking for foreigners to kidnap.

On April 13, our team called on U.S. citizens to put pressure on U.S. forces, through their members of Congress, to cease offensive military action in these Iraqi cities, exercise restraint, and foster dialogue as a means of overcoming the present crisis. This would mean coalition forces talking to and respecting the leadership of community leaders and listening to their recommendations for de-escalating the violence. Local people believed negotiation was possible and had a significant chance of success if international powers really wanted to foster democracy here, but not if they insisted on their own agenda and controlling this society.

Later, U.S. leaders claimed that their ending the siege and leaving Fallujah was a victory. Iraqis in Fallujah said the attacks ended because the Iraqi army refused to keep fighting their fellow Iraqis and that leaders in Fallujah told U.S. forces, "Leave us alone or we will fight you."

Iraqis told us, "Using terror to fight terrorism doesn't reduce it, but acts as fuel on the fire and creates more terrorists." If for every perpetrator killed, a hundred new enemies were created, it diminished the prospect for peace and security.

Meanwhile, Iraqi women and men, with similar concerns, were taking nonviolent action.

4

Nonviolent Responses

"What would justice look like in Iraq?" Hannah asked, paused, and then answered: "When all can be really human, have rights and freedom." She spoke to the group of women and men gathered in late July 2004 in the office of a human rights organization called "Women's Will." Artwork created by women and depicting justice and liberation hung on the walls. For the past year women from different ethnic and religious backgrounds have been coming here to build cross-cultural unity as they nonviolently worked to oppose the occupation and improve society.

"To have peace and freedom, there must be justice for all, including the women and the poor," Hannah continued. "The culture of war in Iraq, perpetuated by the U.S., has meant an increase of violence toward women. Iraqis are now forced to trade Saddam's tyranny for another form of terror. Poor people now have no freedom—it's for the companies and the rich. Women take steps toward freedom when they increase their knowledge and awareness. Women must be on the same level with men and be able to work together with men to bring in the future."

"I got interested in human rights at the age of nine when I experienced war and couldn't understand why people would kill each other," she said. "In any violent situation, I'm for the victim and against the killers." On another visit, she spoke about her longing to unite Iraqi and American mothers in a common nonviolent struggle against the war and occupation. "It will be better for Iraqis *and* for the American soldiers if the soldiers go home," she said firmly.

Part One: Summer 2004—Spring 2006

One of the best-kept secrets of this war in Iraq was the work of hundreds of creative Iraqis like Hannah, who were giving leadership to a widely spread and diverse nonviolence movement. They worked openly and courageously, risking their own lives and careers to solve the almost overwhelming problems they faced and counter the humiliating and crushing effects of occupation on the people's spirit. They built grassroots movements and used nonviolent methods for bringing change. Some joined together to bridge the divisions between Muslim and Christian, Sunni and Shia. Each group with its particular focus, political bent, or methodology had similar goals. In spite of the increasing violence around them, they have not given up the struggle. They maintained a space of hope, even if it simply kept them from being broken. I wanted to bring people from back home here to meet these compassionate people and learn more about their rich heritage and culture, their struggles and dreams.

One day that summer, Musa, a jovial high school teacher and member of Iraqi Human Rights Watch in Karbela, visited our team's apartment and spoke about the work their group had been doing. During and after the March 2003 invasion, he and his colleagues helped people on the streets who were injured in the fighting. They disabled unexploded cluster bombs and grenades to prevent the deaths of those who might pick them up. One day, their friend, Hamza, was killed as he was trying to defuse one and it exploded in his hands. Now their group of mostly Shia Muslim men and women wanted to develop a more intentional and organized peace team.

Musa was part of a group of Iraqi activists who met to share ideas about how to work for justice and peace in their society. Answers they suggested included: "Start at the grassroots level and ask what's needed; dare to think the impossible; get a vision for what could replace violent or repressive systems; don't wait for the people on top to give it to you—start doing it, working together, in networks and coalitions." Many of these leaders were already doing these things.

Maysoon directed a women's human rights organization called Iraqi al-Amal. The organization conducted conflict resolution programs for teenage students and workshops and literacy classes for women—what it called

Nonviolent Responses

"capacity building"—and a civic dialogue among young people about social issues. These programs were offered in a number of cities around Iraq. Maysoon said, "What we are trying to do is to replace the culture of violence with a culture of nonviolence. I'm optimistic; I have hope when I look at the young people. But they also need role models."

"The problem is not any particular ethnic group. It's the culture of violence and using religion as a political tool," Maysoon said as she spoke about the crisis situation in Iraq. "Governments spread ethnic hate, and people are controlled by fear. There's a lot of corruption. Many leaders are pushing federalism for their own interests, while the people don't want it. We need to stop the spread of hate." Her organization backed constitutional provisions to prevent Sharia law from becoming the standard and taking away much of the current rights of women.

"I've had two assassination attempts," Noor, director of the Organization of Free Women, told us. Dressed in traditional Muslim garb, she met with us at her office in the city of Samawah, south of Karbela, in the spring of 2005. Since the invasion, she had been speaking out about the corruption in her community. "A lot of reconstruction money doesn't accomplish anything. We know there's money under the table, because it is a glass table, and we can see the hand."

The women's center worked on literacy education, constitutional rights for women, and aid to battered women. Noor told stories of the mistreatment of women, and women being made homeless when divorced. "Too many young women aren't getting educated because they are married as young as thirteen. These things must stop."

"I have always had these ideas about women's rights," Noor told us. When asked about how tribal and religious leaders responded to her work, she said, "At first they were shocked, but later they began sending their wife or daughter to me for help or to join our programs. You see, the Qu'ran gives complete rights for women. The 'family of Adam' includes both men and women. A caliph can be male or female."

"*Musanat! Musanat!*" ("Equality, Equality!") and, "Where's the human rights?" chanted about a hundred women, children, and men in Firdos

39

Part One: Summer 2004—Spring 2006

Square in Baghdad in a demonstration organized by the Organization for Women's Freedom in Iraq (OWFI). In the crowd were women dressed in conservative Muslim dress and others in Western style blouses and jeans. Babies smiled shyly from their mother's arms. Throughout the morning, women arrived from other organizations bringing more banners in Arabic and English. On one was written, "Full Equality between Women and Men." Another declared, "Separation of State from Mosque." Iraqi and international reporters took pictures and interviews.

"The situation for women is getting worse. Many of the new political and religious leaders limit the public activities of women. And women are not taking more initiative, because they're scared," said Yanar Mohammed, a strong leader of OWFI, which took a clear public stand against the occupation. She was one of the many Iraqi leaders we had worked alongside to protest the treatment of detainees in American prison system since the summer of 2003.

She called for the new Iraqi constitution to be secular, and one that would provide equality for women in all aspects of their lives and all institutions of society. "Our job is to help women rise from sleep. The years 1977–79 were the golden years for women in Iraq. But since then, with the Iran-Iraq war, the 1991 war, the sanctions, and this war, women have lost their fathers, husbands, brothers, and have had to take on family responsibilities."

People at the rally pointed out that the danger of gathering publicly kept more from coming that day. The voice of these Iraqi women, however, was one of strength, determination, and vision. It represented only a small part of the growing women's movement in Iraq.

Banners along the entrance displayed messages such as, "The insurgency has been targeting physicians," "Don't Buy from the Occupiers," and "Iraqi Mothers United Against Sectarian Fighting." Inside the meeting room another colorful banner said, "No Peace Without Justice." It was January 2005, and we walked into a teach-in at the Women's Will office. Hannah and Dr. Jamila spoke to eighteen women and five men. "We could silently defeat the occupation, not by killing, but by refusing to cooperate economically with America," said Dr. Jamila. "America's trying to make this a free market for itself and treating Iraq like another state. We should have our own sovereignty. Even before the tanks came in, the media war succeeded

Nonviolent Responses

in promoting American products. Iraqis' buying cheaper American products has undermined our economy, bringing us poverty."

"There are many things women can do," added Hannah. "Anyone can refuse to buy Coca Cola and other American products. We have our own meats, fruits, and vegetables." She referred to Gandhi's leading the Indian people to spin their own thread and weave their own cloth.

Ashia gave the example of her relative's wedding, where the family served American soft drinks, but the people refused to drink it. They drank Iraqi soft drinks instead. Another woman said that she knew how to make her own shampoo out of natural products. "If they put in a McDonalds in Baghdad, we will boycott it," added another. Hannah concluded the meeting saying, "Women should work through civil society. Working nonviolently can strengthen peaceful structures. Small actions, such as putting up posters, and large actions, like demonstrations, all add up and make a difference."

Months later, about 300 Iraqi men, women, and children gathered at the Ministry of Human Rights (MHR) in a demonstration organized by Women's Will, and other Iraqi groups. "Return Fathers to their Children" and "Release all Innocent Detainees," were written boldly on two of the banners. At one point in the demonstration, a man in charge of the detainee department for the MHR came out and listened to the parents of a missing Iraqi man.

With two representatives of Muktada al-Sadr's organization in Karbela we discussed possibilities for nonviolence in Iraq. One of the men was a doctor of veterinary medicine, the other a member of Karbela's city council. After they spoke about their organization's resistance to the occupation, my teammate, Cliff Kindy, said, "The occupation is wrong, but there are tools to bring justice and lift the truth that are stronger than bombs and tanks."

The men pointed out that though their organization is seen as a violent faction of the resistance to U.S. occupation, most of their work is nonviolent. "We will take up weapons and fight if military intervention and harassment is not stopped, but we try to use political and social development methods and solutions," one said. "We take care of the poor, help illiterate people, and fight with the pen. We try to build unity with other religious groups across Iraq." They had organized nonviolent actions in 2004 to stop the gasoline black market in Sadr City, as well as demonstrations in front of the Oil Ministry in Baghdad protesting the debilitating unemployment.

"The world needs to understand there's a difference between resistance and terrorism," he added. "Iraqis have a right to resist U.S. occupation, we just need to find good tools."

Walking through the Hawar Art Gallery, I was struck by the quality of the paintings and sculptures on display. Hamid, the director, told us, "During the embargo, art was an escape from the hardships and mainly focused on historical subjects. Saddam's government controlled the performing arts, but plastic arts [painting, sculpture, and ceramic arts] could not be controlled."

Hamid pointed out two of the thirty sculptures that were part of their June exhibit depicting the inhumanity of and pain caused by the Abu Ghraib Prison abuses. "In this time of the occupation," he commented, "we fight through art and culture, not by killing." A group we met with at the gallery that day hoped to set up a Peace Education Center in Baghdad that would send out teams to towns and villages to educate about peace. They invited our team to help them make connections with officials and other organizations. Because of increased violence and threats to the lives of their members in the coming months, however, it became more difficult for them to travel, collaborate with others, and carry out their plans.

It was early August 2004, and another crisis flared up in Najaf, sparked by the arrest of Muqtada as-Sadr's representative in Karbela. Sadr's supporters demonstrated in Najaf, and fighting erupted between U.S. forces and the Mahdi Army there and in Sadr City. Once again the Mahdi Army in Najaf retreated into the Imam Ali Shrine. U.S. marines surrounded the shrine and cut it off from supplies. Iraqis warned that if the Shrine of Imam Ali, the holiest site for Shia Muslims, was attacked and damaged, violence could erupt all over Baghdad and southern Iraq. The standoff intensified on August 6, when Grand Ayatollah Ali as-Sistani left Najaf for London to get medical care. Some government officials in three southern governorates called for secession from the Interim Government and the rest of Iraq. Hundreds of government workers and Iraqi soldiers resigned in protest of the attacks. Other Iraqi soldiers left their posts and refused to fire on their own people. I wrote in an article:

> As U.S. forces battle again with Muqtada as-Sadr's Mahdi Army, we do not condone the Mahdi Army's violent activities. Its taking refuge in the Imam Ali Shrine drew the fight into the streets of Najaf, where local residents were killed and their homes and businesses disrupted or destroyed. Disturbingly familiar, however, is the MNF-I's handling these acts of resistance with excessive force.
>
> Excessive violence is a regular part of U.S. soldiers' work here. It's played out in the violent house raids made in the middle of the night, beating, binding, and hooding the men, breaking furniture, and taking the family's life savings and gold jewelry. It's punishing whole neighborhoods or villages for the violent acts of a few, bombing buildings and spraying bullets into large population centers to deal with a small group's crimes.
>
> It stems from the soldiers' intense fear and frustration but also from the underlying goals of the U.S. administration and the orders the soldiers received. The security they've been trying to attain has not been for the Iraqi population, but for its own soldiers and administrators of the occupation, for keeping control and imposing Iraq's economic and political future. And we've seen here that excessive violence, injustice, and political and economic control of another country don't really solve the underlying problems and lead toward peace and democracy, but, instead, cause horrendous suffering and elicit more violence from those occupied.

A call came from Musa, our human rights colleague in Karbela, "We invite you to come in support of a peace vigil planned for tomorrow [August 26]. Sistani has returned and plans to lead a caravan into Najaf to negotiate a settlement and save the holy shrine. Thousands of people are expected to come." Sistani had given a 24-hour deadline for the Mahdi Army and the MNF-I to leave the shrine and the city and asked the Iraqi government to compensate people in Najaf for property damaged in the fighting.

On our trip the next day, our driver explained as he sped faster, "Along here, on either side of the junction leading to Fallujah and Ramadi, is more dangerous. People from those cities come here to attack foreigners traveling along this road." Greg, David, and I didn't relax much on this stretch, but arrived safely in Karbela about 10:00 a.m.

Part One: Summer 2004—Spring 2006

In Karbela, we climbed into a van and two cars along with our colleagues from the Karbela Human Rights Watch and joined hundreds of vehicles headed for Najaf. Flags and banners covered many of the buses, and men were chanting and cheering. We stood out clearly as foreigners, and people were friendly and welcoming, waving and giving us the peace sign. Along the roads, men and women, boys and girls offered water to the hot and thirsty travelers, but I only saw one other woman in the procession. With thousands of Iraqis we gathered on the edge of Najaf and waited until Sistani's entourage arrived. Two cars with tinted windows, full of guards and assistants, came before and after Sistani's car. A chain of men ran along side the vehicles and directed the men on the edge of the crowd to link hands to form a protective barrier.

> Before leaving for the vigil, I went on the roof just as the sun was rising over the horizon. The beauty touched my heart, and a sense of hope replaced my apprehension about what might be given as three of us left Baghdad.

As our cars followed the procession into Najaf, our driver told us that it could be dangerous for us as foreigners if we got close to the shrine where the standoff was happening. We agreed that our drivers would make the decision about how far our cars would go.

Figure 2: Caravan of Iraqis moving toward Najaf on August 26, 2004 for vigil called for by Grand Ayatollah Ali as-Sistani

About a mile and half from the Imam Ali Shrine, the police had closed the streets. They allowed Sistani to go in, but not the rest of the procession. Our hosts decided we should go back. Meanwhile, we heard distant gunshots. As our car turned around, the shooting got closer. We ducked, because people on the streets were ducking and running. We feared for our driver, and no one spoke as he picked up speed. Gradually the gunfire became more distant as we left.

Safely out of Najaf, we stopped with our hosts at a restaurant and debriefed. "At the vigil two weeks ago, the crowd was frustrated and discouraged because no progress had been made," Musa told us. "Today's action gave everyone a sense of hope." As we saw later, it did not resolve the basic conflicts between the followers of Sadr and the U.S. or those between the rival Shia sects, but it did prevent more slaughter and possible damage to the shrine.

I asked Musa, "What should CPT be doing in Iraq?" He said, "Teach Iraqis about nonviolence and peaceful resolution of conflicts. My high school students have never heard of any other way than violence and force. My two sons see mostly violence on TV and in computer games. We have a lot of work to do. Today's vigil demonstrated the power of nonviolent action in a volatile and seemingly irresolvable situation and gave Iraqis an example of nonviolent ways to act for change with strength."

The next morning we heard that Sistani had successfully negotiated an agreement of a five-point plan. The Mahdi Army and international forces agreed to a cease-fire and to leave the shrine area and city and started leaving later that day.

Meanwhile, our work continued to involve responding to institutional as well as street violence.

5

In the Heat of the Summer

THE FIRST BLAST CAME as Doug Pritchard, co-director of CPT, and I sat in the St. Joseph's Chaldean Church in Baghdad's Karrada district Sunday evening, August 1, 2004. It sounded close. I shuddered. There was a stirring around us, yet people stayed in their seats. When the second blast came twenty-five minutes later, just before the service was over, my prayer was for anyone hurt in the explosions, as well as for those who caused them.

Afterward, security guards hurried everyone out and blocked off the streets around the building. People told us that car bombs had exploded at the Armenian Catholic Church two blocks away and at the Syrian Catholic Church six blocks away, both in the direction of our apartment. We were shaken.

Since the fall of Saddam, there had been attacks on mosques and some violence against Christians who refused when conservative Muslims demanded they stop selling liquor or Western videotapes including women in immodest dress, but this was the first time churches had been targeted. As we walked back to our apartment, a middle-aged woman, standing at her gate, noticed that we were internationals and motioned to us to come over. We hesitated. Was she just being friendly? Was she trying to protect us? But when a younger woman, eyes full of fear and visibly shaking, came out of the house and urged us to come in, we followed.

With the electricity out, the woman lighted oil lamps in the darkened apartment. The daughter, who spoke English, wept as she told their story. "My father was killed recently because he sold liquor. I was too afraid to go to my church today. Now it's been bombed. I don't know if my friends there are dead or alive. Saddam was a killer. Now there are many Saddams."

"What are we going to do?" the daughter translated her mother's grief-stricken words. "There's no safety here now. All Christians will have to leave Iraq." Their world seemed to be crumbling around them. We had nothing to offer, but to listen and to care. The mother bravely held her emotions in, but when we gave each other the customary farewell kiss on each other's cheeks, she began to cry. The protective barriers of my heart also fell away and her pain as a wife and mother touched me on a deeper level. In the midst of violence and feelings of hopelessness, we embraced each other as sisters, letting the tears flow.

The next day, prominent Muslim leaders strongly denounced the bombings. Greg and I went to the Saint Peter Chaldean Church on the southern edge of Baghdad, one of the other churches bombed, and saw burnt cars and scattered debris and scorch marks on the grass. As with the other bombed sites, the damage was not to the main church building, but to the outer walls and courtyards, to nearby cars … and to people. "Six people died, and ten were injured," the head priest told us. "My people are afraid it could happen again, so I don't know how many will come for mass next Sunday." He pointed to those working around the grounds and said, "Both Muslim and Christian neighbors, however, helped with the dead and wounded and are helping us clean up." The greatest damage caused by the bombs, I thought, was in the hearts and minds of the people, for whom this instilled more fear and mistrust.

We sent out a news release stating that members of our team planned to attend worship services in area churches the following Sunday and that "We want to be among Christians who said with their actions that they will not give in to fear." The following Sunday evening, the street close to the St. Joseph's Church was closed off to cars, but Doug and I were able to walk in. Only about half the people there last Sunday came today. The leaders asked people on the sides and back to move into the middle section and toward the front, to be farther away from the street. We were thankful there were no interruptions this time.

In the coming weeks, members of other churches spoke about how the bombings had affected them. "Attendance is down because of the heightened fear," a leader in the Evangelical Presbyterian Church told us. He said, however, as did several other church leaders, that Christians weren't leaving the country faster since the bombings, or in any greater proportion than Muslims. It had been a continuous exodus for Christians since 1991. His congregation had not been attacked, but some members received threats or attacks because they were working for Americans or for the government, not because they were Christians. An international church leader working in Iraq agreed with that assessment.

We also spoke to Muslim Iraqis whose mosques had been bombed. They voiced similar expressions of fear. I felt sadness and love for all Iraqis whose daily functioning was affected by trauma from the violence. On top of the difficulties of just getting around the city to carry out their normal activities, the fear, depression, and hopelessness of many had a paralyzing affect on their ability to care for their families, find solutions to their problems, or plan for the future.

Another explosion sounded about 11:30 on an early September morning. From the roof we saw people running down Karrada Street. David and I went to see if we could give support to people involved. At the scene we saw the torn up median strip in the street. Iraqi police were investigating, examining the damage, taking pictures, writing notes, and questioning witnesses. Two shops and a taxi had been damaged and there was blood on the street near the car. The bodies of the two that died in the explosion had been taken away before we arrived.

Soon U.S. soldiers came and repeated the investigation, taking over for the Iraqi police. Then the lieutenant in charge saw David take some pictures. He asked who we were and demanded that David delete the pictures. David refused and told him he didn't have the right to make him do that. We gave him a paper introducing our team and explaining our work. He responded defensively, asking, "What do you *mean* you are reporting abuses in the prison system? Maybe you are part of a group that is trying to obstruct our work."

"I think you would also report abuses if you saw them, and would want such practices reported and stopped," I responded. "In fact, some U.S. military officers have asked us to give them information about any abuse we find." The lieutenant was angry and said he would take the camera if David didn't delete the pictures, but David politely refused. The officer said they might take us to the base for questioning. He asked two American soldiers to watch us while he walked away to call his commander.

While the lieutenant was gone, we chatted with those guarding us and other soldiers who seemed sympathetic but cautious. The lieutenant came back. He had talked to his commander, who said he knew about CPT and that we "were OK." After warning us to stay away from any bombed site in the future, he let us go. As we left, the two soldiers who had guarded us said, "God bless you," and, "Be safe." We responded in kind, "Be safe."

Women in black *abayas* (black robes that fit on their heads without covering their face, and flow around them to their ankles) and men in long robes stood for hours in the broiling late summer sun. In the three lines separated by coiled razor wire they waited to visit family members in the Abu Ghraib Prison. Many of them weren't certain that their family member was inside. One man came from Basra, an eight-hour drive away. A seven-months-pregnant woman stood in the women's line, waiting to see her husband.

"It's better *now*," a man in line told us. "Before the abuse was exposed four months ago, you could only visit every few months. Now, it's every ten days. But all conversations are still just fifteen minutes, through a tiny hole in double glass." Another man said that one reason for the long lines was that people didn't know the identification number of the prisoner they hoped to visit. An official announced that there was a list of prisoners online. The Iraqi man laughed and said, "Hardly any of these people have Internet." The lists were supposed to be at every police station and GIC, but most Iraqis didn't know that.

In our September 2004 CPT Report on Iraqi Detainees, our team was glad to note some improvements in the living conditions in the U.S. detention system. Families had access to more information about detainees' whereabouts through the IAC (now staffed by Iraqis), GIC's, and the Iraqi Ministry of Human Rights (MHR), though they still found it difficult to visit or get that information. Released detainees continued to claim physical and emotional abuse in a variety of MNF-I facilities. Elderly and infirm detainees suffered deteriorating health conditions while in custody. Detainees still reported not receiving receipts for confiscated items, making it hard to retrieve their property or make compensation claims after released. Families continued to suffer economic and emotional hardships from prolonged detentions for which no reasons were given.

By August 2004, the MNF-I established a Combined Review and Release Board made up of six Iraqis and three Americans, to review the cases of all MNF-I held detainees. Their goal was to review each detainee's case every three months, and then either release them, refer them to the Iraqi criminal court system, or keep them in the U.S. system. Major General

Part One: Summer 2004—Spring 2006

Geoffrey Miller, MNF-I's Deputy Commanding General for Detainee Operations, had final authority to approve the board's recommendations. U.S. soldiers still made arrests, but the MHR didn't have access to U.S. military bases to monitor what happened with detainees.

One day, in our neighborhood market, two Iraqi men heard us speaking English and initiated a conversation. They worked at BIAP (Baghdad International Airport Prison) as police inspectors whose jobs were to help decide what to do with the men who came in. "But," one said, "We're just figureheads. American advisors really make the decisions."

Following-up that summer on the seventy-two detainees in our original report, we reported that of the original seventy-two cases, forty-eight had been released, one was still detained, one died while in U.S custody, and the whereabouts of eleven were still unknown—although they had been detained by coalition forces. We were not able to contact ten.

Many of the released detainees we interviewed that summer gave us their testimonies, though some were afraid of reprisals from the MNF-I. Others agreed to give their testimony only if CPT did not publish it, or if their names were withheld.

One who told his story was Jabber, a man who had been detained in Abu Ghraib and Bucca Prison from December 2003 to November 2004. He said he was treated fairly well but never found out what the charges were against him. "I'm broken financially now, because of my detention. I had to sell my car and all my furniture in order to feed my family."

Another was Ibrahim, who had just been released from Abu Ghraib in September after a year and a half in detention. While capturing him in May 2004, a U.S. soldier struck him on the head with the butt of an automatic weapon. As a result, he was partially paralyzed. He had since regained some of the lost motor function, but still needed a crutch to walk and wore a brace on one arm. He said he did not receive any medical treatment or physical therapy except during the first two weeks of his capture. The rest of the time his fellow detainees cared for him. He wanted us to pass his story on to Amnesty International. He said he was forced to sign a paper saying he would be liable for arrest if he talked to human rights organizations or media, but decided to speak out. "I will die before I am taken prisoner again," he said.

In the Heat of the Summer

Kidnappings of international aid workers, that fall, hit us hard. We were thankful when Simona Torretta and Simona Pare, Italian aid workers we had known over the past two years, and two Iraqi aid workers from Italian humanitarian aid organization, A Bridge to Baghdad, taken on September 7, were released unharmed within two weeks. We felt another wave of grief on October 19 when Margaret Hassan, director of the international NGO, CARE, was kidnapped. She had been a friend of our team since before the invasion, and had hosted meetings with many of our delegations. We realized that if CARE pulled out from Iraq, CPT could be the only international NGO left in Baghdad.

Sattar, our interpreter, told us, "It's only a matter of time before something like this strikes CPT." He said, however, that he was willing to continue working with us. Our driver and his wife admitted nervousness about working with internationals, yet chose to continue. We felt conflicted about this. On one hand, it seemed that in such crisis times it was even more important for nonviolent international presence. But we were ready to leave if our Iraqi friends and partners told us that our presence put them in too much danger, or that we could no longer do significant work here. There were no easy answers. After consultation and careful discernment, our consensus was to stay and continue our current projects.

Team members took additional precautions, such as varying travel routes and pick-up locations. Out on the street, women on the team had already started wearing a *hijab* (a scarf fully covering our hair) and a *juba'a* (a long, lightweight coat over our long skirts). The men often wore *keffiyehs*, but had a harder time blending in as Iraqi. Many people in our neighborhood knew who we were in our Iraqi clothing, and gave us knowing smiles. We still greeted and chatted with the people we knew, and acquaintances such as those who sold us food and other goods.

We felt stricken when videos released on November 17 showed Margaret Hassan's execution. The team gathered privately to grieve and honor her life. One teammate recalled, "She worked tirelessly for the people of Iraq, living a life with the people, not a life spent behind concrete barricades and razor wire." Another said, "Margaret and her staff put their energies into improving the future for the people of Iraq, continuing to work even after attackers bombed their warehouse last year. She modeled an extravagant way of living for others."

In our work, we continued to have contact with and hear the differing points of view of U.S. soldiers about their presence in Iraq. One day that fall, two Humvees with two squads on foot patrol were working their way down the street by our apartment, doing random street checks. Two of my teammates went out to talk with them. When one soldier heard that we were working for nonviolent alternatives, he said, "That sounds better than what we're doing." My teammate invited him to join CPT. He answered, "I'd like to. I tried to not come to Iraq, but they made me. I'm not a pacifist, but what I've seen here—this isn't what we're about."

U.S. military units continued to carry out incursions into villages and towns, raiding and ransacking homes, and brutally detaining Iraqis, while Iraqi armed resistance fighters continued their attacks around the country. That fall and winter, we saw more Iraqi Police or Iraqi National Guard (ING). It was common now to see them riding in the back of police trucks pointing out their automatic rifles in a similar posture as U.S. military, but with black facemasks.

An American soldier working in the Green Zone told us that when he was riding in convoys, U.S. soldiers expected everyone else to just move out of their way. "Some did and some didn't," he said. "They [Iraqis] just have to understand where we are coming from."

While accompanying family members to visit a prisoner in Camp Bucca, team members chatted with several U.S. Soldiers at the prison gates. One young soldier from Texas said, "Can you tell me why we are here? It seems that we're just making an awful lot of people mad at us."

When visiting a U.S. military base in early 2005, we had time to chat with some of the soldiers. One said that the hardest thing for him was "being away from my three-month-old child." For another it was "not having personal space." One mentioned the problem of soldiers suffering trauma and then going home and taking it out on their families in domestic violence. I saw soldiers *also* as victims of this war and occupation. I saw them and their families, along with the Iraqis, as bearing the brunt of this war for which U.S. leaders should be held accountable. Most soldiers came here wanting to do something good, but were caught in a violent institution, doing horrific things they didn't really want to do, often over-reacting out of fear and frustration.

Iraqis shared with us various concerns about the presence of U.S. soldiers. "I feel sorry for the American soldiers," a neighbor said. "They liberated us and put their lives on the line—not Bush. We were desperate, and the invasion liberated us. But Bush is not honest when he says the U.S. is bringing democracy and helping us. The American and British governments are evil. I agree with the terrorists on this, but I disagree with their killing innocent people."

At first, twelve-year-old Lara was afraid of me as an American. She told me she had seen soldiers driving their tanks along the street near her home and had heard about soldiers arresting and beating her uncles. "American soldiers kill people," she said. "But Iraqi people don't want you just to say, 'I'm sorry.' They want you to feel our hurt."

In her office, an Iraqi human rights worker said, "The real issue is not about their [the soliders] leaving, but *how* they are operating, and the chaos it causes. Some of the problems come from the legacy of Saddam's regime and his releasing 30,000 criminals from prison before the invasion." Then she added, "Both American and Iraqi leaders want to divide the people in order to get more power—a very dangerous game."

The children at the orphanage gave me an excited welcome. Two-year-old Nura picked up a plastic bracelet with her toes and made a game of rolling away and then back towards me over and over. She could now sit up, stand, and do a kind of shuffle walk on her twisted feet. I missed teasing fifteen-year-old Allah, one of the few children here who could talk. I learned that an American soldier who visited the orphanage arranged to take Allah to the U.S. for therapy.

Then three U.S. hummers arrived and kept guard in front of the orphanage while twelve soldiers came in. They took pictures of each other playing with the children, saying they would put them in their military newsletter. They delivered several boxes of supplies. When one of the female soldiers came in, more heavily armed than the others, a sister told her it would be better for her to stay out in the entry way and not in the play room. Others kept their guns out of view. One of the men asked the Iraqi volunteers how things were going for them. When one volunteer said politely, "not very good—we need electricity, water, and security," the soldier winced.

We knew tensions were building up again between coalition forces and the people of Fallujah.

6

Fallujah Explodes

BY LATE OCTOBER 2004, international and Iraqi forces were preparing for a massive assault on Fallujah, saying that the residents of Fallujah were protecting a group of international terrorists, including Abu Musab al-Zarqawi, head of Al-Qaeda in Iraq. A UN representative told us on November 4 that earlier that week several civic and religious leaders from Fallujah came asking the UN to mediate. The *Washington Post* reported that in October, "local insurgent leaders voted overwhelmingly to accept broad conditions set by the Iraqi government, including demands that they eject foreign fighters from the city, turn over all heavy weapons, dismantle illegal checkpoints and allow the Iraqi National Guard to enter. In turn, the insurgents set their own conditions, which included a halt to U.S. attacks on Fallujah and acknowledgment by the military that women and children have been among the casualties in U.S. strikes."[1] The U.S. command rejected this.

A Sunni coalition also proposed a plan to establish the rule of law in those areas through peaceful means on condition that U.S. forces remain confined to bases during the month before the election. This was a shift from their previous insistence that no election would be legitimate until Western troops left Iraq. Larry Diamond, a former official in the U.S. led occupation authority, involved in establishing the transitional government, said, "This initiative is very significant. . . . If you look at their demands, they're not impossible. . . . If there's a chance that this could be the

---

1. Jackie Spinner and Karl Vick, "Fallujah Talks, and Battle Planning, Continues," *Washington Post,* October 28, 2004.

Fallujah Explodes

beginning of political transformation that could change the situation on the ground, I think we've got to take it."[2]

What could our team do in this volatile situation? We couldn't physically stop an attack, but we could share with people outside Iraq the proposals Iraqi human rights workers made for confronting the problems in Fallujah without excessive force and destruction. Our November 6 release urged people to contact a list of U.S. officials and "ask them to respect the desires of civic, religious, and humanitarian leaders of Fallujah, prevent the attack, and work with the UN to create a non-military solution to the city's security concerns. Options included UN peacekeeping troops going in, an arms buyout, or direct negotiations between city leaders and representatives of the Iraqi provisional government and officials of the MNF-I with UN mediation assistance."

Even after warning residents of Fallujah to leave before the attack, officials estimated that up to 100,000 civilians might remain in the city and suffer high casualties. UN Secretary General Kofi Annan sent an appeal to Iraqi Prime Minister Iyad Allawi and U.S. President George Bush. He wrote, "The threat or actual use of force not only risks deepening the sense of alienation of certain communities, but would also reinforce perceptions among the Iraqi population of a continued military occupation."[3] Unfortunately U.S. Military and Iraqi officials rejected these alternative proposals, so the invasion proceeded, resulting in the deaths of Iraqi civilians, resistance fighters, and international soldiers, as well as a devastated city.

Once attacks on Fallujah started, Allawi established curfews, closures and military law. Iraqi TV reports showed dead women and children in the streets. When civilians tried to flee the city, they were turned back. One of the first things U.S. troops did was to occupy the Fallujah General Hospital. They claimed that the casualty figures it gave out were inflated, and so considered the hospital a "center of propaganda" against the coalition forces.

A member of the hospital staff later told us, "U.S. soldiers forced sick or injured patients to lie on the floor handcuffed. Curfew began at 10:00 each night. The hospital had to close at 8:00 p.m. in order for the employees and doctors to reach their homes. My colleague was traveling home from the hospital one evening when U.S. or ING forces shot eighteen bullets into his car because it was close to the curfew limit. Doctors are sometimes harassed and searched by soldiers on their way home. Air

2. Karl Vick, "Battle Near, Sunnis Make Offer," *Washington Post*, November 6, 2004.
3. Nicholas Kralev, "Annan Protests Fallujah Strategy," *Washington Times*, November 5, 2004.

strikes on another medical clinic killed twenty doctors and dozens of civilians." This countered Geneva Conventions agreements that stipulated that civilian hospitals should not be the object of attack and that medical personnel caring for or transporting wounded and sick civilians should be respected and protected.[4]

We heard reports that white phosphorus, sound wave weapons, a napalm-type material, and other horrific antipersonnel weapons were used in these attacks. On November 8, U.S. forces used eight 2,000-pound bombs. A November 10 *Washington Post* article reported that, "some artillery guns fired white phosphorus rounds that create a screen of fire that cannot be extinguished with water. Insurgents reported being attacked with a substance that melted their skin, a reaction consistent with white phosphorus burns." They were being burned, blinded, or killed. The article also quoted the head of the U.S. First Infantry Division's Task Force 2 saying, "Usually we keep the gloves on. For this operation we took the gloves off."[5]

During the assault, American forces announced they had killed 1,200 "insurgents." Doctors reported finding 700 bodies, including many women and children, but expected that most of the dead were buried immediately by family, according to Islamic practice, and not taken to the hospital or recorded officially. Other bodies may have been in the homes that collapsed in the bombing or that the U.S. military bulldozed. A few months after the attack, 5,000 Fallujans were still missing (out of a prior population of 400,000), so were considered either killed or detained. Some local sources estimated 100,000 were killed. Through monitoring the detainees' SN-numbers in the American system, the Iraqi Red Crescent Society estimated that 6,000 men from Fallujah were detained.

Two weeks into the siege, fighting spilled over into Baghdad and other parts of the country, including around Mosul. Our team heard a radio report of a raid on Abu Hanifa Shrine (the largest Sunni shrine in Baghdad) by U.S. and ING troops, killing four people. A friend of the team was inside the shrine when U.S. and Iraqi troops threw in percussion bombs. Two weeks later they also raided the shrine school. The head sheikh of the shrine asked us to find the captain of the unit responsible at the nearby U.S. military base, and arrange for them to dialogue. When we located the captain, he said that after the first raid, he had met with the head sheikh of the mosque to resolve the tensions before they escalated further. Without

---

4. Fourth Geneva Conventions, Part II, Articles 18 and 20.

5. Jackie Spinner, et al., "Battle into Heart of Fallujah," *Washington Post*, November 10, 2004.

his knowing it, however, U.S. Special Forces went ahead and raided the shrine's school that evening. That led to more violent confrontations between American soldiers and people of the area.

In mid-January, a man in Baghdad told us he had been detained in Fallujah for two weeks after five days of the November bombardment. "Soldiers came into my home, handcuffed me and put a plastic feed sack over my head, and took me away." First he was taken to a big house made into a holding center, which the men called "the chicken house," then to a farm, and then to a site called "Tarik," still inside Fallujah. "Because I spoke English, I was treated better than the others and released earlier. All the detainees were treated harshly, many beaten and given little food, as though they were enemies or resistance fighters. A man there with broken ribs told me a soldier hit and kicked him with a boot."

Our team visited a family who lost four members during the November 2004 assault. One of the young women had watched while U.S. soldiers shot her father and two sisters in their home. With tears streaming down her face, she recalled her father reassuring her during the buildup to the attack, as U.S. forces were coming into the city, saying, "Don't worry, we are a family—they won't hurt us." We left this family feeling haunted by the tragedy of it all. *How much pain can these people bear?*

Thousands of persons were now uprooted and displaced because of the attacks. With members of Women's Will we visited a large building in Baghdad where fourteen extended families from Fallujah (about ninety people) lived. As we sat with thirty men and women on the floor of a large room, they spoke about U.S. forces demolishing their homes in early January.

One said, "To get back into Fallujah now, we have to show our I.D. and a badge with fingerprints and take an iris scan. We can go into our sector of the city but nowhere else, or we might be detained. At night it's dangerous to light even a candle. One might be shot or attacked. To get food subsidies, we have to stand in long lines. Each family is supposed to get 150,000 Iraqi Dinars (about $120) to rebuild, but we haven't heard of anyone actually receiving it."

Most families who fled Fallujah were still living in tents on the outskirts of the city while temperatures dipped to just above freezing at night. American forces prevented them from returning until February. In a tent camp we visited, families crowded together in classrooms of a school building and strung up blankets to provide a measure of privacy. Two babies were born there. Meanwhile, students from the school studied in tents set up outside in the gravel playground.

PART ONE: Summer 2004—Spring 2006

"We have nothing here. How can we take care of our families?" desperately asked one exhausted-looking woman. All the displaced people had tragic stories to tell—their homes destroyed, their family members injured, missing, or dead. Many wept as they spoke.

Twelve-year-old Dunya and her family were among the 1700 families from Fallujah camped inside or around the Baghdad University Mosque. She asked us, "If the Americans are so strong, why didn't they find Al Zarqawi? Why did they destroy my books and games? What did we do wrong?"

This group of internally displaced people (IDPs) said they would remain in their camp until five demands were met: 1. The U.S. apologizes for the indiscriminate bombing. 2. The U.S. gives restitution of $5-10 billion to the people of Fallujah. 3. The people can rebuild their own city (no foreign contractors). 4. Iraqi militias from other areas leave. 5. International organizations and media are allowed to come into Fallujah and report freely. Within a month they were forced to leave their encampment without these demands met. Some returned to Fallujah or stayed in Baghdad, but many were moved to larger displacement camps.

Iraqis told us of other reasons for the U.S. attacks. Where resistance fighters were "successful," as in Fallujah and Sadr City, they maintained "self-governed" or "liberated" anti-occupation areas operating outside the control of American forces or the Iraqi government. They had their own public services, security structures, and power bases made up of local tribal and clerical leaders. Civil management councils of these leaders managed to reduce crime and violence in their areas. U.S. led sieges of Fallujah and other cities were carried out to prevent the spread of such self-governed and anti-American areas, which became more dangerous, "no-go" places for U.S. forces. Such sieges did not restore order, but produced chaos and violence.

Many Iraqis believed that the disaster in Fallujah could have been averted. There had been some precedents in the past year where alternative interventions de-escalated the situation. When resistance to the U.S. occupation reached crisis proportions in Sadr City in April 2004 and erupted into violence, the Iraqi government's offered money for guns and helped to calm tensions. After U.S. forces attacked Fallujah in April 2004, the situation de-escalated when a compromise was reached and a former Iraqi general took responsibility for security in the city. The previous August, Ayatollah as-Sistani's nonviolent intervention in the Najaf impasse enabled the militia groups to withdraw without losing face and the U.S. military to cease their tactics honorably. We knew there would not be real security in Iraq without rebuilding the society, dealing with the huge problems the invasion aggravated, and finding ways for local peoples to have more control over their communities.

In late February 2005 a Sunni Muslim leader told us, "U.S. forces are attacking Ramadi in what they call, 'Operation Euphrates.' U.S. forces have shot many people in the streets as well as those who go to assist them."

I wrote to friends and family:

> I need to share my outrage! I just heard from leaders here and read an article saying that U.S. forces have surrounded the city of Ramadi, about seventy miles west of Baghdad, and are starting to attack it the way they attacked Fallujah last November! They say they are doing this to protect the population from the resistance, which has taken over the city. This is so wrong! We do not protect the 450,000 people of Ramadi (or U.S. soldiers) by bombing their city. Once more, people's lives are hanging on the edge.

U.S. military leaders said they were concerned about the deaths that could be caused by civil war, yet went on to ravage more cities, including Samarra, Qaim, Haditha, Haqlaniya, Hit and Tal Afar, resulting in deaths, injuries, destruction, thousands displaced—and increased rage. We saw, on TV, scenes of U.S. attacks on Samarra. I shuddered for the people there.

When reporting these civilian deaths, officials often used the phrase "collateral damage." I came to see that there is no such thing as collateral damage. All such deaths are murder—the killing of innocent people who feel powerless in these battles created by the powerful.

There was a blackout of news about Ramadi, but in June 2005, I heard that the city was still sealed off, with imposed curfews, and cut off from water, electricity, and other services. U.S. and Iraqi forces told the people they would not get services restored unless they "hand over the terrorists." Troops killed civilians through air strikes and snipers.

Three months later, in September, local human rights workers took us to a camp near Karbela, of families displaced from the northwestern Iraqi city of Tal Afar during the siege. These families told us that until the 2003 invasion, Sunni and Shia had lived together peacefully in Tal Afar. After 2003, violence increased from sectarian strife and from foreign fighters coming over the border from Syria and sometimes killing or forcing residents from their homes. They said that during the current siege,

Part One: Summer 2004—Spring 2006

these armed groups, as well as U.S. and ING troops, were violent toward civilians, causing about 100,000 to flee the city. Many Tal Afar residents wanted U.S. forces to leave; others felt they provided protection. The only hospital in the city had been taken over by the ING, and many doctors didn't come to work, afraid that groups opposing ING presence in the city might attack. The IDPs said that the siege did not protect the common civilians and that the Iraqi Army secured the main road only for U.S. forces.

In most of these cities, there had been ongoing battles of resistance to U.S. troops and bases in their cities. American forces saw themselves as responding defensively, to protect their troops and keep roadways open for safe passage of their convoys. Residents saw themselves as liberation fighters, driving out the occupiers in order to establish "liberated zones," and responding defensively to violent house raids or shooting of their people on the streets.

I believe that wiping out whole cities to deal with a small percentage of residents involved in acts of terror is not justified and will not reduce terrorism. Just ask the people of Fallujah if they feel protected when their homes are demolished, their lives uprooted, and their friends and family members killed. Just ask the many Iraqis who feel that in order to "save" Iraq, the U.S. is destroying it.

> From the roof this morning, I watch the sun come up over the buildings. There is a gentle breeze. A dragonfly perches on the wire near me. A flock of birds makes curves and circles in the sky. It seems like they are doing a dance, having fun, soaring free! It lifts me out of the heaviness I had been feeling. In the midst of the pain and violence—beauty is not lost.
>
> I still see acts of kindness—neighbors helping each other in times of crises, assisting others clean up from an explosion or rebuilding a crumbled wall. I think of Machmoud, who in spite of depression and poverty, reaches out to others in need and shares the little he has. I think of Lamia, who tirelessly goes with families to military bases and offices to advocate for their detained loved ones. I think how hungry people are for tenderness and gentleness in the midst of violence. Love and caring are victorious over suffering and fear.

7

Karbela

Driving to Karbela, a mostly Shia city southwest of Baghdad, was an adventure in itself. In January 2005, Cliff, Maxine, Sheila Provencher, Allan Slater, and I were going there for a nonviolence workshop. At one point, our car turned off the road, down dirt paths to bypass a dangerous intersection. Later, six lanes converged into one to go over a bridge being repaired. I counted eighteen checkpoints. Each time, guards waved us through, not seeming to recognize us as foreigners in our Iraqi attire. With all the obstacles and taking the long way—not the main roads in this area called the "triangle of death"—the trip took four hours instead of two.

Because of increased security leading up to the election, we had to report to a security officer and register as visitors at the edge of the city. At first, our host told us not to speak English outside the car, so we wouldn't be seen as foreigners. The following day we relaxed those precautions in this smaller city, which felt safer and freer than Baghdad.

The five-day interactive nonviolence workshop in Karbela organized jointly by CPT and the Iraqi Human Rights Watch of Karbela (IHRW), for about 26 Shia Muslim men and women, began on January 22. Participants shared in the facilitation and teaching. Each day, they took on tasks, such as convening sessions, videotaping, and creating media releases.

"After the war started in 2003, we went into the streets of Karbela to help the injured," Wa'il, a stocky businessman, began when it was time to share about ways they've worked for peace. Assad followed with his story. "One day in September 2003, several of us interrupted fighting between as-Sadr's and as-Sistani's followers on the city streets. We helped the groups make an agreement not to fight." Later Assad showed us a copy of the document signed by eleven community leaders and sheikhs. Another man said he organized public vigils using large pictures of men who were in prison and asking that they not be mistreated, but given a fair trial.

Then Musa, who we had been with at the Najaf peace vigil last August, spoke. "One day a crowd gathered in the street. Several angry people were trying to incite violence against some nearby U.S. soldiers. I yelled out several times, 'Violence will only cause more problems,' and the crowd calmed down."

Role-plays stimulated the group to explore the methods and power of nonviolence. Participants set the stage of conflicts on the streets that could erupt into violence, such as a man in his car cutting in front of others in a long gas station line. The group tried different outcomes, discussing how and why different responses worked. Together we tried to answer questions such as, how could we respond in ways that would transform a potentially violent situation? How can our actions work to deal with the deeper issues of injustice underlying the conflicts?

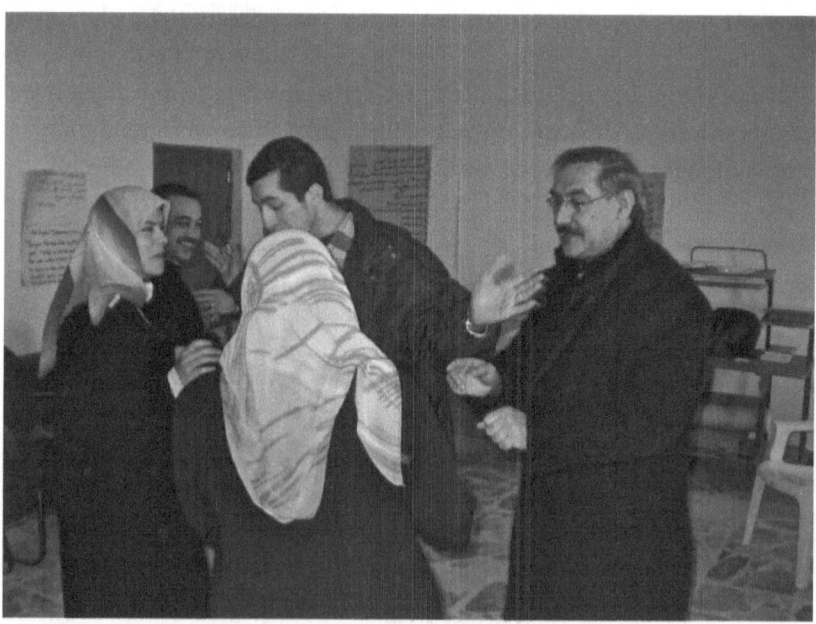

Figure 3: MPT nonviolence training participants role play
a street conflict, Karbela, January 25, 2005

Karbela

In small groups, the men and women discussed the roots of nonviolence in their faith tradition. Several pointed out that Islam has a firm tradition of nonviolence in the teachings of the Qu'ran, the teachings and life of the Prophet Mohammed, and in many historical examples.[1]

On the last day, after a simulated organizing for a public action, sessions on human rights documentation and working with the media, we focused on dealing with trauma while working for peace. Amira, the facilitator for the day, held up a red paper heart and invited others to tell about a time they had experienced violence. She asked them to tear off a piece of the "heart" to symbolize how their spirit was wounded. "Our hearts aren't big enough to carry all the pain we each have experienced," she said. "Every Iraqi could tell stories without end." After a moment of uneasy silence, the floodgates opened. Hameed rose and grabbed the heart. "In the Iraq/Iran War, people died around me. I slept next to my friend's body and then carried it away the next morning. I helped bury bodies after the 1991 resistance to Saddam."

Assad was next. "In 2003, a child was there when another child died violently. He was unable to speak for a year." He tore a piece from the heart and sat down. Abdul, a medic, stood and spoke of his horror when dozens of bodies were brought to the hospital after explosions a month ago. "I walked around for days as a dead man myself!"

Finally Wa'il stood up. "I was fighting in the north in 1975, but then went on leave. When I returned, my entire unit was new. My former companions were dead. I couldn't manage the pain and wanted to kill myself." By this time most of us had tears streaming down our faces.

Then Amira asked the group, "How do we handle this trauma?" Immediately, Abdul responded, "First we cry, with a loud voice, or without a voice. Women and men, we cry." Others shared what had worked for them.

In the later evaluation of the day, Hameed shared, "I walked in here an angry person. I will leave here a different person. I don't want to turn my pain into revenge, but use it to work for reconciliation and healing."

The group considered calling themselves the Iraqi Peace Team to include people from all faiths. But one suggested, "You are part of the Christian Peacemaker Teams. We are Muslim, so I think we should call our group the Muslim Peacemaker Team." Another said, "We believe the

---

1. Books that highlight the tradition of nonviolence in Islam include: Abu-Nimer, *Nonviolence and Peace Building in Islam*; Easwaran, *Nonviolent Soldier of Islam*; Gish, *Muslim, Christian, Jew*; Khan, *The True Jihad*; and Shirazi, *War, Peace and Nonviolence*.

real spirit of Islam is mercy and forgiveness, and we want to work out of our faith."

After choosing a coordinating committee of six, including one of the women, the group began to do the work of envisioning. Long-range goals included spreading Muslim Peacemaker Teams (MPT) throughout Iraq. The group came alive, generating ideas of possible activities. "We should do peace education with children," one said. "Let's form teams to intervene when there's violence on the streets," mentioned another. "We should teach peacemaking to the police and military." "Let's facilitate more nonviolence trainings at universities." "We could work to reduce weapons in our communities." "Why don't we go to the city of Fallujah, help rebuild homes destroyed in the November attack, and build relationships with the people there?" suggested another. For a moment it was silent. Then reactions to that suggestion came fast.

"But we are Shia and they are Sunni. What if they don't accept us coming into their community?" one questioned. "What if they kill us?" Others vented their fears—realistic in this situation. Then Wa'il challenged the group, "But this is what peacemaking is all about, being willing to take risks to break down these barriers and reduce the tensions in our own society."

Later in Baghdad, a Chaldean priest expressed interest in forming an Iraqi Peacemaker Team. He wanted to meet with MPT's leaders to talk about including Iraqi Christians in the organization. MPT became a partner and advisor to our team.

The training was over, but members of MPT who signed up as election observers urged us to stay and work with them on Election Day, only four days away. At the Karbela office of the "Independent Election Committee of Iraq," we accepted I.D. badges as independent observers and planned to work with the IHRW.

All Iraqis would be voting for local Governorate Councils and a 275-member Iraqi National Assembly, which would draft Iraq's permanent constitution and choose the President and Prime Minister. Kurdish Iraqis in the north would also vote for the Kurdish National Assembly for the three governorates of the Kurdish region of Iraq or "Iraqi Kurdistan."

Violence around the country had increased during the two months before the election. On December 19, three members of a Baghdad human rights organization working on the elections had been shot. On January

3, a car bomb exploded at a checkpoint outside the office of Iyad Allawi, Prime Minister of the Interim Government.

We heard mixed opinions about the elections. "I fear they will just lead to another puppet government," a university professor told us while we were still in Baghdad. A member of a woman's center expressed frustration at the list of parties on the ballot. "I want to talk about *policies*, not parties. I'm a poor woman. What are their policies for poor women? Where is *my* list of candidates?" Another friend of the team was more positive. "I've never had the right to vote. Of course I will vote, even if it's dangerous."

Many Sunni leaders had urged the government to delay the elections because threats against candidates or anyone voting kept it from being free and fair. Some Sunni leaders called for a boycott. In mid-January, the general secretary of the Muslim Scholars' Board supported the election in general, but warned that it would "allow the U.S. to circumvent the UN Security resolution calling on the U.S. to withdraw its military from Iraq in 2005, by having the new Iraqi parliament request an extension." The U.S. later turned down the Muslim Scholars' Board's offer to reverse the boycott in exchange for a timeline of U.S. military withdrawal from Iraq.

Now it was Election Day, January 30, 2005. Ninety-year-old Keleje smiled widely as she walked out of the voting center in a school in Karbela, where she voted for the first time in her life. Ahmed, a man near another polling station, expressed his excitement as he said, "We voted democratically. We're happy and hope this will give us a better life." There was a holiday atmosphere. Young and old played on the streets—empty except for police and other official vehicles, bicycles, and pedestrians. Inside the voting rooms of the three polling centers we visited, we saw the stacks of ballots, private voting booths, instructive posters on the walls, and watched voters placing their ballots in two large plastic boxes. Things seemed to be going smoothly. None of the Karbela polling centers reported any violence or disruption.

But not all the responses we heard were positive and hopeful. A man who had been in prison under Saddam Hussein for fifteen years told us he refused to vote. "Nothing will be changed by it anyway," he said." Another man said, "The rosy picture Bush painted of the future for Iraq has turned bloody. And, we don't even know the candidates." Many questioned the legitimacy of this election, or that it would unify the people. Though the elections seemed to go well, we knew they might not bring much change in the quality of life for the common people.

PART ONE: Summer 2004—Spring 2006

Figure 4: Men voting in Karbela on January 30, 2005

The next day, the news reported thirteen suicide bombings at polling centers in Baghdad and forty-four Iraqis deaths from seventy-five Election Day attacks around the country. At least 60-85 percent of the nation's population voted. In places like Baghdad, it was higher (65 percent of registered voters), and much lower in more volatile areas where the boycott was strong (2 percent of eligible voters in Anbar Governorate). In Mosul there were problems with insufficient ballots and polling places that did not open. Eight hundred election workers for that area had resigned under threat.

The Shia-backed United Iraqi Alliance won the most votes, but fell short of an outright majority. Many Iraqis said it was good that one party didn't have a strong majority, because they would have to negotiate and cooperate with other ethnic groups to form the government. Kurdish leader Jalal Talabani was chosen President, and Shia leader Ibrahim al-Jaffari the Prime Minister. A year later, however, in April 2006, amid mounting criticism of his leadership, parliamentarians replaced al-Jaffari with Nouri al-Maliki, also of the Dawa Party.

After the election, al-Jaffari unilaterally extended the invitation to U.S. forces to stay in Iraq without going through the proper channels of the National Assembly. In June, local human rights workers told us that eighty-two National Assembly members signed a protest letter calling for the withdrawal of American and other foreign troops, but Jaffari and the U.S. officials ignored this.

"Our organization, the Iraqi Human Rights Watch in Karbela, has been documenting human rights violations of the former regime," Jamal, a stocky lawyer, told a representative of the U.S. State Department and the U.S. Army Director of Civil Affairs. "We were the first organization to find mass graves after the war." He and two other workers from IHRW (also members of MPT) and four from our team were visiting the Lima U.S. military base outside Karbela, February 1, to learn about the current process for compensation claims. "We have also been documenting U.S. violations against Iraqi people and their property during and after the war," he continued. "We've been helping Iraqis apply for compensation for these losses. Sorry to say, the response has been like a drop in the bucket."

In turn, the State Department representative asked the human rights workers whether they had filed claims for compensation with Sadr's Mahdi Army for the damages *it* caused in Najaf during the fighting between it and U.S. forces last August. The question contained a logical argument that we had not previously considered.

The Iraqi men were quick to respond. "The Mahdi Army *were* the local people, had smaller weapons, and did little damage to the homes of the people around the Shrine in Najaf. The U.S. military were the invading forces, had planes and bigger weaponry, and demolished a lot of homes and infrastructure in the process." The State Department worker challenged that, saying, "But what about the deaths the Mahdi Army caused?" The Iraqi men said those were tragic, but reasserted their belief that the violence on both sides was not equal and that the U.S. forces were more responsible for beginning and continuing the battle that caused the damage.

"So you support the Mahdi Army?" the State Department official retorted. The shoulders of the Iraqi men tightened, but they remained calm. They didn't condone the violence on either side. "We want to respond to all injustice and violence in our society nonviolently," Jamal added firmly. I could see the strain in his face. The tension was not resolved when we left, but I was amazed by the ability of these human rights workers to maintain a respectful manner and not be intimidated by these officials, who to the Iraqis, held the power.

PART ONE: Summer 2004—Spring 2006

Another day, we stood with members of MPT at a site in Karbela where in 1991, fifty men, women, and children had been buried in a mass grave after being shot by Saddam's forces. The government had dropped leaflets from a helicopter telling people to leave the city or they would be killed. They showed us two other sites where 120–130 people were killed when fleeing the city. "Now terrorists are doing the same thing," one said.

"Tomorrow, we'll take you to a mass gravesite caused by the U.S.," the men told us, "where five Bedouin extended families living in tents and killed by U.S. forces during the 2003 invasion, were buried. The families were meeting to decide how to escape the attacks, when U.S. forces bombed them. One man survived but was in shock for several months. He took American officials to the gravesite, but felt that they didn't take it seriously." The following day, MPT members decided not to take us to that site because there had just been bombings nearby.

A highlight of our time in Karbela was the wedding celebration of a relative of one of the MPT members. The women were in one room, the men in another. The bride sat on a large chair in front in her fancy gown.

Looking around at the women, I noticed something in their faces. Their eyes were welcoming, ready to risk, ready to see how much alike we are. In Baghdad, so many eyes were heavy and tense with worry, or averted out of fear or suspicion.

Here at this wedding, the women's eyes conveyed the many feelings dancing around the room. The bride's eyes were nervous as she tried to play this dignified beauty-queen role. Eyes of children flashed with excitement and curiosity, taking in the mysteries of this event. The eyes of the teens were full of dreams and imagination about this day in their own futures. I saw in the middle-aged eyes more realism about the stresses and responsibility of marriage, but also a desire to relive the excitement of these traditions and pass them on to the next generation.

Many pulled off their scarves, revealing stylish hairdos. One passed along a playful wink at me as she began trilling (a high-pitched sound made through a fast rolling of the tongue) and let herself go to the beat of the clapping and dancing. Near me was a row of older women, fully covered in conservative black, unsure about the newer modern styles now mixed in with the old. They were no longer active players, but were beloved and part of the stability of the clan. Some of their eyes were weary and worn, full of strength, some surrounded by countless wrinkles. One of those pairs of eyes looked at me intently, and, for longer than is usual in that culture, our eyes locked. It was long enough for her eyes to reveal her worry, but also acceptance and strength. She tried to tell me something, but her voice got lost in another wave of trilling.

It didn't matter what she said. Something happened as I looked into her eyes. She revealed herself to me. I felt accepted for who I was, another woman who shared the same struggles in life. All the eyes I saw today started the melting of the protective wall I had recently let grow up around my heart in Iraq, but *her* eyes broke through. I let the tears well up in my eyes and allowed the love I've had for the Iraqi people to flow freely.

*In that moment of joy, I savored this gift
that would feed me and give me strength for
the hard things my eyes would see in the days ahead.*

8

Finding Friends in the Midst of Rubble

It was March 20, 2005, the second anniversary of the 2003 U.S invasion of Iraq. Commemorations organized by Iraqis in Baghdad had a strong emphasis on ending the occupation. At the Hewar Art Gallery it took the form of poetry reading and speeches about the war. Three weeks later, thousands of Iraqi men and women filled Baghdad's Firdos Square to denounce both terrorism and occupation and call for a truly free Iraq. "Force the Occupation to Leave Our Country," was written on one banner, "Yes, Iraq! No Occupation!" on another. Partnering groups invited us to be there with them. We walked through the crowd, as demonstrators welcomed us and seemed grateful that the outside world was watching.

Though many Iraqis said the U.S. should stay, increasingly more now said it should leave. "So many people can't bear that the U.S. army is here," said Bertool, a neighbor. "If they leave, there's no one left to fight. It could get better within months." Then she added, "But my heart feels for the American soldiers and their families. So many have been killed. They're also human beings."

At her shop, our friend, Zaleeka, told us, "I like you, but not this American occupation. I heard on the news the other day that President Bush is drawing terrorists into Iraq to fight them here. Why is he doing this? We have suffered enough! How dare he draw terrorists into Iraq to fight them here!"

At a nearby photo shop, the Kurdish owner, Aziz, always spoke positively of American presence. Today he said, "They saved Europe from

Finding Friends in the Midst of Rubble

Hitler, and they saved Iraq from Saddam. Now they will keep us from fighting each other." A year later, Aziz was one of five that were killed by a bomb on Karrada Street. Knowing the person killed made it more real and horrible.

According to another neighbor, "George Bush did one good thing. He got rid of Saddam. But that's it. Why couldn't Americans just get rid of Saddam, give the Iraqis money to rebuild, and leave? U.S. presence has increased the tension between ethnic groups, making civil war more likely. The sooner they leave, the sooner conflicting groups will come together to reduce the violence and negotiate a coalition government."

Another view we heard was that the leaders do not really want peace, but want the conflicts to continue in order to accomplish their own interests. In this view, Shia leaders wanted the unrest to push the country to accept a federal system, Sunni leaders wanted it to keep the Shia government from being successful, and Americans wanted it to justify staying.

I came to the conclusion that the idea that the U.S. military presence was needed to prevent civil war was a myth. The negative consequences of American forces staying on longer in Iraq had been greater than the positive. It was the source of tremendous violence as well as the draw for the resistance and presence of international terrorists in Iraq. It was a stumbling block for Iraq to develop its own democratic society, and perpetuated the pattern of those in power operating with the politics of fear and violence in order to maintain an unjust order.

At this point, there was no perfect solution, free of violence and power struggles, that guaranteed peace or democracy. The greatest harm the U.S. had done here was the *tearing apart of a whole society*. And it's very hard to put back together. The results had been chaos, mistrust, power struggles, fear, and hatred. It's intangible things such as trust, having basic needs met, and care for the common good that hold a society together and build security from the ground up.

I think of how fear works to persuade the American people to support the status quo and the violent policies of our government. Believing the Iraqis out there are terrorists and will kill you and your buddies, if you don't subdue or kill them first, allows our soldiers to do horrific things they would never want to do otherwise. Fear of terrorism or losing our control around the world blocks our seeing life-giving alternatives of justice that lead to peace. There is another alternative—that of being motivated by love, of seeking the well-being of the Iraqi people. This means recognizing that we Americans don't need to be in control. It means removing the blocks we've put in the way of the Iraqi people's taking the practical steps necessary to deal with rivalries, crime, and lawlessness. And it means providing resources for *Iraqis* to rebuild.

Puddles of sewage dotted the street in Sadr City, a poor, mostly Shia area of Baghdad. A tall thin man of about thirty, a representative of Muqtada as-Sadr's organization, briefed our team. "When the sewage system was built here in the 1980s, the company skimped on materials and put in pipes not wide enough to handle the needs," he explained. "The problem has been compounded because cracked and leaking sewage and water pipes lie next to each other in the ground. An Iraqi sub-contractor is now putting new pipes along the main streets, but not the side streets to connect to most of the houses." He pointed to new electrical poles. "They're useless, because contractors haven't brought in new and adequate generators," he said. "We explain this to authorities, but they don't do anything about it."

This job was unfinished because each time it was sub-contracted, huge amounts of money were skimmed off and kept by the contractors. By the time a company actually started doing the work, only a fraction of the money was left, not enough to complete the job. In other cases, companies did a sloppy or incomplete job, and simply pocketed the unused money.

"Any company," our briefer said, "that came into Sadr City to do repair or reconstruction work has been protected by our organization. See here—there's only a chain-link fence around the construction company's equipment to protect the materials from being stolen, instead of concrete walls they'd have if they needed security." This was consistent with what we saw inside the neighborhood—free-flowing traffic and few checkpoints once past the main checkpoints for entering the area. We felt safer in this neighborhood of about three million residents, comprising half of Baghdad's population, than in other parts of Baghdad.

Driving through Sadr City during several visits that summer, we saw vast poverty, narrow, run-down homes and infrastructure. The ditches along the main street remained open, where the sewage pipes had not been completed. Sadr City received two to four hours of grid electricity a day. We heard of a U.S. project to provide 27 compact water purification systems to supply water for 27 out of 375 schools and a small area around them. Only one of these systems had been completed. Members of Sadr City's Governing Council said that "American officials made the decisions about the contracts, and the local people had no say."

Finding Friends in the Midst of Rubble

At a Sadr City hospital office, we sat with the hospital director and five staff members. "About 72 percent of Sadr City residents have a waterborne form of hepatitis because of the lack of sanitation services," the director told us. "Hepatitis A and B, and Typhoid, are at epidemic rates. These diseases spread from water mixing with sewage under ground. Plus, with the overcrowding in the city, these systems are overworked. Most homes are 144 square meters, with twenty or more people living in them." They didn't have vaccinations to give people to prevent the diseases or the typhoid medicine they needed. The death toll was not high, but people suffered with chronic illnesses.

After the 2003 invasion, the UN and other international agencies—but not the U.S. government—helped supply hospitals, yet they continually had a shortage of drugs. According to the director, every hospital in the city received the same amount of supplies and medicines from the government, but the Sadr City hospital served a larger population than others. UNICEF tanked 70,000 liters of water to the hospital daily, but the hospital actually needed 250,000.

The director and the others laughed when we mentioned hearing that the lack of progress in repairing electricity, water, and sewage systems here was due to the security situation. "Of course, that's not true," he said. "I live in a different part of Baghdad and I always feel safer in Sadr City." There may have been security problems for repair workers at times in the past, but it didn't currently seem so. "Another reason for the lack of repairs," the director added, "is that money allocated for reconstruction was spent on security for U.S. troops."

Outside the building, one of the men with us said, "The doctors only told us half of the truth. They're afraid to criticize Iraqi institutions and officials for their role in corruption or not allocating funds for political or ethnic reasons. They want to keep their jobs."

"Hey, U.S. personnel are saying that Fallujah is the safest city in Iraq," Cliff announced after reading one of several news articles on February 20, 2005. "I guess if we want to be safer, we should move there," he added with a sparkle in his eye. I read the article and found its observation about Fallujah sobering. The premise was that it is safe now because the insurgents were gone. It reported that some displaced residents had returned to the city and were cleaning up rubble and preparing to rebuild. But the

Part One: Summer 2004—Spring 2006

journalists also described other conditions: little water and electricity, tight military control, heavy curfews and restrictions on moving around the city.

If Fallujah were the safest city in Iraq, it's not the kind of safety I would want to live with. Real safety won't come by leveling cities. It won't come by killing more American soldiers, or by U.S. soldiers killing more Iraqis. Safety will develop as the destroyed society is rebuilt, by providing jobs, assisting dialogue and unity among different ethnic groups, and taking away an underlying factor for the violence—the occupation of their country.

It was three months since the massive attacks on Fallujah, and local and international media and international agencies had not been allowed inside to document the damage and offer aid to the people. Members of MPT and CPT decided to try to go in, tell the truth about what happened there, and develop relationships or joint projects between Sunni and Shia Muslims.

"Peace teams are of no use, because Bush controls everything," a Sunni leader in Baghdad told us, after we asked his advice for making contacts and arranging a visit to Fallujah. He was respectful, but we saw in his eyes and heard in his voice a lot of anger and pain, held in check. I had a brief glimpse of the tremendous effort it took for so many Iraqis to control these deep feelings, and felt amazed that more violence hadn't erupted here against the U.S. He expressed doubts about what we wanted to do, yet then agreed for one of his assistants to help us—with the provision that he wouldn't take responsibility for us if we got in.

Early morning on March 14, three cars traveled from Baghdad to Fallujah. We were two Shia members of MPT, one human rights worker from Fallujah, five members of CPT, and a Sunni human rights worker from Baghdad bringing donated wheelchairs and medical supplies for the hospital and one clinic still operating in the city.

Our first stop was the cement factory on the edge of Fallujah, where we met with several members of the Fallujah Reconstruction Committee. One told us soberly, "You have a 1 percent chance of getting in today. U.S. soldiers turned back representatives of the Ministry of Religion earlier this morning. Why is entering the city and what happens here being controlled by the U.S. and not Iraqis?" He went on to say, "In the last two weeks, IDP camps have been closed, forcing residents to return to Fallujah, even if they had no home to go back to. About 80 percent have now returned. So far, no one has received any of the compensation money promised for rebuilding, and there hasn't been any government-assisted reconstruction done here."

He said that over 60 percent of the homes were destroyed or so badly damaged that they were unlivable. Another 20 percent were severely damaged, but people could live in parts. A final 20 percent were moderately damaged. U.S. and Iraqi security forces had attacked thirty of the fifty-five mosques in the city and destroyed most of the electrical and water infrastructure. He estimated that it would take at least a year to do the major repairs needed to restore the city. "At this point, Fallujah is still like a big prison."

That, however, didn't deter us from trying to enter. Our cars went to the first of three checkpoints. One of our Iraqi partners spoke to Iraqi soldiers and then an American soldier, showing the medical supplies, her I.D., and giving the name of the doctor at the Fallujah General Hospital. "We aren't supposed to let you in without a permit, but just this once. Next time you will need to get the permit," the soldier told us. At each checkpoint, we all got out to be searched.

What we saw in the city was shocking. Almost every building was damaged. People were busy cleaning up rubble and patching holes in walls. A few cars were on the street. We stopped at a house with its roof caved in. Two girls invited us in to see how they lived in the two rooms that were left. We wanted to take medical supplies, including five new wheelchairs, to the hospital that had been most severely damaged in the attacks. The only way to get there, however, was by foot over a bridge across the Euphrates River, closed to vehicular traffic, and then along rubble-cluttered streets. Rather than trying to carry the folded wheelchairs, we pushed them, carrying the other medical items, looking like a parade to the surprised people around us.

In a damaged mosque in another part of the city, the sheikh gave a grave account of the devastation of the city and its forced isolation during the past four months. "The Americans were trying to find al Zarqawi, but where is he? They knew he left on the first day of the attack. America is a superpower, but didn't close our borders in 2003 to keep terrorists out. We hold the U.S. responsible for this tragedy."

PART ONE: Summer 2004—Spring 2006

Figure 5: Pushing wheelchairs over bridge in Fallujah, March 14, 2005

We asked him how people from outside might support the people of Fallujah. He answered, "If you come to show what good you Christians are, we don't need your help. If you come as human beings to share our tragedy with the world, you're welcome. The most important thing you can do," he said, "is to let people outside know about the destruction here and the suffering of our people. Western countries and international organizations have shown little respect to Islamic societies. Religious leaders and political authorities should dialogue to build more open, respectful relationships between Muslims, Christians, and other religious groups. There might not be terrorism if they did." As we mentioned the difficulties of contacting him from Baghdad, he told us, "Our hearts are open, but the borders are closed."

In the southern area of the city it looked like an earthquake had struck. Air attacks and bulldozers had leveled most of the homes, and even schools. Where homes had once been, there were piles of rubble. As we approached clusters of tents in the Gebeil area we didn't know what to expect. Some Iraqis in Baghdad had warned that if the word got around that there were Americans in the city, our lives could be in danger. We were surprised, therefore, when members of one of the families walked out, greeted us warmly, and invited us into their tent.

Finding Friends in the Midst of Rubble

Figure 6: Tents in the midst of the rubble in the Gebeil area of Fallujah, March 14, 2005

On a small gas canister burner in the corner of the tent, used for the family cooking, the women heated water for tea. We sat on the floor of the tent with many of the twenty-five family members (including a number of small children) that shared that space. The father told us their story, revealing in his eyes and voice his deep pain. "Our family left the city after American forces warned of impending attacks. All our homes were standing then, and there were no resistance fighters left in the area. We went with other Fallujans to stay in a school in the nearby village of Halabreh. Three families shared a room."

"A month ago, Iraqi and American authorities forced our family and others to return to Fallujah. But this is what we found. See that pile of rubble next to the tent? That was our home. The Red Crescent provided us the tent and four blankets. It was cold, so we pulled out our broken furniture from the rubble to burn for heat. I don't know how we will ever rebuild."

After an hour of sharing back and forth, we felt drawn into the warm fold of their family circle. But then it was time to get up and leave. "Thank you," the women said to us as they fervently hugged and kissed the women in our group. We all had tears in our eyes. Walking away in awe, I felt humbled to receive so much love from this family.

Part One: Summer 2004—Spring 2006

Figure 7: Visiting family inside tent in Gebeil area of Fallujah, March 14, 2005

Here we were, Iraqi and American, Shia, Sunni, and Christian. We had done nothing to change their situation, but simply listened and cared and said we were sorry for the damage and suffering our country caused—the first step toward healing. Five of us were from the country that had destroyed their city and home, so they had every reason to see us as their enemies. Instead, the power of love broke down the barriers between us.

We left, overwhelmed by what we experienced, but sober about the tragedy of the situation and the daunting task the people of Fallujah had of rebuilding their lives. I was outraged to think of the consequences of my own country's continuing this excessive military approach to eliminate the resistance and acts of terror in other Iraqi cities.

Eight more times that year, our team went into Fallujah with members of MPT and other human rights workers. On April 27, we had a series of meetings with leaders there to get information and test possibilities of collaborating on some common projects.

In a barren office, the director of the hospital, the only in-patient care facility in the city, said they still didn't have an X-ray, ultrasound, or ECG machine. They had seen cases of typhoid, salmonella, and malaria over the past month as a result of the poor sanitation and water treatment

Finding Friends in the Midst of Rubble

conditions. Last month they could pay no salaries. The U.S. military had promised, but had not helped rebuild or supply the hospital.

"And then there are the travel restrictions, which prevent people in villages outside from coming into the city to the hospital," the director said. "They're dying of treatable illnesses because they can't get through the checkpoints and have to drive long distances to another city to receive care. During the 10 p.m. to 6 a.m. curfew, anyone on the street could be shot. A person needing an ambulance calls one of the three emergency care facilities. Emergency personnel have to call for a military escort and wait until it arrives before going to the patient. It's better to take them in a civilian car than in an ambulance, because the troops delay and search ambulances more."

"Only one quarter of the city has electricity," he continued. "Many areas have no water. People have to walk up to one kilometer to get water from tanks U.S. contractors brought in containing water from the river, which isn't safe to drink."

A former Fallujah Police officer explained that after the first assault on the mostly Sunni city in April 2004, he and other Sunni officials were removed and replaced with Shia officers and troops mostly from southern Iraq. Many of them were associated with Shia militias, such as the Badr Brigade, and were abusive to Fallujans. "U.S. and ING soldiers here are more aggressive than in Baghdad," he said. "They are quick to fire at cars that get too close to their convoys. Soldiers drive fast, ramming into other vehicles. People fear house raids. If the wanted persons are not at home, soldiers take their relatives. In our society there's tremendous shame for a woman and her family if she's imprisoned."

"The Iraqi Committee of Industry and the U.S. Marines based in Fallujah estimated the damage at $493 million," a doctor said on another visit, "The U.S. Military and Iraqi government promised to rebuild the city, but have given only $100 million in aid money. Families received only one-fifth of the promised compensation. Many are still homeless. U.S.-controlled funding from Baghdad has stopped, shutting down garbage collection in the city and delaying sewage and water line repairs." Several months later, in November, about 15 percent of the destroyed homes had been rebuilt. The doctor told us that even then only about 20 percent of the $500 million, promised by Prime Minister Allawi for reconstruction, had been allocated.

Part One: Summer 2004—Spring 2006

On May 6, fifteen members of MPT and three of CPT joined local residents of Fallujah for a workday. They worked beside men from the Al Furqan Mosque and workers from the Department of Public Works, helping to clean rubble from the street. Everyone shared a meal together, and at the Friday prayers a sheikh called them to unity. Members of the mostly Shia MPT read their statement: "We are among our brothers and sisters in the city of Fallujah to recognize our solidarity with you. God willing, this project will be the beginning of many projects that will show the world that we are truly one people. We hope to counter the increasing Sunni-Shi'a sectarian violence in Iraq."

"We need a similar kind of peace organization as MPT and an ongoing CPT presence here to counteract the terrorist actions of the MNF and Iraqi ING," a doctor we were in regular contact with in Fallujah that summer told us. He invited team members to stay at his home for "a week or a month" to observe what was happening, collaborate on projects with Sunni and Shia Iraqis, and explore forming a peace team. Repeatedly, however, our planned trips were canceled when gun battles or other violence in Fallujah led to extra curfews there.

On a visit in late August, the doctor explained that he and others in the neighborhood were detained by the ING for two days, after an ING soldier was shot outside his office. After this, over half of the twenty-five doctors practicing in this medical center closed their offices and some left the country. He said the situation was still too tense to create an MPT group there.

By the time of the anniversary of the November 2004 assault, many people in Fallujah planned to commemorate with a fund drive to aid the victims of the earthquake in Pakistan." A Sheikh explained that "in Islamic culture it's important to first seek to aid others before caring for your own needs."

We wake up to a dull orange sky, dimming the sun. Every breath we take is full of dust. Buildings across the street are hidden in the haze. During the night a dust storm had rolled into Baghdad. The streets are quiet, without the usual traffic jams. We postpone a trip and catch up on writing and team planning.

Finding Friends in the Midst of Rubble

It's reminiscent of the dust storm in the early days of the 2003 invasion of Iraq, when the sky turned a dull red, and then a deep orange. The dust jammed war machines, and for a time, the fighting stopped. Many of us saw God's hand in it, saying "no" to this tragic onslaught. Even if just for a day the world's strongest army could not stop the wind and sand.

Today the sandstorm temporarily freezes a different scene, a society beaten down and bound up by frustration and fear. It freezes the day for the mother hanging out her laundry, the child wanting to play outside or on the roof, and the maintenance workers on the streets. But it also freezes the soldiers' automatic weapons, the gears on the Humvees, and the visibility of those setting bombs in the streets. We guess, however, that it failed to freeze armed players from planning future attacks.

By the afternoon there's a thick coating of dust on the trees, sidewalks, and inside homes. It reminds me of the heavy weight of power-seeking groups and governments, exploiting and terrorizing their own people. It freezes and weighs down, but doesn't change the persistent longings of an ancient people still wanting God's hand to intervene in a deeper, long lasting way.

Much of the truth here was not pleasant,
but it was important to let people know the truth.

9

Continuing the Legacy of Torture and Abuse

Under a tent in front of a hospital, several doctors stood around talking to anyone walking by. "Members of the Iraqi Special Forces stormed into our hospital last week and killed a doctor," one told us. "We're demanding that no one with weapons be allowed into any hospital."

It was summer 2005, and we were hearing horrific stories and recording testimonies of Iraqis who were arrested, tortured, or killed by Iraqi Police and the newer Iraqi Special Police Commandos. Those that had been released said it came after lengthy torture or a large pay-off. More and more tortured or mutilated bodies were found on grounds around urban areas. People voiced their fears of an increased police state, as bad as, or even worse, than under Saddam.

In May 2005, after their three sons had been arrested by Badr Brigade soldiers, we sat in the living room of a family in the Sakani Palestinian refugee compound—also called the "Baladiyaat Camp"—a complex of buildings in the Baladiyaat District of Baghdad. The parents' faces were grim, and their story, disturbing. "Iraqi forces raided our apartment twice and were abusive," the father of the three said.

Their ordeal started when Badr Brigade soldiers arrested an emotionally unstable man and threatened to slit his throat if he didn't give them names of others involved in terrorist activities. In desperation, he gave the name of a neighbor upstairs from the family of the three brothers. Then while raiding the building around 11:30 p.m., May 12, the soldiers took that man, but also took the three brothers who lived downstairs, though they didn't know their names. Another neighbor heard a soldier ask his commander, "Are four Palestinians enough?"

The following evening, they watched a TV program for alleged terrorists to confess their crimes, called, "Terrorism in the Grip of Justice," and there were their three sons, their upstairs neighbor, and another man. The men seemed confused, but admitted involvement in a car bombing in Baghdad Jidida the day before. One of the three sons had several cuts on his face. The face of another appeared badly beaten on one side.

Several days later, the upstairs neighbor they had seen on TV with the others, was released. He contacted this family to tell them their sons were in a Ministry of Interior (MOI) prison run by the Wolf Brigade. He said they were all "tortured badly" and forced to sign a confession. Family members were certain that the three sons did not commit the crime.

We had heard that Special Police Forces were targeting Palestinians, who were Sunni Muslim, and that the government often arrested people to show it was making progress against the insurgency. The family was afraid to go to any government office to ask for help, feeling more vulnerable to random detention and mistreatment. They asked us to go with them.

After the family inquired at the Ministry of Human Rights (MHR) and searched lists of prisoners at the MOI, another man who had been detained with the men told them their sons were being held in the Rusaafa prison in Adhamiyyah, Baghdad. The family hired a lawyer, who found the brothers and was able to go in and talk with them.

"After their arrest they were taken to the MOI and turned over to the Wolf Brigade and tortured," the lawyer told us. "Under threat of more torture they were forced to make false confessions on TV that they were working with and financed by a terrorist and had taken part in the bombing. From there they were taken to the MOI 'high-crimes directorate,' where they were tortured with electric shock, strung up to the ceiling, sometimes upside-down, burned, and beaten."

The lawyer spoke about a system of extorting money from the families of victims—coercing them to pay thousands of dollars to keep the prisoner from being tortured more or forced to confess on TV. An official in the office of terrorism at Rusaafa prison had threatened to torture the men again if they did not pay a bribe of $5,000.

PART ONE: Summer 2004—Spring 2006

"There are two ways one can proceed to free the men, the legal way or the 'payment way,'" the lawyer said. "The legal way likely means more torture and imprisonment." The "payment way" means the family sells what they have to get money and other Palestinian families contribute. Palestinians knew that after watching the TV shows, Iraqis would conclude that Palestinians were behind terrorist attacks, resulting in more danger of attacks on all of them by civilian Iraqis.

"The American Forces caused the whole mess," the lawyer said cynically. "At an Iraqi police station, I once paid a U.S. soldier $50 to release my client. The whole system is corrupt."

After discussing having a doctor examine and document the effects of the torture on these men, we suggested taking information about the three brothers to the Ministry of Human Rights so they could press charges against those involved. Maybe it would help "crack" this system and prevent torture of other prisoners. "No," said the lawyer. "That would make it more dangerous for the brothers. They would be tortured more or killed." Then he added, "You would *trust* the Iraqi government? It's because you're foreigners. We don't have any trust for our government. If you're looking for human rights in Iraq, you won't find any. You'll soon get tired of this. I have many clients who have been tortured by Iraqi security forces. The reputation of Iraqi Palestinians here has already been destroyed by this television show."

This was a frustrating dilemma. Exposing the abusive system was necessary for change, but there was a legitimate basis for the fear and cynicism of the lawyer. Four months later, however, in September, Palestinian leaders at the Baladiyaat Camp asked us to publicize the house raids by the Wolf Brigade, as well as the injustices suffered by Palestinians in Iraq in general. At that time, the family of the three still detained Palestinian brothers spoke with international journalists and U.S. Embassy officials and gave members of Amnesty International permission to publicize their case and make inquiries with the Iraqi authorities.

During the summer, leaders of the local Palestinian Human Rights Association mentioned other Palestinians being detained or killed. The ING entered the camp several times a week, searching four or five homes. Many residents were afraid to leave the camp because Iraqis verbally abused them and accused them of being terrorists. "Our religious leaders are careful not to talk about politics during their sermons out of fear of retribution from the government," one said. "We tried using nonviolent action, but now more of us are being killed. After writing two articles for a newspaper, U.S. and brigade soldiers came and told me not to write any more. We're walking the line between protesting and survival."

During the Israeli-Palestinian war of 1948, Iraq welcomed Palestinian refugees. Others came in 1967. The United Nations Refugee Works Agency (UNRWA) built camps for them, but didn't register them as refugees because the Iraqi government said it would provide for their needs. These promises, however, were never fulfilled. Palestinians could not obtain Iraqi citizenship, vote, or buy property, though most were born in Iraq. If they left the country for two months they lost the right to return. One told us, "We have been here for fifty-seven years, but with no rights." Now many of the estimated 23–30,000 Palestinians in Iraq were afraid and wanted to leave but didn't have the necessary legal papers.

Our team was working along with Iraqi organizations who were also addressing issues of torture, such as the Voice of Freedom Society, Women's Will, the Adhamiya City Council, the Muslim Scholars' Board, and the Organization for Human Rights in Iraq.

In late June, we began a series of visits to the MOI to find Iraqis we were looking for, but also to learn about treatment of detainees in Iraqi prisons. One official told us about atrocities being committed by the Iraqi Police Commando units the Minister of Interior formed in June of 2004, and which later received arms and logistical support from the U.S. He said the Commando units arrest, torture, and kill Iraqis with impunity, particularly target Sunnis, and that U.S. officials are well aware of these abuses.

He described Iraqi Special Operations teams under General Adnan Thabit that worked with U.S. Intelligence officers and the U.S. Army—with the knowledge of the U.S. Embassy. Some of these teams were created, trained, and equipped by the U.S. At least a fourth of the fighters had a history of criminal activity. The teams had imprisoned about 700 people, of which 650 were Sunni. They operated above the law, raided houses at night, blackmailed, kidnapped, tortured, and killed Iraqis. Sometimes they simply took a person, asked for a ransom and then killed him. The brigades received names of people to arrest or assassinate from Shia political parties participating in the government or from the MOI. The official attributed the killings to the divisions between Sunni and Shia rather than opposition to the occupation.

PART ONE: Summer 2004—Spring 2006

Months earlier we had seen the January 9, 2005 *Newsweek* article by Michael Hirsh and John Barry called "The Salvador Option," reporting that the Pentagon was debating instituting the "Salvador Option" in Iraq. This referred to the U.S.'s training and equipping death squads in El Salvador in the 1980s to fight the guerrilla insurgency. Such squads were involved in terrorizing leaders of progressive movements or those resisting the U.S.'s economic role in their society, through brutal and gruesome killings. Now, it seemed as though the "Salvador Option" was well underway here in Iraq.

The officer at the MOI confirmed that the television show on which supposed criminals confessed to crimes was "faked." No warrants were issued for those detained, and they had not been charged, tried, or brought before a court. Instead they were interrogated for days, tortured, and then put on TV to confess. Sometimes they were released after their confession.

Another official told us that each department of the MOI operated independently on a separate floor. There was a cell room the size of his office in which 500 men stood packed together, with no room to sit. On the sixth floor and in the basement, prisoners were regularly tortured, with American personnel present.

At the MHR, an official said he knew of more than one hundred cases of kidnapping, torture, or murder by Iraqi Security Forces. In prisons controlled by the MOI and the Ministry of Justice (MOJ) and within the High Crimes Directorate prisons, the detained had no access to lawyers. The MHR was attempting to inspect the prisons and stop such treatment.

It was difficult trying to navigate through the maze of complex institutions, which seemed to run independently of each other without overall coordination or consistency. We visited the MOJ, where officials said that their prisons (housing about 6,000 prisoners) were legal, but the prisons by the MOI and Special Forces (holding 300-800 prisoners) were illegal. They said the Ministry of Defense (MOD) was responsible for maintaining a list of detainees held by Iraqi Security Forces, but families had to go to the MOJ to arrange visits.

An official at the MOD told us what we by now realized—there was no centralized list of prisoners held in their prisons or standard procedure for families to get information. Each prison kept its own list, which wasn't available to the public.

A few weeks later, at the front desk in a prison run by the Iraqi Special Forces, we talked with an Iraqi woman who was looking for her stepson. After we left the office, the woman told us that U.S. and Iraqi troops had searched her house but didn't find anything suspicious. An hour later they came back and took her stepson, without knowing his name. In prison, Iraqi guards beat him and knocked out four of his front teeth. He said they tortured one of his friends in prison by drilling a hole through his foot. About a month after the stepson was released, he was shot in random gunfire of Iraqi Security Forces on the street. He was taken to a hospital where he stayed for ten days. The family saw him there several times before Iraqi Police came and took to prison him and others they had shot that day.

Repeatedly, the woman came to this Special Forces prison to find out if her stepson was there, but the men at the front desk always said, "No." Eventually one man who worked at the desk took her aside and told her that he would help her. That night he called her and confirmed that her stepson was being held in that prison. When she came to the desk today, she thought officials gave her this information because internationals were standing there, witnessing all.

Around that time, a National Dialogue Commission made up of Sunni and Shia Iraqis had complained to the U.S. Ambassador about police commandos targeting Sunnis. The Commission claimed that the Al Dawa and the Supreme Counsel of the Islamic Revolution in Iraq parties created arrest lists of Sunnis engaged in terrorist activities. Of the approximately 3,000 people detained by Commandos, 97 percent were Sunni and 3 percent were Shia. The Commission called for an end to house raids and to removing Sunni officers from the MOI, and for better control of the Commandos' activities. The Ambassador suggested the commissioners meet with the Minister of Interior. At first they refused, because "the Minister has so much blood on his hands." When the Commission finally met with the Minister, he agreed to its requests. Afterwards, however, Iraqi human rights workers didn't see a change.

A United Nations Assistance Mission for Iraq (UNAMI) human rights worker told us, "We also have a hard time getting information about conditions in the MOI prisons and specific cases of human rights violations." UNAMI had started conducting trainings with Iraqi security forces and other officials, trying to break the cultural expectation that you must torture a prisoner to convict, rather than gather evidence. Unfortunately, we saw that the U.S. treatment of Iraqi prisoners reinforced this mindset of torture rather than helping the UN to change it.

UN workers were not allowed to go out of the Green Zone to document what was happening unless accompanied by armed guards and at least two U.S. military Humvees, so we began to meet regularly with this worker in his office to share information. He suggested we write a report on abuses by Iraqi forces, which they could use to press the Iraqi government to stop torture and abuse by the Iraqi Special Forces.

Iraqi human rights colleagues gave us information about cases of torture and extra-judicial execution by Special Police Commandos, and by early fall, our team recorded torture testimonies of three men. We didn't know what kind of influence such a report could have on this entrenched system, but we knew the first step was to tell the truth about it.

On June 2, 2005 investigative writer Max Fuller published an article on the Centre for Research on Globalization website titled, "For Iraq, 'The Salvador Option' Becomes Reality."[1] He published another study, November 10, 2005, called, "Crying Wolf: Media Disinformation and Death Squads in Occupied Iraq."[2] He claimed that the increasing number of tortured and mutilated bodies found around Baghdad and other cities since May 2005 was not just a tit-for-tat revenge killing between Sunni and Shia by rogue, independent militia groups or Al Qaida. Instead, it was mostly the work of the Wolf Brigade and other Special Police Commandos, which were founded and under direction of the Iraqi MOI and its National Security Service, so could be seen as "state terror." He also regarded it as a CIA intelligence supported operation.

Fuller documented the direct role of the two main U.S. advisers to the Iraqi MOI, with CIA connections, in developing and equipping these Commando brigades and in collaborating by producing death lists. James Steele had been a U.S. Army Special Forces operations officer in El Salvador, training death squad units responsible for 60 percent of civilian deaths during the height of the civil war in the 1980s. Steven Casteel worked in Colombia during the drug wars of the 1990s with operations that led to the formation of the death squad, "Los Pepes." This was the forerunner to current paramilitary death squads, responsible for 80 percent of Colombia's most serious human rights abuses. He was now the most senior U.S. advisor to the Iraqi MOI.

Three reporters, Steve Vincent (*The New York Times*), Yasser Salihee (Knight Ridder), and Fakher Haider (*The New York Times*) were murdered in Iraq in 2005. They had one thing in common. The story of the U.S. connection with the death squads was the last story they covered before they were shot to death.

1. Fuller, "For Iraq, 'The Salvador Option' Becomes Reality."
2. Fuller, "Crying Wolf."

Fuller's documentation led him to the conclusion that these death squad killings were not only a prime cause of sectarian violence, but were designed to sow seeds of sectarian strife that was mostly non-existent prior to the invasion. What was now labeled "civil war" would distract attention from the brutalities of the occupation and mask who was really behind the deaths of those who resisted the neocolonialism and economic shock treatment underway in Iraq. Already by March 2004, more than 1,000 professionals, intellectuals, and trade unionists had been killed, and thousands had fled the country.

We could not prove Fuller's conclusions, but what we had seen since the invasion supported what he said. We knew about the economic restructuring laws and privatization of state industry that Bremer declared in the first six months of the occupation. We knew that there was resentment among Sunni Muslims toward the new Shia-dominated Iraqi government that reasserted power for the Shia after being oppressed under Saddam. We knew this sparked some backlash violence by Sunni toward Shia civilians and government. We also saw that the structures of occupation provoked sectarian violence and heard testimonies about marginalizing and targeting of union leaders and other professionals who criticized U.S. policies in Iraq. It was clear to us that the longer U.S. troops remained in the country, the more dangerous and violent the society became. Fuller's assertions also fit with what officers at the MOI told us about Americans being present in parts of the MOI where torture was being perpetrated.

Around that time, I was visiting our neighbor, Basma, who worked in a government office in Baghdad. "What do you do all day? Just talk together?" she asked me. So I shared about our work with detainees and reporting excessive violence and abuse. She looked at me with apprehension and said, "But we must *stop* those who are terrorizing our people! Do you just hear one side of the story from the prisoners?" "We also get information from officials," I answered, "and we don't try to determine prisoners' guilt or innocence, but believe they should be given a fair trial and not be abused or tortured." She responded, "Maybe police and guards *need* to beat people to get the truth from them." I said, "When you beat people you get lots of false confessions—anything to stop the torture." Most Iraqis had bought into the belief that violent forces were needed to keep terrorism in check. We didn't agree, but I was glad for her openness.

PART ONE: Summer 2004—Spring 2006

In early September, two team members were present as 500 Shia Muslims gathered for a memorial service for Othman Ali Beite in Karbela, a service organized by the Iraqi Human Rights Watch and members of MPT in Karbela. Five days earlier, August 31, 2005, during Shia holy days, mortars had exploded on a Shia procession to the Imam Musa Al-Khadim Shrine, in Khadamiyah, Baghdad, and killed sixteen worshipers. Later that day, as thousands amassed on the Al-Aima Bridge over the Tigris on their way to the Shrine, a rumor spread among people on the bridge that a suicide bomber was in the crowd. This set off a stampede, leaving almost a thousand people dead. Hundreds were crushed, while others jumped into the Tigris River to escape, but drowned. Othman Ali Beite, a Sunni Muslim, was near the scene and jumped into the water. After pulling seven Shia Muslims safely to the shore, he went back for the eighth. This time, however, he got exhausted in the effort and drowned. Now he is honored as a hero.

Iraqis around the country responded with actions demonstrating ethnic solidarity. A Sunni sheikh from Fallujah donated blood to help Shia survivors of the stampede. Others in Fallujah collected funds and supplies, and Kurdish groups organized to send relief to the victims.

I had already left for the U.S. on a break when on November 13 the air raid siren sounded from the Green Zone across the river, followed by a loud explosion and the sound of breaking glass. Minutes later my teammates realized a mortar had exploded on the roof of our apartment building. It destroyed water tanks and satellite dishes, and sprayed shrapnel that tore through the metal railing of the roof and the neighbor's metal water tank twenty yards away. About half of the windows on the top floor were broken. Fortunately, no one was on the roof at the time.

Iraqi soldiers came to inspect the damage, and a patrol of Iraqi Police arrived about a half-hour later. "That type of mortar had a firing range up to twenty-seven kilometers," they said. "It was probably aimed at the Green Zone."

My colleagues spent the afternoon cleaning up. Neighbors expressed relief that no one had been hurt. Our landlord seemed tired and discouraged as he fixed the windows, and repaired the roof and water system. Once again, we were thankful for our team's safety.

*But who of us guessed what was yet to come
in just less than two weeks?*

10

The CPT—4

"Four members of the Iraq team were abducted today!" CPT's co-director, Doug Pritchard's voice sounded strained over the phone. "I don't know what that means for your coming back." This shocking call came on November 26, 2005, while I was in the U.S. on my break and visiting our son, Dale, and his family in San Francisco. We always knew it could happen, but it was shaking when it did. In two days, Art and I were scheduled to fly back to the Middle East to work with CPT, Art in the West Bank, and I in Iraq.

Tom Fox, full-time member of the team from Virginia, Jim Loney, Program Coordinator of the CPT Canada office and Canadian citizen, and two delegation members—British citizen Norman Kember and Canadian citizen Harmeet Sing Sooden—had just left a meeting with an Iraqi organization to collaborate on documenting abuses of detainees in the Iraqi prison system. Two cars moved in to block their van. Three men with pistols jumped inside, forced out the driver and translator and drove away with the four, later abandoning the car.[1]

At first, international officials in Iraq advised the team not to make the kidnapping public, since this could increase the value of the hostages and make it harder for the abductors to release the captives more quickly. But after the media picked it up independently, it seemed like putting public pressure on the captors could be helpful.

---

1. For more about the team's experience those first days and weeks and the work of other members and friends of CPT, and the impact of this event on countless people and communities around the world, see Brown, ed., *118 Days*.

The CPT—4

Besides shock and concern, my next feeling was that I wanted to be in Baghdad to support the team. It was like wanting to be with my family in a time of crisis. The team had hope that within a few days the four would be released and this would all blow over, so instructed me to go to Amman, Jordan, and do media work from there until it seemed good for me to come on to Iraq. Art and I flew to Amman together, but then said goodbye the following morning when he left to travel into the West Bank to work with CPT's Hebron and At-Tuwani teams.

The team in Baghdad, Anita David, Greg Rollins, and Maxine Nash, began contacting and asking religious and secular leaders for help, posting information in the Iraqi media and over the CPT website about the men and their work, and appealing for their release. In Amman, I did this with Middle East media. The Hebron and At-Tuwani teams began extensive media work there and a week later sent a member to help me in Amman. The Chicago and Toronto CPT offices organized a crisis team that coordinated media work, reached out to support the families of our four colleagues, and increased support of the small team in Baghdad.

> It was time to say goodbye to my son, Dale. It was especially hard this time. I wanted to share with him the love I have for him and others in our family, but also about the inner callings and the deep love I've been given for the Iraqi people that compelled me to leave my family to work in Iraq. But my attempts were clumsy. My heart felt torn apart when he said gently, but soberly, "Mom, I've already come to accept that you and Dad might die in the Middle East doing this work."

The outpouring of love, support, and prayers of people all over the world for our four men was heartening. Peace groups, other CPT teams, and friends of CPT organized vigils in places such as London, Toronto, Ramallah, Jerusalem, Colombia, and New York. Tears of gratefulness welled up in me when I saw pictures on the Internet of Palestinians in a circle with signs supporting our captured men. This helped me deal with the TV showing that evening, of the disturbing video of the four, put out by the captors, who called themselves the "Swords of Righteousness" and claimed our men were spies. The second video, released December 3, demanded that all prisoners in Iraq be released within forty-eight hours or they would kill our men.

It was moving when Muslim organizations and leaders, such as Annas Al Tikriti, leader of the Muslim Association of the UK, and Ehab

PART ONE: Summer 2004—Spring 2006

Lotayef from the Canadian Islamic Council, spoke out for the release of our four. Then they both came to Iraq and met with Muslim groups around the country, asking them to make public statements pressing for the release of the four. I saw on TV a leader of the Association of Muslim Scholars from Ramadi, Iraq, forbidding hurting the men, saying that we were peaceful people and they have no problems with us, just with the coalition forces. We were particularly touched when three *Muslim detainees, Mahmoud Jaballah, Mohammad Mahjoub, and Hassan Almrei, who had spent years in solitary confinement in Canadian prisons without charge, called for our Christian hostages to be shown mercy and set free.* In their appeal, they said, "We care about their freedom more than we do our own."

> I vacillated between being weighted down by fear and grief and times of calm. I felt more peace when I could accept that I couldn't control what happened, and that I didn't have the strength and faith on my own to keep doing this work. Then I was able to ask God to give me the love and strength I needed. It would be grievous for all of us if it ended tragically, but whatever happened, I believed God was caring for everyone involved.

We set up press conferences and gave interviews to worldwide media. We distributed press packets of information and pictures about the work of CPT in Iraq and the four to humanize them, in contrast to the images of them in the abductors' videos.

Themes of Advent spoke to us in this time of uncertainty and waiting. I wrote on December 15, 2005:

> It's hard to wait now, as we hope for the safe release of Jim, Tom, Harmeet, and Norman. It's hard for their families. It's hard for us, not knowing where they are, how they are holding up, or when they will be released. We pray, we cry, we care deeply about them, yet feel the same urgency for all Iraqis who suffer fear and pain because of the disappearance, killing, or imprisonment of *their* family members.
>
> Advent is a time of waiting and longing for something to happen. People, at the time Jesus was born, cried out for healing and release from the oppression or captivity they knew. They, too, had heard God's promises, but had not seen them fulfilled. Many were able to keep walking ahead in faith, expecting God to break in and work in seemingly impossible situations.
>
> Waiting does not mean being passive. We're called to an active waiting. We can act boldly because God is with us giving

us hope. Even death, persecutions, or violent forces of power "will not separate us from the love of God"! If we follow the way of Jesus—of nonviolent suffering love—we will expect hardships and suffering. We may have to grieve and cry together, and support each other more deeply, but we keep going and working where God leads us.

Meanwhile, the Baghdad team also worked for the release of our team's two Iraqi interpreters, Sattar and Azhar, and two drivers, who had been put in jail for the investigation. At times, fear, strain, and tension gripped the team. The team was also responding to state department representatives from the three home countries of the four, assigned to investigate and assist in foreign hostage situations.

On December 19, the day after a major speech President Bush made about Iraq, I wrote to my family and friends:

> In his December 18, 2005 speech, President Bush gave a very different picture of the U.S. legacy in Iraq than what I've seen in the last three years. His perspective and proposals seem based in political and economic self-seeking, *not* concern for the well-being of the Iraqi people. When *Iraqis* hear Bush say the U.S. needs to "stay the course" in Iraq, they understand that to mean continuing the house raids, bombing civilians, illegal detentions, torture and abuse. Bush continues to generate fear so that the American people will sacrifice the lives of our young people and social well-being for the poor, to continue this war.

One of the effects of kidnappings, killings, and bombings, whether done by the resistance or the state, is to instill fear in the people. This fear leads to feelings of helplessness and paralysis and drains away hope that change is possible. People become afraid to speak out and take action against injustice. As peacemakers, we often feel pressure from others to be more realistic and see the world's economic, military and governmental structures as so strong and entrenched that they are impossible to change.

We know that when we work for change, we can be eliminated any time our work is seen as threatening to those wielding power. The world's networks of violence appear all-powerful, but we must not be seduced into believing that they are invincible. I continue to believe that the power of truth and love is stronger than these forces. This does not mean that there won't be struggle and suffering. It's when the dissent is having a powerful effect and the structures of power feel threatened, that the greatest crackdown occurs. We are encouraged when we work alongside courageous Iraqi people who daily take risks to eliminate injustice and corruption.

Part One: Summer 2004—Spring 2006

> Our current crisis grieves us greatly, but has not blunted our commitment to intervene nonviolently in conflict areas of the world. We choose the way of Jesus, acclaimed during this season as the Prince of Peace, which means to be willing to lay down our lives for our brothers and sisters around the world (including our enemies). This is a time for us to rely more deeply on our resources of faith. I return to Iraq this week, feeling a deep love for the Iraqi people and that it is important to walk with them.

The good news that day was that our Iraqi employees were released after two weeks in jail. Two days later, I flew into Baghdad and was glad to be back even in such circumstances.

Our employees debriefed about their detention. Sattar[2] called it a "nightmarish experience" and spoke of the humiliation he felt. One of our drivers was very emotional about it, saying, "It's the first time I experienced such a terrible thing. These police and guards are savage. They eat each other's flesh."

Since being back, I noticed that some Iraqis were more hesitant to relate to internationals because it was more dangerous, but people in our neighborhood, who know us and what we do here, remained friendly. They often stopped and asked whether or not we had any news about our men, or expressed concern for our safety. Muslims and Christians told us they were praying for the captives. They knew what it is like to worry and wait or have family members injured or killed. Some Iraqis had become bitter and willing to take advantage of their fellow Iraqis during this chaotic time, but most continued to be gracious and generous in caring for each other.

Our Iraqi friends had different views about the kidnapping. One thought the kidnappers were politically motivated, not a criminal gang. Another said the talk on the street was that U.S. Intelligence agents instigated the kidnapping, even if Iraqis carried it out. They would do it to scare us away and distract us from our work of exposing death squads, torture, and the U.S. connection. We didn't know if that was true, but it was possible. That scenario felt ominous to me and made it less likely our men would be released and that our work in Iraq could continue.

In spite of the gravity of the situation, we found ways to bring some lightness to the team, such as bringing home a potted Christmas tree and sharing meals with our neighbors. On Christmas Day, I received phone

---

2. At the time of preparing this manuscript, our team was sad to hear about the death of our beloved translator, Sattar Hatam, of a heart attack while he was in Amman, Jordan preparing to come to the U.S.

calls from family members and our team spent some time together. I had personal plans for the rest of the day, but then Maxine and I accepted the invitation of a religious leader from Tal Afar, that our team met last summer, to meet with him and other leaders from the National Iraqi Foundational Council. This was a coalition of about thirty Islamic parties and organizations, Sunni and Shia, which opposed the occupation. They were willing to put more information about our kidnapped men on their website and in their newsletter and contact other leaders around the country.

"Kidnapping and terrorist acts do not come from Islam," one of the leaders told us. When we asked about our team's continuing to work here, they answered, "Your work is very important. Many Iraqis find it amazing that you're still here." The leader from Tal Afar spoke about his city since the U.S. attack last summer. "Tal Afar is broken," he said. "There's still no functioning hospital, only three doctors left, and a few medical clinics with little equipment. The municipality is not functioning, and few schools are open. There's a shortage of water, petrol, and electricity. Tension remains among the main four ethnic factions."

The holidays were over, and we still didn't know where our four teammates were and who had them. What were they going through? How were they dealing with it? How would we sustain ourselves if this continued a long time? How could we be proactive as well as respond to events as they occurred? We had countless meetings to discern the best approach and responses. It was easier to think about the possible positive outcomes and things we could do if and when the men were released. We hoped one team member could accompany each of the four, as they left Iraq, as far as to their homes if they wanted. It was harder to plan for the negative possibilities. One of the hardest scenarios would be a long time of silence, hearing nothing. In the event of death, we wanted to accompany their bodies to their home countries.

Two different persons claimed to have separate links to the captors and told us repeatedly that the men were about to be released. Each time, nothing happened. These "links" did not give us evidence of being legitimate and initially did not convey demands. These communications got our hopes up only to have them crash. Soon we mistrusted them. When we contacted the families to discuss what we were doing and answer their questions, we told them about the two link claims, but also about the contradictions and our doubts about them.

Part One: Summer 2004—Spring 2006

Officials from each of our kidnapped teammates' countries, comprising what was called the Hostage Working Group, continued working to find and free them. They related to us to the degree they thought it would help them accomplish their goals, but clearly saw themselves as the experts and those in charge of this task. After several meetings to see if there were things to learn from them or ways we could be helpful to each other, we continued contact but affirmed our need to move ahead more independently out of our consciences and in our own way of operating.

One of our differences was our not wanting to use military force to release our men. We told the officials about the precautions we took as we worked around Iraq, but that we were not willing to carry weapons or have armed guards. We didn't believe that using violent forms of protections would make us less likely to be hurt or kidnapped. We knew that a military raid would greatly increase the chances that our colleagues, their captors, or those carrying out an armed rescue, would be injured or killed. We didn't want others to be harmed in the process of releasing our men. The government representatives said they would do whatever they needed to do with the safety of the hostages in mind. They would also prefer a nonviolent solution, but wouldn't rule out a violent raid.

Being seen going into the Green Zone (GZ) added to our danger, and there were times these officials' actions were deceiving or put us at risk. This added to our wanting to distance ourselves from them. One time, without notifying us, they sent men to our door with GZ identification tags visible, loudly asking to come in and drawing the attention of people on the street. At times, they tried to pressure us to cooperate with their intelligence work. They misrepresented to the families things we said and misrepresented the words of family members of the kidnapped men in ads they put in the media. They misled us when telling us we would be able to stay with our colleagues as much as we mutually wanted, if they were released to the GZ, or accompany their bodies home if they were killed. All this created dilemmas for us, even though we found caring people among these officials.

We often felt overwhelmed by the pressures to make decisions that could have serious consequences when there was so little certainty. When it seemed impossible to decide, someone in the group would call us back to grounding ourselves in our faith and our commitment to nonviolence. Other times when we felt weighed down with stress, we did silly antics like singing goofy songs or acting out funny characters.

One break from the stress for me was visiting at the orphanage. I was glad to see Yasser walking with a walker and braces on his legs. Nura, at first, was pouting at everyone. I sang the "itsy bitsy spider," however, and soon the "spider" was crawling on Nura, Yasser, and Jacqolina. Then with the head sister, I shared more personally about the kidnapping, our work, my family, and why I come to live and work in Iraq. In turn, she shared more about the Sisters of Charity of Mother Teresa, about her background, becoming a nun, and the places she had worked. She showed me pictures of her family in southern India, and I showed her my family pictures. Before I left, she took me to their chapel. I felt her loving care as she prayed for me.

Walking home from the orphanage, I thought about the heartbreaking conditions of these children, but felt grateful for the love and joy they were able to maintain and share. As with the children, it was important to look beneath the appearance of things and the tragedies of this society, handicapped and stunted from years of oppressive dictatorship, sanctions, and wars, and now devastated by the current hardships and violence. When Iraqis opened up windows into their lives and struggles, we experienced their basic love and goodwill. An Iraqi woman once told us that even though she had suffered, she didn't want to center her life on being a victim. Their finding strength to move forward in spite of horrendous adversity spread hope to others.

When new videos of our kidnapped men appeared on Al Jazeera TV, we put out media releases and responded to phone interviews. After the one dated January 21 appeared, showing them somber and thin and with beards, we said the following, "Yes it's a little shocking to see Jim, Tom, Harmeet, and Norman looking tired and thinner than before, but we are thankful that they are still alive and holding up." We chose to look at the positive side. The video prompted worldwide leaders and organizations to make a second round of statements supporting the four.

In another video on Al Jazeera, dated February 28, Norman and Jim asked for the Canadian and British governments and the governments of the Gulf States to help secure their release by cooperating with their abductors' demands. They looked all right, but Tom was not with them. It only showed and referred to three men, never mentioning Tom. Canadian officials thought it was a strategy to disturb people so they would be more open to their demands.

PART ONE: Summer 2004—Spring 2006

We felt "jerked around" by the video, but I felt more connected to the three when I looked briefly into their faces and saw they were basically OK, not crushed by their ordeal. It was disturbing that Tom wasn't with them, but I clung to hope. I felt for their families, especially Tom's family and the fear and pain they must be going through.

In CPT circles, there was talk about the possibility of U.S. Intelligence involvement in the abduction. At times I felt like I was walking deeper into a sinister web of state terrorism, into the den of evil forces—like Frodo walking into Mordor with the ring to face the forces of evil.

*But we tried not to lose sight of the good
and the beautiful also around us.*

11

Seeing the Broken and the Beautiful

Azhar, our friend and interpreter, got out his guitar and started playing and singing as we sat around our living room one evening. We sang along with songs we knew. I soon forgot where I was. It was a wonderful break from the stress. I realized how uptight I'd been much of the time. We looked for ways of having special times with the people around us.

Du'a and Marwan dressed up in adult clothing and pretended to be their parents or "the Americans." It was delightful to be silly while visiting with Miriam and her children.

A human rights worker came to visit with his wife and five-year-old grandson, Hamid. We discussed a human rights abuse case, but most of our time was spent having fun. We showed pictures of our families. Beth Pyles made and flew paper airplanes, and Hamid's energy was contagious. Allan made a pinwheel on a pencil and put it on top of paper folded to look like a helicopter. Our spirits were refreshed.

As much as we could, we tried to continue our work of accompaniment, reporting what we saw happening on the ground, and working alongside Iraqis as they spoke out against injustice nonviolently, rebuilt trust among ethnic groups, and brought factions together to resolve major conflicts. It felt good to return to the UN human rights office in the Green Zone to exchange information. We gave him copies of torture testimonies we had taken and agreed to turn in a small report to the UN when we finished others.

One day in January (2006), we stood outside an Iraqi military base—Hikmat (a seventy-year-old Iraqi man), an Iraqi human rights worker, a filmmaker, and a lawyer, and three from our team. Hikmat was looking for his wife and daughter-in-law. They were taken away in a U.S.-Iraqi raid of their home five days ago, along with four sons who were accused of involvement in violent resistance and kidnapping a relative of a government official. "There are no women here," the guards at the base told us. We persisted, and kept asking to talk to a higher official. Finally, a spokesperson told us to come back the next day.

The following day, guards took our group right in, and we met with the top commander, an Iraqi general. After we told him why we were there, he launched into a long discourse about the Iraqi Army's need to fight terrorism. In response, Anita spoke about the problems the U.S. had caused in the detainee system and the need to use humane treatment in military operations.

After about an hour, the general had an assistant bring in Hikmat's wife and daughter-in-law and said they had been detained because they had information about violent acts but refused to give it. We guessed they were being held hostage to put pressure on other family members to give information about people in their area involved in the resistance.

Then the general brought in two of the sons and accused them of killing many people and of being involved in a kidnapping. One was accused of killing his own sister for political reasons. We were troubled by the way the commander tried to shame the men in front of us, and we wondered whether our presence there was doing more harm than good.

Moving closer to the oldest son, who had difficulty walking into the room, we saw signs of physical mistreatment. Quietly to us he said that his feet were swollen because of beating, and that he was beaten all over. Looking more closely, we saw scars and marks on his hands, wrists, and forehead. Out loud, to the people in the room, he said that he had just scratched himself.

The general refused our request to talk with the son or the women alone. As the discussion continued, the general changed the reason for detaining the women, saying "it was to protect them from the family who might harm them." Before we left, he promised to release them in two days. Three days later, the family called to tell us that the women had been released.

Seeing the Broken and the Beautiful

It was late January. Michele Naar and I walked through the high-ceilinged hallways and sparsely furnished rooms of the hospital that served the Najaf region. The doctor, a member of MPT in Najaf, showed us the broken or outdated CT scan, MRI, and other equipment. "People need to drive to hospitals in Baghdad for services we can't offer here, though many are afraid to drive that route," he said. "Only three of the original seven floors are useable. We care for 1,500 outpatients a day. Only twenty-four patients can stay overnight."

"The hospital had been taken over by international forces for a year after the invasion and then given back to the hospital administration badly damaged," the doctor explained. "U.S. officials said it would be rebuilt and refurbished, but the progress has been slow. They paid for the reconstruction of three floors, but not to replace equipment."

Members of the new Najaf branch of MPT, that we were visiting, were working on projects to build inter-ethnic cooperation and deal with justice issues in their community. Some sponsored sports matches between Shia and Sunni children. Some were monitoring human rights in local prisons, which involved observing conditions, talking with prisoners, and giving workshops for prisoners and for police.

That night, we were rewarded with a feast with both men and women of MPT. Before the women of our team settled in on our sleeping mats in a room with women and girls, we sat and talked some more. One of the women asked us about our continuing to work in Iraq. I told her, "I keep coming back because Allah sent me and gave me love for the Iraqi people and a longing for reconciliation and healing of the people and the land." Her eyes lit up as she responded, "That is like a peaceful jihad, a struggle or mission that Allah gives."

The next day I said to Nahla, a member of MPT, after she showed us around a clinic that she and other doctors were building to serve the poor of the area, "Shukran jazilan! (Thank you very much) for taking good care of us here. We're impressed by the work you're doing." She answered, "Your eyes are beautiful." Nahla saw the puzzled look on my face and explained. "This expression is often used to respond to a compliment. It means that you see things as good or beautiful, because there is already goodness and beauty in you or in your eyes."

"What a lovely expression," I thought at the time, but I continued to mull it over as we traveled back to Baghdad. It explained why those of us

Part One: Summer 2004—Spring 2006

who repeatedly return to Iraq see it as beautiful, in spite of the violence permeating Iraqi life. Love for the people did shape our vision about Iraq, but the people were still beautiful in their own right, and the work Nahla and others were doing was still impressive, whether I saw it through eyes of love or not.

Other ways beauty and love were connected came to focus. There are those, who, with loving eyes, see the beauty beneath layers of character flaws and twisted egos of those around them. Their seeing and calling forth beauty hidden in others evoke healing and transformation. I thought of Iraqi volunteers at the orphanage that patiently assisted Yasser, a child with cerebral palsy, practice walking. There were those in our neighborhood who befriended and cared for the homeless or poor in that area. I thought of leaders of women's organizations, who helped empower other women in spite of the surge of repression of women since the war.

I meet so many people here with eyes of love, who not only help to keep hope alive in the people they serve, but also lighten the heaviness in my own heart from all the pain I have seen.

I thought of the hospital in Najaf when Michele and I revisited the IAC in the Green Zone a few weeks later, now called NIAC (National Iraqi Assistance Center). Two U.S. officers spoke about the work they were doing, including sending seven children to New York for open-heart surgery and seven for eye operations in Turkey. One officer said, "There's a backlog of over 6,000 persons, who can't be treated here, to get out-of-country medical treatment approved. They are waiting for a charitable organization to sponsor them." He was excited that a Spanish NGO had just agreed to take eighty to one hundred children to Spain and cover the costs for one parent to accompany each child.

We were glad for those who have been able to get this kind of care, but couldn't help thinking about the neglected regional hospital in Najaf, which thousands relied on for care. We pointed out that after being responsible for the major damage of the medical facilities in the country during the invasion and occupation, the U.S. had done little to rebuild and supply medical centers. In return, the officer said, "We must support the Iraqi government as *they* build up the medical system, using the motto, 'Iraqis helping Iraqis,' and 'to empower Iraqis.' They set their *own* agendas and goals, just as they are working on building a professional police system, one Iraqi people can trust." The officer went on to talk about the problems of unemployment, and the need for safety to allow international corporations to bring in capital to stimulate the economy and provide jobs.

We listened, but wondered where this resolve to let the Iraqis set their own agenda was when it was most crucial—in the months and year after the invasion, when U.S. officials were making major decisions about reshaping their society. Where was it when Iraqis were finally told they could form their own ministries, but the U.S. appointed international advisors who had veto power over ministry decisions? Why was the advisor appointed for the Ministry of Health soon withdrawn? What did that say about the importance American administrators assigned for Iraqi health needs? Why couldn't the U.S. provide resources, but allow Iraqis to oversee medical development?

And where was the concern for unemployment and the economy in those early post-invasion months when it was safe on the streets for rebuilding and Iraqis were crying out for jobs, but the contracts were given to international corporations? These corporations delayed starting the reconstruction for a year or more, after millions were siphoned off with multiple sub-contracting or into the pockets of corrupt leaders or construction firms. There were the billions of dollars allocated for reconstruction that were diverted into security for the U.S. military, and then the U.S. policies gutting Iraq's economy and imposing on Iraq a new free-market economy that benefited foreign corporations rather than the Iraqi economy.

Late January, in the wake of the Danish newspapers publishing controversial anti-Muslim cartoons in September 2005, several churches in Baghdad were attacked by car bombs in retaliation. On February 1, our team released the following statement of concern:

> We, the members of the Christian Peacemaker Teams in Iraq, are disturbed by cartoons from twelve different artists, connecting the prophet Mohammed with terrorism, published in September by Denmark's daily paper, the *Jyllands-Posten*. The publisher claims the freedom of speech to publish the cartoons, but we believe the cartoons spread hate and bigotry.
>
> To those who believe and act as if terrorism is an essential part of the Islamic faith, we say No! Stop! We cannot stand by and remain silent when our gracious Muslim brothers and sisters are being defamed. Some members of *all* religious and

cultural groups have taken up the way of violence, killing innocent civilians for political causes. Christian leaders of our countries have been carrying out such domination and oppression, yet we, as Christians, do not want others to see our faith as one that advocates dominating and oppressing the poor and weak of the world.

Those of us working in Iraq see the suffering and pain that acts of terror cause. Terrorism is wrong, though it is hypocritical to label Muslims as terrorists when our own countries have been the greatest perpetrators of terror and violence around the world.

Instead of spreading prejudice about another faith, we call on artists, publishers, religious leaders, and all people to put their creative efforts into exposing and eradicating the deeper injustices that foster the use of terror. We must open our hearts and minds to listen and learn from the riches of each others' cultures and find ways to build bridges in our fractured world.

An Iraqi human rights worker translated our statement into Arabic and arranged to have it published in the *Al Sabah*, a large Iraqi newspaper, and three organization newspapers, and to have it read on Dar a-Salaam Radio.

Three weeks later we went to a church where a small bomb had exploded and damaged the outer wall. "I guess it takes a bomb to bring our friends here to see us again," the priest and friend of our team said with a twinkle in his eye, as he welcomed us to the Sunday afternoon mass. "It was frightening," he said, "but, fortunately no one was hurt. Yes, it was shocking, but we need to continue on with our life and work."

In our visit today, we grieved for the Christian and Muslim victims, who should not suffer for the wrong caused by others of their faith. We were encouraged by people of all faiths who worked together for mutual respect and cooperation, as well as victims of violence who refused to get caught up in cycles of hate and revenge and were able to "continue on."

A few days later, two Iraqi human rights workers we had worked with a year earlier, calling themselves "Independent Activists," came to our door to show us a leaflet asking the kidnappers to release our four men. Without our knowing, they had had two public demonstrations and a press conference on our behalf. At their next vigil in Firdos Square, they planned to hand out copies of their leaflet and of our Danish cartoon statement. They advised us not to join them because the presence of internationals might attract danger to the whole group.

Seeing the Broken and the Beautiful

"There's no reason why your people should be kidnapped," one told us. "They came here to help the Iraqi people. We want you to know you still have friends here!" We were grateful for their expressions of love. We'd had the sense that God had been watching out for us here, as well as our Iraqi friends. We will never know how often.

It was late January 2006 when Allia called, saying that her husband and six other Palestinian men from Baladiyaat had been detained during nighttime raids. In the following days, our team visited detention facilities and U.S. offices with Allia, trying to find where the men were being held and on what charges, but without any success.

A week later, several Palestinian men came to our apartment and reported that Allia's husband was found murdered and buried in a sewer in Najaf. The grief-struck community agonized about what they should do. Should they try to leave the country? They asked us to send two people to stay with families over the next two nights to be there in case police came and harassed them.

That night, Allan and I stayed with Nasser's family in the Baladiyaat compound. Many others came and spent the evening with us, showing pictures and telling their stories. They said that at least 150 Palestinians in Iraq had been killed since the invasion.

The next morning Ryah, Nasser's mother, told us the story of her family leaving Palestine in 1948 and coming to Iraq when she was eleven. For two years they lived at an old military base in Basra, where families were crammed in old barracks. "It felt like living in a jail," she recalled. From there, they moved with others to Baghdad into places where Iraqi Jews lived before leaving for Israel. The Iraqi government subsidized the rent of others. The UN built the Baladiyaat compound. Many Iraqis had the mistaken belief that the government built it for them, so resented those who lived there.

Nasser was one of 400 Palestinians in Baghdad who recently received deportation orders, which he thought was intended to scare the family into leaving. While saying goodbye that afternoon, I saw tears in his eyes, and behind them, deep pain. I wanted to cry out for a safe refuge for these strong and courageous people who simply wanted to live in peace.

PART ONE: Summer 2004—Spring 2006

On February 22, violence broke out throughout Iraq when the Al-Askari Shia shrine in Samarra, north of Baghdad, was blown up. Gun battles erupted in many Baghdad neighborhoods. Police closed bridges. Around the country, groups of angry Shia men gathered to march and protest or retaliate by attacking Sunni mosques and leaders. People were afraid this would escalate into sectarian war. Iraqis called the day of the shrine bombing "our 9/11."

On the streets, people lined up at food shops to stock up before they closed for the three "days of mourning" declared by Prime Minister Jaafari. He called on Iraqis to "close the road to those who want to undermine national unity." Grand Ayatollah Ali as-Sistani termed it "Black Wednesday" and called for seven days of mourning. We sent messages back home, asking others to join us in prayer for the Iraqi people.

The following day was calmer, but reports of widespread violence were sobering. Sunni leaders reported ten Sunni Imams killed, 168 Sunni mosques attacked, and forty-seven men pulled off a bus and killed in Baqubah. The morgue in Baghdad received eighty new bodies, and in areas east of Baghdad, fifty were killed. Even in the following days of curfew, sporadic violence continued.

The news that did not get circulated as widely, however, was about the actions to curb ethnic warfare and foster unity. Sunni and Shia crowds marched together from the al Mansour neighborhood to the Khadamiyah district in Baghdad, calling for peace. In another Baghdad neighborhood, Shia residents protected a Sunni mosque. Sistani urged Shias not to attack Sunnis or their holy places. Muqtada as-Sadr also called for an end to the sectarian violence and commissioned the Mahdi Army in Basra to protect the Sunni mosques.

Iraqis believed that those who bombed the shrine were trying to incite more division and hatred between Shia and Sunni. When I asked a neighbor who might be behind it, he said, "All the leaders would use this to grab more power. Sistani had been speaking out against civil war or violent jihad, which could damage Iraqi society even more."

Within the next week, several Iraqi television news programs, including Baghdadiya TV and the Iraqi Islamic TV, reported that the usual guards of the shrine had been sent away by a large group of U.S. military and Iraqi police the night before it was bombed, implying U.S. involvement. The next morning, two shrine guards were found alive but handcuffed inside. A few days later, two of our team met with the Minister of Housing and Reconstruction, who said it would take ten men about twelve hours to set up enough explosives to do this kind of damage. The U.S. offered to rebuild the shrine, but the Iraqi Islamic Party asked that repair be delayed until an independent investigation could be done. About four months later, U.S. officials claimed that a man named Yousri Fukhar Mohammed Ali confessed to organizing the bombing, but this didn't resolve the issue for many Iraqis.

On March 5, the eve of the 100th day of the kidnapping, our team gathered and voiced our prayers for Harmeet, Jim, Tom, and Norman . . . for good to come out of this bad thing, for God's love to flow powerfully in them and uphold them, and for them to be released soon.

This helped strengthen us for what was yet to come.

12

Tragedy and Keeping Hope

Friday, March 10, proceeded as a restful day off, until about 9:40 p.m. when we got a call from Doug, CPT's co-director, and then, from a member of the Hostage Working Group. That morning, Iraqi police found the dead body of a Caucasian man that could be Tom's in a garbage dumping area along the road going to the Baghdad airport. They planned to send the body back by military transport to Dover, Delaware Military Base forensic lab for forensic data, DNA, and identification.

We asked U.S. authorities if we could identify the body, but they said it was already sealed, and they didn't have any photos. We learned that if a body was found on the streets, Iraqis had jurisdiction over it. If they determined it was not Iraqi, U.S. officials took possession. We would not be allowed access to his body if it were Tom's. Only the family had that right. Later that night, our director called and said that fingerprints confirmed Tom's identity. We were stricken. We grieved for Tom and his family. *What had Tom endured?*

Iraqi friends came for visits to comfort and support us, since for us this was a death in our family. Fears for the other three gripped us—*what if they meet the same fate?* We desperately wanted to prevent this, but felt helpless and weak.

Should we go ahead with the two meetings scheduled at our apartment the next morning, that we had waited so long to have because of the perpetual curfews? We agonized. One was with MPT leaders, a Sunni human rights worker, and a Christian priest, for building a coalition among ethnic groups to prevent sectarian violence. The second was to connect members of MPT with Palestinian Iraqis asking for accompaniment to travel to one of Iraq's borders. While emotionally it was hard for us to host these meetings, we decided it was important to proceed.

Beth had a frustrating time trying to get permission to accompany Tom's body to the U.S. She contacted U.S. State Department and military officials in the U.S. and Iraq, who went back and forth for two days, granting and then denying permission. When it looked like she could do it, she went to the Green Zone and got on a flight to the Anaconda Air Force Base near Balad, the site of the largest U.S. base mortuary in Iraq.

At the last minute, Beth was not allowed to travel with his body, but was able to offer blessings for the bodies of Tom and an unidentified Iraqi man killed while in U.S. custody, also being sent to Dover for forensic examination. After their bodies were put into a cargo plane, she read aloud from the Old and New Testament and the Qu'ran. She commented later, that, "Even in death, Tom accompanied an Iraqi safely to his destination."[1]

There had been rumors that Tom had been tortured. Those viewing his body at the Dover Military Base saw a bullet wound in his right temple, a bruise on his face and were told there had been a number of bullet holes in his chest, but no signs of torture.

> I struggle with the darkness that wants to creep in and take over—not the darkness of evil, but of pain and discouragement, and some anger. This is the hardest test, I think, when we have to face death in our own "family." But every crisis we've gone through here has had its own challenges that have pushed me to the very edge of my own strength and forced me to seek help beyond myself. I have to reclaim my faith that God is still with us, guiding and caring for our three captive men, their families, and us. I long to run into the woods and hills at home and greet the beauty of springtime as buds begin to open, and forget this bad dream. But it is real and we are experiencing more of what Iraqis experience, not just carrying it vicariously.

"If I understand the message of God, we are here to take part in the creation of the peaceable realm of God . . . and that is to love God with all our heart, our mind and our strength and to love our neighbors and enemies as we love God and ourselves. . . ." Allan read during our memorial service

---

1. Brown, ed., *118 Days*, 199–202.

Part One: Summer 2004—Spring 2006

for Tom at a local church in Baghdad. These were Tom's words, written days before he was kidnapped. At the front of the sanctuary was a large picture of Tom, a bouquet of fresh flowers, and burning candles.

It was rewarding to see in the congregation the caring faces of so many Muslim and Christian Iraqis who had loved Tom. The parish priest gave a tribute to Tom, saying he not only laid his life down for Jesus, he also welcomed people of all faiths, honoring the one God we all worship, whether we use the name, "Allah" or "God."

"Tom was clear that if any harm came to him he didn't want anyone to act out of revenge. He called us to follow Jesus's example of loving and praying for those labeled enemy," I said in the beginning tribute to Tom. When I came to the part about Tom's captivity and death, the words were harder to get out. Maxine read excerpts from Tom's writing in which he spoke of his struggle to not let rage take over, become numb, or suppress the pain he encountered, but to learn compassion while staying with that pain. Our tribute to Tom ended with the words we heard expressed by so many Iraqis in the past three days: "Tom, we will greatly miss you!"

Afterward, some of our Iraqi friends voiced their feelings about Tom. One Muslim Peacemaker Team colleague said, "When Tom was killed, I and others in my organization cried. Many said that Tom came to Iraq to do a good thing for Iraqis, but Iraqis refused it and killed him. I told them I was sure he would go to God, because he was working for peace. Others disagreed, saying, 'but he's a *Christian*.' I countered this, saying, 'but *he gave his life for us*.'"

A neighbor said that she could understand if the kidnappers killed him in the first two weeks, thinking he was a spy, but "who could kill such a gentle person after being with him for three months?"

We followed the Iraqi custom of having black cloth memorial banners made to hang in public. Iraqi friends hung two near the place where Tom's body was found. Written on them in Arabic was, "In Memory of Tom Fox. In this place Christian Peacemaker Teams declare, 'We are made for God and we return to God' [from the Qur'an]. To those who held him, we declare, 'God has forgiven you.'"

Amidst media interviews and other tasks, we received loving care from Iraqi and international friends and colleagues through visits, phone calls, and e-mail messages. We prayed for the other three captives and honored Tom's life by continuing the work he was a part of. It did not take away the sorrow, but it helped remind us why Tom was in Iraq and willing to give his life.

Tragedy and Keeping Hope

A few days later, journalist Henry Porter, in his article, "Tom Fox, Death Squads, and the Dogs of War,"[2] referred to the gruesome reports of atrocities discovered in the basement of the Interior Ministry (men killed with electric drills, etc.) and wrote, "These Special Police Commando units were created, trained and equipped by the U.S. These units represent the operational implementation of the so-called 'Salvador Option' being championed by some people in the Pentagon. It is reasonable to ask if the CPT-4 kidnapping was related to their investigation of death squads. Unfortunately, Tom Fox is not the first American murdered while investigating U.S.-sponsored death squads in Iraq." We didn't know if the U.S. was involved, but we knew the U.S. has been responsible for such activities as part of intelligence operations in other parts of the world.

"Ten of my friends have been killed," Ziad, a young Palestinian man, told us with a look of anguish. "Our family has decided to leave Iraq. I don't want to wait until I lose my brother, father, or sister." "All hell is breaking through!" Nasser declared. Two Palestinian men had been killed two days before, and the head of one of them was thrown back into the compound. Yesterday, four were killed. Two brothers, in their twenties, were taken from a barber shop and their bodies hadn't been found yet. "We want to leave by Saturday," Nasser told us. Our team had accompanied nineteen Palestinian women, men, and children to the Syrian border in October 2005. After six weeks they were moved to a UN refugee camp inside Syria. Our team now decided that two of us would go with this group wanting to go to Jordan.

Early morning on March 18, eight days after Tom's body was found, Beth and I left Baghdad with eighty-eight Palestinians from the Baladiyaat compound. On the two buses headed toward the Iraqi-Jordanian border were sixteen families, including forty-two children. Before leaving, we spoke on the phone with United Nations High Commissioner for Refugees (UNHCR) staff in Baghdad and the field officer and coordinator at the Ruashiayd Refugee Camp in Eastern Jordan, who offered their assistance.

On the bus we got acquainted with many of the families and had fun joking with four teenage boys in the seat in front of us. Three-year-old Hibba kept peeking up over the back of her seat to us, with big bright eyes and a trusting smile, then snuggling down between her parents.

---

2. Porter, "Tom Fox, Death Squads, and the Dogs of War." See also Porter's "Wikileaks Documents Confirm Tom Fox Died for Our Sins."

Part One: Summer 2004—Spring 2006

At the second of three Iraqi military checkpoints between Baghdad and Ramadi a masked Iraqi soldier entered the buses, walked along the aisle looking over the people and the overhead baggage racks. We saw eight U.S. military convoys along the way, often causing traffic to stop or slow down. One convoy escorted traffic past Fallujah and Ramadi and then turned off. It was 9:30 when we saw the lights at the border crossing, then closed for the night.

"You will not be allowed to enter the border crossing and leave Iraq unless the Iraqi MOI authorizes it," a border official told the group the next morning. After some time, however, the eighty-eight Palestinians were allowed in the gate and slowly went through the processing steps. Border officials stamped their travel documents, "no re-entry into Iraq."

About noon, the buses entered the "no man's land" area in between Iraq and Jordan. They didn't go far before Jordanian police and officials, standing in a line across the road, stopped them and demanded that they turn around and go back to Iraq. We got off with the Palestinian leaders, and together spoke with the chief of police and other officials about the threat that prompted the Palestinians to leave their homes and their being unable to re-enter Iraq. The Palestinian leaders finally agreed to go back closer to the Iraqi border gates to set up camp.

As the buses were turning around, a Jordanian policeman insulted one of the Iraqi drivers. The angry driver stopped the bus and jumped out yelling and ready to fight. The Palestinian leaders quickly got off the bus. Beth and I, and then others, followed. Soon there was a line of Jordanian soldiers and police on the Jordanian side of the road holding their guns, and a line of Iraqi soldiers and police with their guns ready, along with about twenty Palestinians.

Quickly Beth went to listen to and help calm down the bus driver. I went to the Jordanian police chief and urged him to ask the policeman to apologize to the driver and tell his men that insulting the driver was not acceptable. The police chief said he would, but not there in public. Others helped calm down tensions enough for the Palestinians to get back on the bus and be driven back to the Iraqi border.

On the barren desert ground just outside the Iraqi border gate, each Palestinian family made a pile of their belongings. They erected the one tent that the group brought along, saying it would be for women and children. The leaders made a list of persons in the group for us to take to the UNHCR office in eastern Jordan.

Tragedy and Keeping Hope

It was hard to say goodbye to these families. One of the mothers came to us and asked desperately, "What will we do now?" We listened as she shared her fear. We told her and others we would do all we could to help them after we left. The worried but determined women, men, and children braced themselves for an approaching sandstorm. Iraqi guards also offered to let the women and children sleep in the small mosque just inside the border gates and use the toilet inside. Feeling torn, we left.

As Beth and I walked toward the Jordanian border, three Jordanian border officials stopped us, the chief of police, chief of intelligence, and chief of customs. "Why did you bring these Palestinians here?" they demanded. We explained why they came and our role in accompanying them. "The refugees must go through proper channels to emigrate," they insisted. "They do this by getting application forms from the Jordanian Ministry of Interior."

At the Ruashaiyd Palestinian Refugee camp on the way to Amman, we gave the UNHCR official the list of those camped inside the border. She said we should advise them not to give their documents to any Jordanian officials or to fill out forms for the Jordanian MOI. If they did, the information would be used to make security files on them, and possibly to harass them.

The more I thought about the plight of the Palestinian refugees, the clearer it became. There was no good option for them to find safe refuge. The proper channels were not in place for them to leave their dangerous situation and go to another country. Workers assisting refugees operated under limitations set by UN agencies under pressure from governments not wanting more refugees coming in. Basic policy and structural changes needed to be made in how nations and international organizations responded to groups of people fleeing extreme threat, so that new possibilities were created.

We saw our accompanying this group as violence prevention. These women, children, and men left to escape death. How do people under threat, who lack the power to escape situations of terror, break through a closed system? Sometimes it takes confrontational actions or civil disobedience to change the status quo and make a statement that positive options must be found. Even though it did not fit the rules and was inconvenient for the officials, nonviolent resistance and pushing the system to change seemed these Palestinians' only available route.

With International Committee of the Red Cross (ICRC) and Iraqi Red Crescent Society (IRCS) officials in Amman, we were able to discuss these issues, as well as seek aid for the refugees.

Part One: Summer 2004—Spring 2006

Early the next day (March 21), our press release sparked calls from BBC and AP journalists to interview leaders of the group camped out in the border, resulting in a number of articles in international media. International aid organizations gave the group tents, food, water, and other supplies, and made a relocation plan. After six weeks between the Iraqi-Jordanian border, Syria agreed to allow them, and some other Palestinians who had come to the Jordanian border, entry into a refugee camp in Syria.

March 23, the day after I returned to Baghdad, was a happy one. After being held for 118 days, Norman, Harmeet, and Jim were freed by British and American forces and were in the Green Zone (GZ)! We had a whirlwind of phone calls from media and friends congratulating us.

Officials from the Hostage Working Group didn't allow us to see the three released men at the British Embassy until 4:00 p.m. We went prepared to stay with the men, as earlier promised, but were now told we couldn't. It was great to see them, but officials allowed us only an hour with them. They were thin, but seemed strong, alert, and in good spirits. Jim said their captors didn't physically abuse them, but they didn't get adequate food. Harmeet said they were able to exercise and move around the room, and were not bound all of the time. Jim shared that during the kidnapping Tom prayed for us. When they discussed whether the team had left the country, Tom told the others, "If it were me, I would stay." All along, he believed we were here.

Jim gave us a brief overview. On the eighth day of captivity, December 8, Tom and Norman were separated from the other two and taken to another house. They were all brought back together on December 11. Then on February 12, Tom was taken away. The guards told them they were all going to be released one by one, but they weren't. Then the guards said they were going to announce that Tom was killed, but wouldn't really kill him. The three feared that something happened to Tom on March 11, when they saw Tom's and their pictures on TV and heard something in Arabic about Tom. Their guards said it was a feature on Tom, but that he was OK. They didn't know definitely that he was killed until the morning they were freed.

The three said their release was confusing. Their guards left the building just before MNF-I forces arrived, making them think the rescue was coordinated between the forces and their captors. We were thankful it didn't involve a shootout.

Tragedy and Keeping Hope

The next day, we returned to the GZ for a second visit with Jim and Harmeet, knowing that Norman had just left the country to return to England. The promised four hours with them was shortened to a little over an hour. They were able to share what they called "just a scratch in the surface" of what they experienced. It was frustrating that our position as their teammates and representatives of our organization wasn't respected and we didn't have the time to really hear what they went through personally.[3]

Harmeet and Jim gave us a message to give to a press conference we had arranged for that evening: "We are deeply grateful for all who prayed for and worked for our release. Our heads are in a swirl and we have no words to describe our gratitude and joy. When we are ready, we will talk with the press." A variety of international media personnel attended our press conference. I read Jim and Harmeet's statement and then our team statement that expressed our gratefulness for their release, the outpouring of compassion and support for members of our team, and then called on all not to vilify those responsible for the kidnapping.

Reporters asked about the men's condition and their captivity. They also raised some difficult issues, such as the false accusation that the three had not thanked the MNF-I for their part in the release. "Isn't it contradictory to be against military presence in Iraq, yet accept military rescue?" one asked. I explained that though we had not wanted military intervention, we were thankful to all who helped to free them.

We were deeply grateful for their release, to see them in such good shape, and to have this nightmare over. But we knew they needed to heal and pull their lives together. We would also have to deal with the pain, fear, and grief that we still carried. We needed to figure out what this meant for our team's future. I didn't know what it meant for mine. *Also, I had no idea that in a little less than a year, I would also need to heal from my own kidnapping in Iraq.* In the meantime, we needed to wrap up things here and prepare to return to the U.S.

The next fall, Iraqi authorities arrested several Iraqi men for carrying out the abduction and Tom's murder and asked Harmeet, Jim, and Norman to testify at the trial in Iraq's Central Criminal Court. On December 8, 2006, they made a public statement unconditionally forgiving their captors, while acknowledging the suffering their captors caused them. They linked the "catastrophic levels of violence and the lack of effective protection of human rights in Iraq" to the U.S. led invasion and occupation and

---

3. For their accounts of their captivity, see Loney, *Captivity*, and Kember, *Hostage in Iraq*.

Part One: Summer 2004—Spring 2006

understood that their captor's actions, though not justified, "were part of a cycle of violence they themselves experienced."[4]

What now for our team—after our three and a half year presence here? It was essential that we hear from Iraqi friends and partners we worked alongside. Over the years they had offered us support and love, while advising us, warning us, and challenging us.

They were now worried for us. Many suggested we leave or change location until there was a stable government or until public attention on CPT subsided. One colleague, however, said, "I believe you're very useful here, so wonder why you would leave." A human rights worker suggested we relocate near or in the Kurdish region and focus on building bridges between the Kurdish north and the central part of Iraq. Another advised us to move to the south. A Chaldean priest who had been a friend and adviser said, "I would feel bad if something happened to you, but I would be angry if you disappear. If you care for us just in the good times, I will forget you. If you take care of us in the bad times, I will remember you. *You die when you do nothing, but live when you do something. Everyone dies, but not everyone lives.* When we lost our friend, Tom, the suffering was hard, but it gave us courage. When they bombed my church, it didn't weaken us; it made us strong. Iraq's recovery may take ten years or more. But we can't wait until the tragedy is over to work, laugh, and hope."

It was April 6 and I was on the airplane, flying back to the U.S. I was now in a place of safety, away from a country of fear and struggle. Thinking over the past months, a dam inside me burst, and tears of grief and pain could not be held back. In Iraq I felt I had to put aside and submerge much of the pain, grief, and anger I experienced in order to survive emotionally and keep the fear in check. I became a rock in the midst of it—not uncaring, but guarding my emotional vulnerability. I thanked God for being safe, for taking care of me and others, and for enabling me to start the healing work I needed to do. I grieved, however, for Iraqi people caught in a desperate situation and not able to leave and have the luxury of safe spaces for healing.

4. Loney, *Captivity*, 394–96.

Part Two

Summer 2006—Fall 2011

13

We Are Kurds First

IN JULY 2006, THREE months after our team left Baghdad at the end of the kidnapping ordeal, we met in the U.S. to debrief and make decisions. In a letter explaining our team's planned return to Iraq, I wrote,

> We go, believing that with the increased violence, it is still important—maybe even more important—for international people to be there to witness and tell the truth about what is happening, and let Iraqis know that others still care about them. We need to learn and grow from these painful events, but I hope that Tom Fox's death doesn't lead us to turn away from our willingness to take risks to walk with the people here. Not only do I want to see nonviolent intervention make a difference in world-wide situations of violence. God has given me a deep love and concern for people in Iraq and all over the world living under threat and fear.

When I said goodbye to my husband, Art, it was a difficult moment. All the "what ifs" came to mind, but his last word of advice was, "Don't let fear control you."

It was three months after our team left Baghdad at the end of the kidnapping ordeal and then met in the U.S. We took our Iraqi colleagues in Baghdad seriously when they said that working with or living near us put them in too much danger. And because last January, authorities in Baghdad stopped giving visas to other team members trying to come in, we thought it might be hard to enter the country there. We decided to move, at least temporarily, to the city of As-Suleimaniya (usually called just "Suleimaniya," or "Sulaimani") in northeastern Iraq, an area the local

Kurds called "Iraqi Kurdistan," or sometimes "Southern Kurdistan." A Kurdish woman working for a human rights and development organization helped us get visas, find housing, and became a legal sponsor for us until we could register as an international NGO.

One of our questions was answered when we got a call a week later from a member of the Muslim Peacemaker Team (MPT) in Najaf. "There was an explosion in the city this morning," he told us. "Security's become worse. Outside groups are coming in to destabilize the country. Passenger cars are being attacked along the road from Baghdad to Najaf. It's not a good time for you to come south."

Along a gravel path, up steep stone stairs, and through picnic sites terraced on the side of the mountain we climbed, at a vacation area called Zewe. Under a canopy of shade trees, where it's cooler, extended families talked, ate, and listened to music. Everywhere people greeted us warmly.

A group of men convinced us to stop and sit in their circle of folding chairs. Skewers of lamb pieces roasted over a grill to our side. "Until the 1991 war, Saddam's military controlled this and other vacation spots in the Kurdish area of Iraq and closed them to the public," one of the men explained. "I'm thankful to the U.S. for getting rid of Saddam. He destroyed the humanity of the Iraqi people and caused division among us." Then he stopped. "But let's not talk about politics," he said as he passed around juicy wedges of watermelon followed by other food.

Walking on farther, we stopped to admire a group of women's brightly colored traditional Kurdish dresses, and they lured us into their circle. They just happened to have extra dresses in a bag and invited us to try them on. We couldn't resist. After picture taking, they pulled us into a Kurdish dance, in a large circle, interlocking hands and arms.

This day in the mountains was refreshing in the midsummer heat, and we experienced the welcome of Kurdish hospitality. It wasn't hard for us to contrast life in the Kurdish North with other parts of Iraq. We're thankful that people here don't have to deal with the same daily violence as in the South. They've known relative peace for many years, allowing for more openness to strangers and lightness in their laughter and fun.

Our Kurdish sponsor showed us around Suleimaniya and taught us greetings in Kurdish. "We see ourselves as Kurds first, then Iraqi. Kurds are the largest ethnic group in the world that doesn't have its own country," she said as she briefed us about Kurdish history and culture.

We Are Kurds First

We learned that the Kurdistan Regional Government (KRG) was the semi-autonomous governing body for the northeastern governorates of Dohuk, Erbil, and Suleimaniya. The KRG had its own parliament, but was also under the Iraqi Central Government in Baghdad. This semi-autonomous status became possible after UN Security Council Resolution 688 (April 5, 1991) established no-fly zones in northern and southern Iraq and guarded these three northern governorates in October 1991 to protect humanitarian operations from Saddam's forces.

On May 19, 1992, Iraqi Kurds held their first elections and established the KRG. Since then, there have been many political parties, but the Patriotic Union of Kurdistan (PUK) and Kurdish Democratic Party (KDP or PDK) have been the main power holders in this region. Rivalry between the two parties erupted into fighting in 1994, called the "Kurdish civil war," and lasted until September 1998, when party leaders Jalal Talabani and Massoud Barzani signed a peace agreement. In 2002, the KRG Parliament resumed meeting. At the time of our arrival in July 2006, Massoud Barzani was the President of the KRG and head of the KDP, and his nephew, Nechirvan Barzani, also KDP, was the Prime Minister.

Kurdish people readily shared about the tragedies they've experienced. We learned about the process of "Arabization," which forcefully displaced Kurdish families to other areas of the country and brought in Arab families, changing the demographics of the oil-rich northern region around Kirkuk. This started in the 1920s after the fall of the Ottoman Empire, but accelerated under Saddam. People spoke about "the Anfal," the Ba'ath government's genocide campaign against Iraqi Kurds in the late 1980s.

One of our interpreters grew up in a village near Halubja. His family traveled over the mountains into Iran and stayed in refugee camps after the chemical bombing of Halubja on March 16, 1988, returning to Iraq after the end of the Iran-Iraq war in 1989. They fled a second time during the Kurdish uprising against Saddam in March 1991, when three million Kurds fled to Iran and Turkey, in what he called the "exodus." In the coming year we had a chance to record more in-depth accounts from survivors of these events (see stories in chapter 17).

From the doors of our hotel in the center of the city, we stepped into streets teeming with people walking and shopping, and among men selling their wares—anything from fruit or underwear to batteries or goat cheese. Women sat on the sidewalk selling grape leaves, parsley, and dried herbs in neat piles on burlap bags. Down the street was an old indoor "bazzar" with hundreds of stalls crammed side-by side. Here one could find clothes, housewares, fabrics, spices, and jewelry.

On the street, women's dress ranged from conservative Muslim black abayas to Western-style clothing, or something in between. At parties and picnics, women often wear Kurdish dresses made of bright, shiny material with sequins. In the city, about a fourth of the men wear traditional Kurdish baggy pants, with or without a long-sleeved open top jackets with a thick sash around their waists. Older men often wear a keffiyeh or other cloth wrapped around their head in a semi-turban style. Kurds in rural areas wear more traditional and conservative clothing.

Kurdish Iraqis are mostly Sunni Muslims, with a minority of Shia Muslims. Relationships between Sunni and Shia are better in Kurdistan than in other parts of the country. Other smaller ethnic or religious groups include Yezidis, Shabakh, and Christians—about 1 or 2 percent of the population. There are two Christian churches in Suleimaniya. Kurdish is the main language, with a minority also knowing Arabic. We learned that it is safer here than in other parts of Iraq, but there's less freedom of speech and action. People complain, but seem to accept this, believing this is the price they have to pay for more security.

Like other parts of Iraq, electricity is on only four or five hours in a twenty-four-hour period. Cars wait in the same long lines for gasoline for a cheaper price. Men sell black-market gasoline along the streets for a higher price. There's an undercurrent of social unrest and occasional public protest about the rising costs of fuel and the shortage of electricity and public services. We were approaching the hottest time of the year, August, when in Suleimaniya it would be 115–125 degrees Fahrenheit, in contrast to 125–135 degrees in Baghdad.

As we drove through rugged hills and windy mountain passes, we whizzed by fields of sunflowers, melons, or terraced rows of grapes, and then villages with stone and mud houses. We were driving to Erbil (commonly called "Hawler" by Kurds), the capital of Iraqi Kurdistan, to learn from and build relationships with other NGOs working in the region. Much of the terrain reminded me of areas of Nevada or Utah. Now in the dry season, the land looks parched. Just north of Suleimaniya, our translator pointed out the Fernaldi U.S. Military Base and the Susia Prison that was still under U.S. control. Our car passed through many checkpoints, where guards wanted to see our passports.

The fortified UN Compound, on the edge of Erbil, was surrounded by high concrete walls, and multiple checkpoints for vehicle and personal searches.

According to a UNAMI (United Nations Assistance Mission for Iraq) official, "The new challenge we're facing is the displacement of people by threat and violence. Christians are moving out of Mosul to villages north and east of that city. Muslims from Mosul are coming to Erbil. People from Kirkuk and Baghdad come to Erbil and Suleimaniya. Five hundred families moving into a village cause overcrowding and hardship for all the people. Political parties are trying to change the demographics and affect the future status of Kirkuk. Kurds fear that more Arabs coming from Baghdad will increase tensions in their region. There's peace here, but it's a delicate balance that could be upset at any time."

"Mosul is split in half by the river," he continued. "In the east side is a mixed population of Shia Arab, Kurdish, Christian, and other religious minorities such as the Shabak and Yezidis. Most of the fighting, bombing, and assassinations take place there. In the west side, Sunni Arabs police themselves and do not allow the U.S. and Iraqi military in. Officially the U.S. has turned security for Mosul over to the Iraqi military, but in actuality, the U.S. is in charge." He explained that American soldiers travel daily back and forth in tanks between the U.S. base in the south of the city and the U.S. Embassy and the UN compound in the north. "They're often attacked as they do. Because of this, tank drivers drive very fast and often crush people as they go. There are about ten to twenty such accidents a day, killing or injuring people. The soldiers don't stop to help, for fear of being attacked. This causes a lot of pain and anger."

"One of the problems in Tikrit is that former Ba'athist soldiers, fired after the invasion, don't have retirement income or compensation," he said. "If the U.S. had been smart, it would have continued their retirement salary and there would be less fighting or accepting money from the resistance to take in fighters. Terrorists from Syria, Yemen, or Saudia Arabia pay families $500-$600 a month to forge ID's for them, and live with them as one of their family. When the MNF has been presented with one easy and one hard solution, they have chosen the hard one."

Part Two: Summer 2006—Fall 2011

UN agencies interact regularly with the U.S. military and share information. American forces accompany UN staff when they travel outside their compound. Some of their projects are similar, but never done jointly. He expressed concern about the military's humanitarian efforts, which may be positive, but blur the military's main role. It also put workers of humanitarian groups in more danger, as people who take out their anger in hostile actions don't always differentiate between the military and humanitarian groups, or think they're all connected. We heard a similar concern from the director of ICRC (International Committee of the Red Cross) in Erbil.

Staff from other NGOs moved around freely and safely in Iraqi Kurdistan. Some traveled within what they called the "gray areas," contested areas outside the KRG with a mostly Kurdish population, such as Khanaqin, Makhmour, and Sinjar. Several thought the Christian communities north and east of Mosul were safe for internationals to visit, but not to live or work in. "In Mosul or Kirkuk, many would suspect you worked for the U.S. government or CIA," one said. Working with internationals in those areas was dangerous for Iraqis. Having Christian in our name would be a stumbling block for some, until we built a reputation of trust and good work.

"This is the first time my wife told me she was glad I was leaving!" Muthana, our friend from MPT in Karbela, told us with a laugh. A month after we came to Suleimaniya, he arrived for refuge after he received threats on his life and was shot at in front of his home. Rumors had circulated that he was working with the U.S. occupation. Others in MPT also received threats. He was OK, but was obviously shaken by the assassination attempt. We grieved for him, but were thankful to see him alive. He didn't know what he would do, or where he would go. "It's hard to think under such stress," he said. Many of his family were now begging him to return. He felt lost here without his work. After three weeks, he went home.

Other friends from Baghdad kept us in touch with what was happening there. "It's hard on our five young children," one told us. "We keep them inside for their safety and don't take them out. Your old neighborhood in Baghdad is fairly open and functional, not much different than when you left, but there's barbed wire many places along Karrada Street to keep cars from parking in front of shops, for fear of car-bombs. Only some of the neighborhoods have walls." Other friends in Baghdad said that militia and criminal gangs were in control of many of the city's neighborhoods. In a former translator's neighborhood there were daily gun battles on the street. The husband of a member of the Women's Will organization was killed.

In August, Fareed, a former neighbor from Baghdad, was in Suleimaniya on business. He had worked for the U.S. until about six months ago when his life was threatened. He had survived a kidnapping and assassination attempt. Soberly he talked about the mortar and car bomb explosions in the Karrada neighborhood on July 27, killing 71 and injuring 150. "My family's OK, but Re'ha [his wife] was very close to one of the mortars when it exploded."

"Whole buildings were leveled and burned, not just the small damage made by the kinds of mortars and bombs used by the insurgents," he added. "We Iraqi men have been in many wars and know these things. In the rubble from the mortars, people found fragments that said 'USA' on them, so many Iraqis believe that the U.S. was behind it." He said, "Americans want to keep things destabilized in order to stay a long time. Now everyone wants American troops to leave."

When Fareed returned two weeks later, he showed us pictures of his daughter, son, and wife. Re'ha appeared to have aged dramatically and was depressed since their nephew died in an explosion last April. Another nephew didn't talk unless spoken to. Fareed was upbeat in his outward manner, but his eyes and voice betrayed inner pain.

> These friends are family! It's painful not to be able to be with them at this horrendous time or be able to do more to help.
>
> During our morning meditations, we mentioned them by name. We spoke of hope, but hope seemed like something out of reach. "Right now it's hard to have hope for the future of Iraq," a teammate voiced what we felt.
>
> *This* is the struggle the prophet Isaiah was addressing, I thought, when he spoke of God bringing forth springs of water in the thirsty ground (Isa 35:6–7). Just like water in dry lands, hope is a precious commodity in war-torn places.
>
> If our hope is based on *our* ability to stop this horrible violence, we are lost. When our faith is rooted in *God's* ability to work in seemingly impossible situations, we can rise above despair and allow hope to strengthen us and lead us to action. When we dare to hope, we can dare to act. This is the hope I pray for and want to walk in.

Part Two: Summer 2006—Fall 2011

We knew that 12,000 additional U.S. soldiers had been deployed into Baghdad to help Iraqi forces crack down on the insurgency and terrorism, an operation called "the surge." On August 7, 2006, U.S. and Iraqi forces began a series of attacks targeting Muqtada as-Sadr's Mahdi Army in Baghdad's Sadr City neighborhood. According to news accounts, women and children were among those killed in the raids.

Farrah, a Baghdad friend, sent us an e-mail telling us that she was visiting friends in another neighborhood when U.S. marines surrounded the area, shutting off streets. For hours they were not allowed to leave while the marines battled the Mahdi Army. She said, "Any day, I expect our neighborhood to be in the middle of such battles." Referring to the added U.S. troops conducting house raids and fighting in the streets, she said, "This increases our hell."

U.S. forces claimed that their violent interventions were necessary to prevent civil war and protect the people. A Kurdish friend here also told me these actions against militias in Baghdad were necessary in order to bring stability to Iraq. Residents of Baghdad, however, whose families were caught in these battles, had difficulty seeing how this was helping them. To them, these interventions were just adding fuel to the fire.

Why did the U.S. assume that continuing military presence and bringing in more soldiers would substantially help? After three and a half years, this had not dealt with the basic problems and needs or prevented civil war in Iraq, but had made things worse. I believed it was time for some new thinking and new choices to be put on the drawing board.

Months later, there was some reduction of violence in Baghdad that the U.S. attributed to "the surge." People from Baghdad told us there were other reasons for it. The U.S. military put up walls between some neighborhoods. By this time, most of the forced "ethnic cleansing" of neighborhoods in Baghdad had taken place. The U.S. military was paying former Sunni insurgents, groups called the "Sons of Iraq" or Awakening Movement," to fight against terrorists groups and maintain order. Some of those terrorist groups just relocated to other parts of the country (mainly in north central and northwestern Iraq). Also, Sadr had called a six-month ceasefire for his militias on August 29, and extended it in February 2008.

These were short-term solutions with possible negative long-term consequences, so even though it seemed somewhat stabilized, the ethnic strife was not resolved. Iraqis feared that the recent decrease in violence was temporary and not indicative of a substantial strengthening of society and governmental unity.

We Are Kurds First

A friend from Kirkuk told us that the U.S. was giving 7,000 weapons to Sunni Arabs just south of Kirkuk to fight Al Qaida, but that this wasn't a good idea. "They don't really know who there are giving these weapons to." We saw on Iraqi TV that the U.S. military bombed an area of Baghdad, destroying forty houses in that neighborhood, saying they were targeting Al Qaida. After such raids, U.S. officials usually labled all those killed in the raids "terrorists," even though the majority would be non-combatant civilians. It was another reminder of what anti-terrorism really means here on the ground. Such attacks resulted in suffering for residents not involved in acts of violence and didn't really get rid of terrorism. This is the nature of war. Since so many Americans reading those reports trusted that such military actions would give them more security, it seemed imperative to expose these lies and tell the truth about the situation.

Being transplanted in Iraqi Kurdistan, we developed new friendships. One night we went with a friend on a Ferris wheel and other rides at Azadi Park. For a time, we just had fun being "children" again. Azadi Park had been founded on a site of a former infamous Ba'ath Party military base and Red Prison (Amna Suraka), where many Kurdish people had been buried alive. It was destroyed in 1991, after the Kurdish uprising against Saddam.

Visiting a friend's home, we met his wife and their new baby. They lived with her two sisters, two brothers, and parents. We sat around a cloth on the floor for a special meal. The meat served came from a sheep they had sacrificed in a traditional ceremony for the well-being of the baby. The Kurdish people were quickly working their way into my heart.

It wasn't long, however, until we saw some of the fissures in their society.

14

They See Saddam

"A DEMONSTRATION IS JUST about to happen in the city center," our sponsor told us by phone one morning in late August. "I advise you not to go there, because police often shoot into the crowds. You need to take time to understand the situation and build a foundation of relationships before deciding whether to get involved." She explained that while it's the people's right to protest, the Ministry of Interior (MOI) rarely gives the needed permission to do so. The group today had not been given a permit and on TV officials warned people not to participate.

The protest took place near our hotel, so we heard the chanting of the crowd as it marched down the middle of the street. From our tiny balcony we could see the scene below. Groups of police and Iraqi military were positioned around the MOI building. Crowds of bystanders gathered, and people stood on balconies and roofs to watch. Police in riot gear stood in lines with the other police. An hour later, it ended peacefully.

Several of the leaders we interviewed that week said the protests called on the government to provide adequate fuel, electricity, and water, get rid of government corruption, and allow the people a way to publicly voice their concerns. One said, "We're not making unreasonable demands, but simply asking the government to provide services it has promised." An organizer who had been imprisoned for his involvement told us, "After all these years of being freed from Saddam, living conditions should be better. Where did the government spend all the money it had? People are angry at the inequalities, especially when those in the government live rich lifestyles." Another protest leader said, "Authorities say we're violent, but in all the demonstrations around the area, no security person was ever injured, only protesters. Usually a few days before a demonstration, authorities arrest those believed to be the leaders."

Over the next two weeks, others we met with shared their views. A university professor defended the government's actions. "Kurdish leaders welcome constructive criticism. Kurds have long been repressed, but now they're free. Student groups produce newspapers and can say whatever they want. Those demonstrating, however, don't know how to use democracy." Another professor voiced a different view. "The police try to break their dignity and treat them in ways that provoke violence." A radio station manager told us, "The government tries to discredit organizers of the demonstrations by calling them Communists, or supporters of Iran."

"There's widespread corruption on all government levels," a professional woman said. "Over the years, billions earmarked for building and maintaining these services were pocketed by those in power. They threaten anyone trying to expose it." Also referring to the corruption of the parties and government, a businessman stated, "They don't want to change, but some day they will be forced to. It's better for it to happen now peacefully, than later through violence."

An editor of a Kurdish independent newspaper acknowledged that he didn't feel completely free to publish what he wanted, and described this society as "something in between democracy and a police state." If a government or party official was offended, the official might start rumors against him and try to damage his reputation. "If you file charges concerning freedom of the press, you will lose, because the parties control the courts. Our leaders' excuse in the past for restricting freedom of speech was Saddam. Now it's the fear of terrorism."

The director of the Dinga Neue Radio station in Halubja, the first women's independent station in the KRG controlled region, told us that the station didn't have complete freedom of speech, but it can say a lot if it is careful about it. "One can say there's corruption, without mentioning names of individuals or groups," she said. "This is still a step forward, because there was *no* room for free expression before."

Protest leaders also described the prisons run by the Asaish, where they had been held. One said, "The conditions are very crowded, and there's no room for everyone to sit or lie down. Prisoners are threatened with beating or death if they say anything incriminating to the ICRC staff when they visit the prison." Many long-time prisoners have never been charged, and some people have been held since 1994. Others working in the prison system confirmed what we heard about oppressive conditions at the prisons belonging to the two main political parties—extremely crowded cells, with inadequate food and medical care for prisoners. "The parties deny their existence because they're illegal, but the people know they exist," one explained.

"The U.S. government is our rescuer," a Suleimaniya University professor told us. "Most Kurds believe the U.S. should stay in Iraq, or in the North even if they leave the rest of Iraq. I don't think we could solve the border problems without Americans here to back us." In Kirkuk, a woman told us, "Kurds are afraid that when the U.S. leaves, Arabs will take over our city and there will be more violence. U.S. presence keeps a balance."

It struck us that the Kurds in this region generally have a more positive attitude toward U.S. military presence than Arabs or even Kurds in other parts of the country. We also realized that people in the KRG hadn't experienced the invasion and occupation by American forces like the rest of Iraq. Even so, the longer we were here, the more criticism we heard.

A Kurdish Christian couple in Suleimaniya described the U.S. as "coming for their own interests, not Iraq's." They saw America exploiting countries around the world. One day a Kurdish human rights worker told us, "Your government doesn't see Iraqis as full human beings. Our lives aren't worth as much as lives of Americans or other Westerners. In the U.S., there's more sorrow about an animal's death than when an Iraqi dies. They want power in this region and to keep Iranians afraid. America didn't really care about us when Saddam's government killed thousands of our people by chemical gas, but used this as an excuse to invade Iraq in 2003. International troops now need to give the people a timeline plan and then leave Iraq."

One day, we were walking with a Kurdish friend along a main street in Suleimaniya when three U.S. military Humvees drove by. A gunner, perched on top of one, pointed his gun toward the people as he passed. This was the first time we saw U.S. military on the streets in the Kurdish region, so were surprised. Our friend commented, "If they [U.S. forces] want people to like them, they would stay out of the city. If they want people to hate them, they'll continue doing this!" A year later, I saw the same type of convoy driving down the street toward the Ministry of Interior (MOI) plaza and asked my Kurdish friend about it. "Yes, U.S. officials come in like that about twice a month and have meetings with officials at the MOI," he answered. "People have gotten used to it and accept it."

They See Saddam

When we spoke to a U.S. State Department representative—a Provincial Action Officer for the Regional Reconstruction Team (RRT) for the Kurdish region—he explained that he rides into Suleimaniya in a caravan of three black cars and that "the civil affairs staff that rides in the Humvees don't like having to do that." He called himself "the eyes and ears of the U.S. Embassy," who allocates USAID money "for winning hearts and minds," and was a liaison between the U.S. and KRG. He said that many KRG ministries have American advisors. Other U.S. personnel here trained Iraqi prison guards, police, and soldiers.

Through a green valley between two mountain ranges, we drove later in the summer to the city of Kalar, on the southern border of the KRG controlled region. In Kalar, a representative of the Directorate of Human Rights Office briefed us about the internally displaced persons (IDPs) in that area.

"Their situation is good," he claimed. "Both Kurdish and Arab IDPs get the same help—a plot of land and provisions to get started with. The children are able to go to school. There are tensions between the IDPs and the local residents, but no violence yet. We're trying to educate our people to accept IDPs. Our main problem is financial, but we work with the UN and international NGOs to provide for their needs. We worry that they might bring in terrorism, sexual immorality, and drug trafficking, which will destroy our society." He estimated that four to seven displaced families arrived daily. Arab Iraqis coming to Kurdistan needed to have sponsors. Only those with financial means could rent a house. Others lived in their host's home. Poorer IDPs stayed in tent camps outside the cities.

The village of Harmota, near the city of Koya in the Erbil Governorate, dated back to the fourth century. There was some crumbling in the walls of the 200-year-old church. A Chaldean priest and leader of a group called the Christian Displaced Person Committee walked us past family vegetable gardens and women sitting on the ground hand-winnowing rice and wheat, to meet with some of the displaced.

We sat in the priest's home with a circle of displaced persons who had fled the violence in southern or central Iraq. They voiced their needs—a water tower, a deep well, resources to build homes, help with medical care, and a school taught in Arabic for their seventy children. In one house many families lived together, each family crowded in one room. "The families with more money go to Einkawa on the edge of Erbil, and receive a stipend equivalent to $80-$120 a month, while the poorer families settle in the Koya area and get nothing," the priest explained. "The Finance Minister of the KRG, responsible for providing resettlement money, has only given financial support to IDPs in the areas controlled by the KDP, but not to those in the Koya area under the PUK. These people do not face violence or threats, but need financial support to build houses and community buildings and basic infrastructure."

Later, in the fall, some of this group was finally able to meet with the finance minister and secured some financial assistance for family stipends, water, agricultural, and some infrastructure projects, but not for housing.

In the coming months, we heard expressions of fear and pain from both Kurds and Arabs around Suleimaniya. Realizing I was American, a Kurdish shopkeeper one day lowered his voice and confided, "We trust Americans, but not Arabs." When our team was looking for a house to rent, one of the owners said he didn't want to rent to Arabs, but would to us. A Kurdish friend told us, "Of course Kurds should receive Arab people and allow them to rent homes and have jobs, but Arabs shouldn't be allowed to *buy* property. We don't really want them to *stay*." We listened respectfully, but when possible and appropriate, we questioned or countered prejudicial statements. We also met Kurds who seemed welcoming to their new Arab neighbors.

"I feel humiliated," Sabah, an Arab woman from Baghdad, told us. She had come to teach at Suleimaniya University. "The man who hired me does not treat me respectfully. When I walk down the street or into the market, people talk about Arabs or jeer at me."

Clusters of men stood around a large mosque each day, waiting to be hired as day laborers. Of the 50,000 IDPs in Suleimaniya, about 6,000 of them were single workers whose families remained in the south. Many had no place to live, so crowded inside the mosque at night to sleep on the floor or outside on the pavement when the mosque was full. I saw discouragement and worry on their faces, and shivered as I thought of the cold weather we'd had the last few days.

They See Saddam

Animosity between Kurds and Arabs had existed for decades. At the end of World War I, the British contributed to this when they divided the Ottoman Empire. In the 1920 Treaty of Sevres, the Kurds were promised their own country. In 1923, however, the Turkish leader rejected the treaty, and the British divided the Kurdish areas among Turkey, Iran, Iraq, and Syria. Officials in many of these new nations forced Kurds to give up their seasonal migrations with their herds, abandon their language and cultural practices, and conform to the ways of the majority. Saddam's regime fostered divisions, corruption, and hatred, especially during mass killing and displacement of Iraqi Kurds in the 1970s and 1980s. Kurds still carry a collective trauma from the genocide and displacement campaigns under Saddam. "So now," a friend told us, *"when they see an Iraqi Arab, they see Saddam."*

The social unrest, power struggles, and increased violence resulting from the 2003 U.S. invasion and occupation of Iraq caused Iraqis to migrate to the safer Kurdish region. Some Arabs saw Kurds as responsible for inviting and cooperating with the U.S. to invade Iraq. It was hard for Kurdish communities to welcome people they connect with their past sufferings, and it was hard for those who were uprooted out of the desperation or hardship of war. There were no easy answers. Stability and peace, however, could only come through collective reconciliation, sharing power and resources among all Iraqi ethnic groups, and through foreign powers working for the well-being of all Iraqis.

One organization building relationships between local Kurds and Arab IDPs living in a tent camp on the edge of Suleimaniya was the Darstan Group for Children Media Organization. "Arab and Kurdish youth in our program made a video interviewing each other," the director said as he showed us magazines they produced focusing on messages of peace and friendship.

> This morning I reread the story of a South African woman forgiving the man who was behind the brutal murders of her son and husband. I had read it before, but it was more meaningful to me in this context. It spoke of the power of forgiveness to heal and offer healing to those who did horrible things, something so difficult and impossible—that one could never demand of another—but can be given as a gift. I also thought of the many smaller hurts in my life that I have had a hard time letting go of and forgiving, but instead allowed resentment and pain to wound my spirit. I prayed that people here in Iraq could find that power and be instruments of healing of the hatred and strife.

Part Two: Summer 2006—Fall 2011

Five members of the Muslim Peacemaker Teams (MPT) from Karbela and Najaf sat around our apartment in Suleimaniya in early September 2006. We met new members and caught up on what was happened with their group in the last six months.

"Last spring, we took a survey of 5,000 people concerning the dangers of small weapons," Sa'ad reported. "Now I hope to mentor youth in peacemaking." Achmad spoke about educating people on the dangers of children playing with violent toys. He also wanted MPT to publish booklets and writings to "increase people's awareness of the importance of peacemaking and its roots in Islam."

We discussed networking with other organizations, and training others in peacemaking and reconciliation tools. We couldn't work together as closely as we did before we left Baghdad, but they spoke about occasionally coming north to collaborate on projects.

As with other Iraqi organizations, the increasing violence and instability around them has made it difficult for them to work. They've also struggled with organizational problems. Their strengths have been in their ability to intervene in violent situations in their own community, their reaching out to different ethnic groups, and rooting their work in their faith. And while many others in Iraq are losing hope that any positive change can take place, they hold on to their vision for a peaceful world, believing it is the only sane choice they have.

Four months later, we got a call from an MPT leader telling us that one of their members, the father of another, and the director of the regional hospital we had met a year ago, had recently been killed. Plans for our organizations working together were put on hold. Besides the extra stress they were under, it was not the time for them to relate closely with internationals.

People swarmed into downtown Suleimaniya in mid-December. Shops displayed artificial Christmas trees and decorations. Shoppers bought gifts for New Years and the Muslim Eid (feast days) connected with the Hajj pilgrimages to Mecca.

On December 28, we woke up to a cold apartment, where we had just moved. Outside, the rain turned to snow, and we saw dustings of white on the mountains around the city. There was no electricity until evening. We had a kerosene stove and learned to run a small generator a few hours a day so we could have lights and use computers. Here, we're living like most local people, with no hot water in the tap and one to three hours of city electricity a day—some days with none. Our building had a well, so we could pump up water into a tank to use when there was no city water. Without this we would only have had water every three days. Today, we understood more personally the frustration behind the protests.

It wasn't until three years later that most neighborhoods in the city got "neighborhood generators," which added another four to six hours of electricity to most days. There was still a four-to-seven-hour stretch of time every morning with no power, and every week or two there were evenings without any electricity, when we worked by candlelight like we did in Baghdad.

On the last morning of the year, we were surprised to find the electricity on—the day of the Eid al Ahad. I turned on the TV and discovered that Saddam had been hung just before 6:00 that morning. It caught people by surprise. We heard that Iraqis in the cities were cheering and dancing in the streets, but also of car bombs in Baghdad. All day, the news focused on pictorial accounts of his life and commentary by leaders around the world.

> Christmas morning we attended services at one of the two Christian churches in Suleimaniya. Peace was the theme of the sermon—peace for Iraq and other troubled areas of the world. The priest spoke of the promised one, Emanuel, which means "God with us."
>
> Many here have a hard time believing the presence of God *is* with us, considering the escalation of violence and the way that corrupt governments and leaders are able to maintain their power. So many things here (and elsewhere) have not turned out the way I have thought God should have wanted them to. Yet, I recall times of struggle and pain during our work in Iraq when it was clear to me that God was present, strengthening and caring for us, bringing good news of reconciliation and hope.

PART TWO: Summer 2006—Fall 2011

Figure 8: Banner in Suleimaniya calling for severe
punishment for Saddam, September 9, 2009

In Suleimaniya, we heard mixed responses. Some said that even though Saddam did horrible things, he should not have been killed. Many Kurds, however, were glad Saddam received his "due reward." Many Sunni Muslims saw this as a slap in their faces. Highly religious Muslims were offended that he was killed on a holy day. But there was also revulsion about the disrespectful way it was done and shown on TV. Some thought Iraqi government officials wanted to decide what happened to Saddam and were afraid the U.S. might take him away in their custody. I didn't see how killing Saddam would foster reconciliation or peace.

In early January 2007, the UN released a report noting that a total of 34,450 civilians were killed in Iraq in 2006, an average of 97 civilians a day,

> One answer is that we don't have to have all the strength, knowledge, power, or whatever it takes to solve the problems here. We just need to bring the small gifts and strengths we have and be willing to be vulnerable, give ourselves, and God will use the little we have. This faith is the source of strength for many Iraqis who have allowed their gifts to be used and have done this under threat or sacrifice.

and 36,585 civilians were injured. I kept asking what we can do in these horrendous times of violence, chaos, and injustice.

What we had been able to do is to live and work alongside Iraqi people as they did the work of rebuilding their society. At times the most we coud do was to love the people in their beauty and their pain, and through our tears pray for them as they struggled even to live.

The New Year also brought us a new crisis, shaking the foundation we were building for working in northern Iraq.

15

A New Crisis

"*N*O, DON'T STOP!"—*I WAS about to yell as the driver of our car slammed on the brakes, but it's too late.... I can't believe he stopped!... I guess he feels culturally obligated to help this man—my mind racing now.*

Parked along the side of the road was an older red VW hatchback. A young man with a red and white keffiyeh wrapped around most of his face stood outside the driver's door motioning to us. But we had had it pounded into our heads to follow careful safety measures when traveling in the disputed areas outside the KRG protected areas, and we had discussed these measures with this man who had invited us on this trip and was now driving. But it all happened too fast.

As soon as our car stopped, the young man pulled an automatic rifle out of his coat, opened the front passenger door of our car, jumped in next to our translator, and closed the door.

We were returning home on January 27, 2007, from spending three days in an under-developed and impoverished and area of northwestern Iraq. At the invitation of the director of a community center and editor of a local newspaper, we came to see the living conditions of the people, and explore possibilities for future work. In our meetings prior to the trip, the editor spoke of the poverty of the people and the lack of help from authorities. "Even if you can't help with financial aid, I believe a hundred people might be interested in taking part in a nonviolence training to prepare for addressing their concerns and needs to authorities," he had said.

That region was considered one of the "gray" or "disputed" areas outside the KRG, considered mostly safe with occasional violence and where a majority of the population is Kurdish. While UN forces started protecting the three Kurdish governorates in the KRG from Saddam in 1991, the "gray" areas remained under his regime.

Several partners we consulted raised concerns, but many thought travelling there would be OK with caution and gave us advice about areas we shouldn't go to or routes to take or not take. (After the trip we learned, from other key organizations we should have consulted, things that would have changed how we proceeded with the trip.) We decided that Will Van Wangenen and I would go. Our host assured us that he would follow safety precautions and that we would have phone connections with Anita, remaining in Suleimaniya. We left on January 23 for what we thought would be a three-day trip.

In 1975, most of the villages in that area had been destroyed and the people forced out by the Ba'ath Regime, during the "Arabization." After the fall of Saddam in 2003, many of those Kurds came back to build what they called "replacement towns" near their old villages.

Living conditions and infrastructure in these vast rural areas were more depressed than the rest of Iraq. People cried out for basic water and irrigation systems, and educational and medical services. Most families cooked over wood fires or stoves. The life of women seemed particularly hard, with little opportunity for personal development or expression.

Our time there was spent visiting families, organizational leaders, and community centers. In a girl's school, there were ten teachers for 1,255 girls, and up to 200 students in a classroom. Only half the children had desks. In a town of 30,000 people, there was only one doctor, but one who didn't treat women, so in a medical emergency females needed to travel two hours to get care. "Because of that, many babies and mothers die in childbirth," said a community leader. "There's no university in this area. We have few jobs, so many go to the cities for work. Neither the KRG nor the Central Government wants to give us services or help until the referendum decides if we will be part of the KRG. About four years ago the Central Government dug seven wells in this area, but there's not enough water for the people's needs."

Kurdish and Arab villages and towns in the area were plagued by prejudice and resentment toward the other. Kurds told us that some of the tensions they had with Arabs in this area stemmed from the invasion. "We welcomed the Americans and don't fight or kill them, so Arabs consider us cowards and will kill us," one said.

The trip was frustrating in many ways. In order to get phone reception and call Suleimaniya, we had to go to the top of the nearby mountain range. Other times we were able to borrow a Syrian network phone. Our hosts took us to areas where we were cautioned not to go. On Friday we were told an emergency came up with family members, so we couldn't meet with the women's groups.

In our Friday meeting with leaders of area organizations, one man summarized their requests. "Now that you've been here and seen our problems, we expect you to tell other people and organizations about us and try to find ones that will give us material aid." We encountered a sense of helplessness, believing the main thing they needed was outside assistance. In my response, I attempted to counter this by highlighting the positive things, the possibilities, and the inner resources of strength and leadership we saw here. Will talked about the possibilities of their organizing to build schools or soccer courts themselves. The meeting did not lead to planning future collaboration on nonviolence campaigns, but seemed stuck on how we could make contacts for them. I mentioned that some funding organizations were interested in projects that help build bridges and reduce tension between ethnic groups in communities.

Then, the promised Saturday morning departure didn't happen. Our host said his driver's cousin died, so the man had to pay respects to his family. We insisted we find another driver and still go today so we could get back to talk with Anita before she left the country the next day. We waited while our host was on the phone, trying to work out a ride. Finally he said he would drive us back with his cousin's car.

It was 2:00 p.m. when we left. There were four of us—our host who was driving, our translator, Will, and me. As on the way here, I covered my head with a scarf to avoid being recognized as an international. It was about a half hour later when the young man by the side of the road waved for us to stop and our host braked and pulled over next to the other car. It was not uncommon to see men wearing keffiyehs wrapped around their mouths as well as their heads to protect themselves from the sun or dust. I was still alarmed that our host stopped, and even more alarmed by what happened next.

Now in our car, the young man demanded that our driver follow the red car, with two men in it, as they drove up the road, and then turned off to the left, onto paths in the desert. He told us, "We are police and are just taking you to our headquarters to check you out." I didn't believe him and the bottom dropped out of any sense of security I thought I had.

Once I realized we were captive, I did two things instilled in me by my training in nonviolence, my experience with CPT, and my faith: pray and become super-observant of what was happening around me—of our surroundings, direction, and our captors. Looking back later, I realize that these things helped me not get paralyzed by the fear I felt.

For about a half hour we navigated the desert paths, maneuvering to avoid gullies and rough ground. At one point, the two cars stopped, away from any human habitation. Our three captors ordered us to get out and took away our mobile phones, our coats, and duffle bags. Two of them drove our car away and directed us to get into theirs. The driver ordered the men to put their heads down, but I was able to watch as he turned into a family courtyard on the edge of a small village. He rushed us into the first building on our left and into a rectangular sitting room, lined with mats and pillows, where we stayed for the rest of our captivity.

Two of the other men brought in our duffle bags, took what they wanted from them, but never looked through my purse, body-searched us, or took our passports. Our guard warned that if we tried to escape, other men with guns surrounding the compound would shoot us. We sat on mats in the end of the room away from the door. Our guard, with his automatic rifle, sat next to the door at the other end. All this time, none of us had our hands bound or eyes covered.

At different times of day, a middle-aged woman in traditional Iraqi garb brought water, tea, or food to the door and our guard brought them in. He later told us she was one of his two wives. At night he brought in a blanket for each of us, and we slept on the mats.

When our guard was with us, we spoke with him in Arabic, trying to become real people to him and to ease the tension. He told us some things about himself and his family, but we didn't know how much of what he said was true. We told him about ourselves and our work.

When our guard was out of the room, we talked more freely among ourselves, checking in with each other about how we were doing and trying to encourage one another. We talked about our families. We told stories. Our driver and host from the area shared about how it felt as a child when Saddam's forces destroyed his village and everyone was forced out. My teammate and I spoke about the pain this abduction would cause our families and how bad we felt that our translator was kidnapped just for being with us. We questioned some of the ways our team operated and made decisions, and commiserated about our fear that this would mean the end of the Iraq team.

I didn't know what would happen to us. I remembered the taunts of the man who challenged me back home. Would my commitment to nonviolence hold up now that I was in the hands of terrorists? During quiet moments, I mulled over what we could do and how we might relate to our captors, but intentionally did not let my mind dwell on all the possible outcomes. Our translator regularly did his Muslim prayers; my colleague and I prayed silently, in our own ways—for strength, clarity, and safety for us and our other teammate back in Suleimaniya, for our captors, our families, and for others in CPT who would be affected by this.

At times, I had a clear sense of God's love and care for us, but in other moments would be more aware of underlying anxiety. I thought about Tom, Jim, Harmeet, and Norman and what they went through. I thought of Allia and other Iraqis who found the strength and courage to keep going in terrifying times. I found strength by silently singing songs such as, "Be Not Afraid," and "How Can I Keep from Singing" ("No storm can shake my inmost calm, while to that rock I'm clinging . . ."). I knew that didn't mean for me the absence of fear. It meant not sinking into the terror that lurked in the wings, but staying in the present and keeping hope.

Once again, I was in danger. I was pushed to the very limits of my faith and had to go beyond it. No theological statement of beliefs would carry me. There was no firm footing, no clear path to follow. I had to walk into a space of the unknown, a place that was uncomfortable and hard. Now, as before, I wanted God's presence to be more clear and dramatic, to have more assurance and no fear. But it wasn't that way. At such a time there was no other choice. I had to hold on to every thread of faith I had inside and let faith carry me as I walked ahead.

We were Sunni Muslim, Yezidi, and Christian, captive together. Our religious differences weren't a problem for us, but suddenly became a big deal to our guard when he questioned each one of us about our backgrounds. This induced an extra measure of fear in my Iraqi companions. Their religious identity could mean life or death, depending on the biasis of our captors.

When our guard asked me if I was a Christian, I simply said, "yes." But when he repeated his question, I sensed in it a deeper question as well as a veiled threat. I knew I needed to say more. I wanted to be sure our guard would understand, so I asked our translator to translate the words that came to me next. "You are holding us here, and you would do us harm," I said. "I *am* a Christian, and because I am, I will *forgive you*!" Our guard seemed taken aback, and then responded defensively, "No, we will not harm you! You are like my mother."

A New Crisis

I was startled at the clarity and force of my own words, aware of some anger toward these men that held us. I had no idea what they would do with us. And I *wanted* to be able to forgive them, but I knew I was not at that place now.

On the second day, our guard told us in a threatening way that their group might pass us on to another group that would treat us worse. This produced some cracks in the outer appearance of strength I was trying to maintain. I couldn't hold back all my tears.

A little later, the guard said that our translator would be released the next day. We were glad for him, but also realized that we could each write a message for him to take and send to our families. Writing that note was agonizing and brought up tears of grief. *What should I say when this might be my last words to those I love deeply?*

My anger surfaced another time. After our guard said they would release our translator and we thanked him, he said something to the effect that he doesn't have the power to release us all and was helpless to do more. The other three responded, *"You are a good man."* I couldn't believe they were saying this! This felt like cheap pandering, so I countered the others, without it being translated, "No, he's not so helpless or good! He kidnapped us! He brought us here! If he wants to do something good, he would release us all!"

Will, who could speak Arabic much better than I could and had taken the lead in building a human connection with our guard, started another conversation. He told the guard several stories to illustrate the work of the CPT team in the West Bank, including the one about my husband, Art, standing in front of and stopping an Israeli tank which was destroying the main Palestinian produce market in Hebron, in January 2003. I thought a moment, and then said, "I have the picture of that with me." I found in my purse the envelope of family pictures. Will passed the picture of Art over to the astonished guard. Then I brought out pictures of my children and grandchildren and said, "My husband is supposed to come here in three days, but now I won't be there to see him." For a moment, he seemed taken aback.

One of our Iraqi companions asked the guard to release me too. The guard left the room and in about fifteen minutes returned smiling. He told us that he just convinced the other men in his group to also release me in the morning! Once again, he said, "You are like my mother." It's hard to know, but it may have been for a combination of reasons. One factor seemed to be that he was sympathetic to me as a woman or even that he saw keeping a woman as more of a hassle.

Part Two: Summer 2006—Fall 2011

I was thankful, but I would be leaving Will there! It felt wrong to abandon him and not be there to support him through whatever happened. If anyone else left with our translator, it should be him and our driver/host because they were younger and had a longer life ahead of them. I'd lived a good life. Will insisted, however, "You *must* go. You could help get me released."

Sitting in a car the next morning with our translator, on our way to Suleimaniya, grief and pain flooded me. This would probably end the work of our team. So much had happened in the past several hours—heart-wrenching discussions with Will before leaving, tearfully saying goodbye, getting into a car that took us to a place in the desert where men in another car met and took us to our host's town. There we got into the car of a man hired to drive us back to Suleimaniya.

In Suleimaniya, the ordeal wasn't over. Overshadowing the gratefulness I felt for being released unharmed, and for Art's coming and supporting me two days later, was the knowledge that Will was still captive. Also, a lot of condemnation was directed toward *us*, the victims of the crime, for being abducted. The top Asaish official yelled at me for taking the trip without notifying him. He said U.S. authorities had reprimanded and held him responsible for us, even though it took place outside the jurisdiction of the KRG. This was an "embarrassment" to him. Then for four days an Asaish officer interrogated me for their investigation. U.S. state department officials questioned me and made false, negative implications about Will and me.

Meanwhile, our organization formed a "crisis team" to assist and support us. We consulted with them daily. We spoke with members of other organizations that had contact with leaders in the area where we were abducted, who tried to work toward Will's and our host's release. We contacted authorities to persuade them to not use violence in any rescue effort.

My heart sunk when our translator, who had gone through this traumatic experience, was arrested and put in the local Asaish jail while officials investigated whether he had a role in the kidnapping. We went repeatedly to the Asaish office asking for his release. On one visit, we met his worried parents and spent time outside the jail supporting each other. We wrote a letter saying we didn't hold our translator responsible for the abduction and that we gave up any claims against him. Then, with the advice of Kurdish friends, we hired a lawyer to work on his behalf.

A New Crisis

Six days after my release, February 4, our abductors released Will and our trip's host. Three days later, after completing only one day of interrogation by the Asaish, Will and Anita flew to the U.S. for a needed break. Two other team members, Joe Mueller and Beth, arrived.

We knew we needed to go home for healing and debriefing with our team and organization, but decided we must stay long enough to assist our translator and deal with the problems created by the abduction. Harder than the tasks themselves was dealing with differences on the team about how to proceed. We were all working in a situation of high stress.

I was thankful for the way our pastoral support person and our team support person were able to really listen to and take me seriously when I said I believed it would be healing for me to stay there longer and work to release our translator. It was a bit like "getting back on the horse" after falling off. Healing activities for me included talking by phone with CPT support persons, walking to a hill with trees, writing, looking at pictures of close family and friends, and rereading loving messages many had sent or given me over the last few years.

We met with workers from several international NGOs to give them information about the kidnapping, but also to learn more from them about how they deal with trips outside the KRG-controlled area. We consulted with trusted partners about the possibilities of continuing our work. The predominant advice was that continuing to work here would not be a security risk to us or anyone working with us if we stayed within this region, but that we should take more careful security procedures when traveling outside the area.

On February 18, we felt great relief when, after two and a half weeks, our translator walked out of the Asaish jail and went to his family's home. We felt thankful, but also regretted that working with us put him through that ordeal. Four days later, he came to our apartment, and we debriefed about the kidnapping. We were able to thank him for his good work and all the help he gave us. He said that at least while he was in jail he was not tortured or mistreated. "I learned a lot through the experience," he said. "God gives us difficult experiences that can actually strengthen us. People can imprison your body, but not your mind. Many times I closed my eyes and imaged being other places, and resisted despair or fear from taking over my thoughts."

Remaining in Suleimaniya longer was good for me. One day, Art and I had a lively talk with several university students while riding a bus. Later that day, a young girl called out to us on the street. She had grown up in

England and wanted to speak English with us. I found myself laughing and opening myself up, without the walls that had been forming around my heart. This softened some of the wounds in my spirit and replaced the negative with more positive interactions. I flew home on February 28, feeling love for the people here.

It had been a difficult and shaking experience. We were thankful that this crisis lasted only eight days, and that no one was killed. We will probably never understand the whos and whys, and incredibilities of all that happened. Intertwined with the disturbing memories, I recalled the moments of grace given in the midst of threat, and remembered Iraqis who were gracious and helpful throughout my years of working in Iraq. Once home, I went on retreat, shared with friends, did physical healing work, walked in the woods, worked in the garden—activities that gradually renewed my strength. I felt thankful for the many gifts I've received in these years of working in Iraq. *Once more, my life had been given back as a gift to me!*

So what did this mean for my life, for my long-held beliefs in the power of nonviolence, and my future work? In the process of healing and returning to life in Athens, Ohio, my mind and heart sifted through these questions. To do the reconciliation work we are called to, we need to be prepared to face difficult or threatening situations, even death. Nonviolence isn't always "successful." It doesn't guarantee safety. At any time, we could become the victims of the violence, desire for revenge, or power grabbing unleashed in war and occupation. We have been living among the Iraqi people, willing to stand with them and share their suffering, yet have experienced only a small piece of what Iraqis face every day.

But it is still hard when violence against us happens. It disrupted our work and our lives. When I came home, I had to pull back awhile and deal with the pain, grief, fear, and anger it produced until I felt like my feet were on solid ground again. I had to regain openness. I resisted fear settling in and keeping me from being able to re-enter situations of risk.

I wanted to more fully forgive. I knew it couldn't be forced—I couldn't make it happen, but I could choose to take that path. Looking back, I see that the anger I felt during the kidnapping was a gift and was part of the forgiving process. It helped me combat the utter sense of helplessness and gave me strength to speak boldly. After I was released, it kept me honest and real about my need for healing. It was when I faced my weakness and inability to forgive, and cried out to God for help, that forgiveness was given as a gift—not all at once, but over time. I began to release the anger

I was left with. I did not plan, however, to get rid of anger toward injustice, senseless violence, and greed. This kind of anger has emboldened me, helping me to speak clearly in other situations of injustice.

From deep inside I came to these conclusions and wrote in my journal:

> When we do walk ahead and give ourselves to love in action, we can know that we do not walk alone, even into the most frightening experiences. Even when we can't feel it, when we are stumbling along blindly in the darkness, God is close to us, giving us strength, wisdom, and love for those around us. Even if it would have ended in death, God was with me.
>
> Of course violence can kill or crush persons. Trauma doesn't just go away. It can be passed on from one generation to another in many negative ways. I carry scars on my spirit—wounds of fear and pain that are healing now, but can be opened by another hurtful event, and can overshadow the lightness and spontaneous joy I want to feel. I could not have kept returning to Iraq had I not learned in a personal way, that when we are hurt while doing such work, we *can* heal and through our pain be given greater compassion and strength.
>
> So many wonderful gifts have come out of times we took risks to do the work we felt compelled to do. Being free to die gives us this freedom. The purpose of any act of terror is to weaken our confidence, strength, and resolve—to make us feel and say, "I can't." *But we will not let these forces claim such power over us.*

16

Voices of Change

"MY EXPERIENCE ABROAD MADE me think that no one wants to hear us [the Kurds]," Khadr, a business man, commented as we hiked with him and his wife in the hills looking down over the city of Suleimaniya. "If you could inform the international community about our situation and viewpoints, that would be helpful." It was refreshing to walk among the trees. Other families and groups of young people were walking or having picnics nearby.

It was late October 2007, and our team had just returned to Suleimaniya. That summer our team wrestled with whether to return to Iraq and work mainly in Iraqi Kurdistan. We took seriously the burnout, trauma, and problems team members experienced, yet concluded that the reasons for returning outweighed the dangers. Our Kurdish sponsor encouraged us to come. We still had concerns and uncertainties—*though had we ever waited for complete certainty, we never would have worked these last five years in Iraq.*

One of our main concerns was the potential danger for our interpreters and drivers. There was no way to guarantee safety, but we would try to decrease their danger by studying Kurdish and following a revised list of security procedures for how we travelled and did our work. We would also engage our translators, drivers, and local partners more in our team's decision-making process. We informed new interpreters and drivers about the kidnapping, so they could weigh the possible risks of working with us.

While we got our entry visas extended in the Residency Office, a young Kurdish woman, Shad, offered to interpret for us. We developed a close friendship with her and her family as she became our fulltime interpreter, made connections for our team, and advised us about work and travel. We met Mohammed Salah, an English teacher in an elementary school, when our sponsor arranged for him to pick us up at the airport, help us find a place to rent, and be a part-time driver.

On another walk with our friends in the hills, our conversation ranged from bits of history, to plants native to the area, to culture and political concerns. "The U.S. got rid of Saddam," Khadr, said, "but then they made huge mistakes here. Even we in Kurdistan are shaking our heads at it and can't believe Americans, with so much intelligence and education, could mess it up like that. I don't know if it is due to individual errors or policy—if it was accidental or planned."

This same question came up a week later while getting together with other Americans in the city one evening. "Did top decision-makers in the Bush administration intentionally make decisions that were destructive for Iraq without caring about the harm it caused, or were they just ignorant about the negative consequences of their policies and actions?"

Some argued, "They just have blinders on and don't see the harm caused, or really think it's for the best for Iraq." Others disagreed and said it seems to be a systematic pattern of relating to countries around the world. Some of us working in Iraq for long periods of time had read Naomi Klein's *Shock Doctrine: The Rise of Disaster Capitalism*, and found her description of U.S. policies in Iraq consistent with what we saw here. In that book and her article[1] she states that the U.S. deliberately gutted and attempted to redesign Iraq's economy and imposed rapid and wrenching economic adjustments in the aftermath of social upheaval, when the people were too stunned and preoccupied with survival to resist it.

One American in the group said he had problems with people in the peace movement who can't see the humanity of the people in the U.S. government and the military and so demonize them. "Yes, this happens a lot," I said. "We need to see the good and the possibility for change in any person, yet be realistic about how entrenched power structures are and the difficulty for anyone invested in them to break out of them."

"How do you like Suleimaniya?" Heider, a teenager and secondary student who hoped to be a lawyer, asked us while we visited his family. When I

---

1. Klein, "Baghdad Year Zero," 43–53.

said that the people were friendly and hospitable, he answered, "Visitors don't see the many problems here. The rich people, like those who build the tall buildings, say that things are good here, but you'll hear something different from those who barely have enough to live on."

"Because there aren't enough schools, some buildings hold three shifts of classes a day," he explained. "It's free to attend the university if you do well in your exams, but you can't choose your field unless you have high enough scores. We want to live in a society where we have more choice."

As we walked by one of the parks in the city another day, we noticed a cluster of tents and a group of young adults, mostly university students, milling around. They had been living in these tents since early September, calling on the government for policies that benefit young people. "Kurdish youth here have little hope for the future," said Zara, one of their leaders. "The government's corrupt. To get a good job and other social services you have to join one of the two main political parties." Among their demands was an end to that practice, and an office that would help youth find employment.

A few weeks later we got a call from Zara, saying the Asaish closed down their tent camp and detained the leaders overnight as a warning not to continue their work. We saw a deep tension between those who wanted to grasp onto their political power and the economic and social benefits this gives them, and those who recognize that changes in the economic and political structures are inevitable and need to come. Many people we talked to seem to understand that change is necessary to keep Kurdish youth from *leaving* their society, and that the youth are a creative and important resource for *birthing* that change.

"I expect to be killed if I stay here," Raman declared. He was among about twenty men and women journalists who, in mid-November 2007, sat around the meeting room of an office we rented along with Gulzar Mustafa Madher, director of the Women's Alliance for Democratic Iraq (WAFDI). The journalists were discussing how to prevent a bill from being passed in the Kurdish Parliament in December that would further restrict their freedom of speech. They asked us to bring international attention to this legislation and talk to some of the Parliamentarians before the vote. Members of the Committee for the Protection of Journalists (CPJ), an international organization based in New York, had recently visited the Kurdish region, and called the restricted language in this proposed bill incompatible with the kind of democratic society Kurdish officials have publicly embraced.

The bill acknowledged the "legal right to criticize the government," obligating government leaders to disclose "public information," and imposing a fine rather than imprisonment for violating the law. The fine, however, could be heavy for public statements that "disclose any negative personal information about government leaders, even if it is true," or that "encourage breaking the law" or acts of terrorism. The language in the bill was vague or "elastic" enough so that a nonviolent demonstration or any other public criticism of government officials could be called a "disruption of security" and be prosecuted in counterterrorism courts and result in a life sentence. One member of the Parliament (MP) we spoke to the following week told us, "We're also concerned about the vagueness of the proposed law and that it could be misused." Four days later it was passed with only minor changes to the wording. Only seven voted against it.

In an open-air press conference and public forum in Azadi Park the next day, about 200 gathered to protest the law. "This new law will send journalists to prison, ban newspapers, and allow for outrageous fines under various pretexts," the editor of an independent Kurdish newspaper stated in his speech. An MP who voted against the law said, "This law means silencing journalists and intellectuals who criticize the government and its mistakes."

Our team sent out an urgent action appeal, calling on the international community to contact the Embassy of Iraq in their countries, or email the President of the KRG, Massoud Barzani, asking him to veto the new law. Three days later one of the journalists said that Barzani refused to sign the censorship bill and sent it back to parliament for further deliberation. Weeks later, however, Barzani signed it.

Within a week of the bill's passing, an independent newspaper in Suleimaniya received threats of being closed down. Bahar, an independent journalist in Halubja and secondary school teacher, was arrested for writing an article accusing a government official of corruption when he took, for his own use, some land that an individual donated to the city. It was after the houses were built, and two days after Bahar's article was published, that the municipality gave the official permission to take the land.

Weeks later, the official charged Bahar with slander. Bahar won the case because he had a computer disk on which he recorded the donor of the land saying that he given it to the municipality and not to any individual. The official had no legal ownership papers. A month later, however, the official brought the case back to court. This time he had a document that officials signed in retroaction, stating that the municipality had given him the land and permission to build on it. He claimed that Bahar originally accused him because he wanted the property himself. Bahar lost the case and was given three years probation.

Ayoub, another journalist in Halubja, stated in an article that all Peshmerga were corrupt. Eight days later, the head of the Peshmerga filed a complaint against him, and he was jailed for two hours. The Asaish told Ayoub he was being held for his own protection, since many Peshmerga were angry and threatened to hurt him. They said he had two options: He could retract his statements and make a public apology or face the charge. Ayoub refused to retract his statement, and was charged with "Slander and Damaging Reputations."

Before Ayoub came to trial, four men wearing Asaish uniforms forced him into a pickup truck, then took him to a remote area where they beat him and threatened to kill him. They took his cell phone, put a bag over his head, tied his hands behind his back, and drove him to a rural area. The men tied his feet and threw him into a ditch and beat him some more. He heard a gun cock, and was told to promise that he would not write anything slanderous again. Under threat, he agreed to this. They untied his hands and left.

After Ayoub walked forty-five minutes to the nearest village, a family called his parents, who came and took him home. He was hospitalized for his injuries and put, on a computer disk, pictures of the bruises on his back. The next day he filed a complaint with the Asaish for the abduction and published an article about his ordeal. The Asaish denied any responsibility and refused his request for an investigation. He asked to have his trial changed to Suleimaniya, because he did not feel safe in Halubja, but this was also denied.

Along with five independent journalists and human rights workers, three of our team traveled to Halubja for Ayoub's trial. About twenty people, including his wife, family, friends, journalists, and other local human rights workers, gathered at the courthouse to support him. The investigating legal officer told us that, if found guilty, Ayoub faced a five-year prison sentence. After half an hour, the attorney informed us that the judge postponed the trial because he had to take his son to the hospital. Some guessed the judge wanted to avoid international publicity. Ayoub's supporters however, arranged an alternative plan for him to meet with and directly work out the complaint with the head of the Peshmerga.

At the Halubja Cultural Center, an hour later, about thirty people sat in a circle with the Peshmerga leader. The director of the center facilitated the meeting, giving anyone in the room an opportunity to speak. After about a half hour of discussion, the Peshmerga leader said he would drop the charges if Ayoub changed his statement and agreed to write only with specific evidence about the Peshmerga. Ayoub agreed to modify his article to say that some of the Peshmerga are corrupt, being careful not to compromise his convictions. The Peshmerga leader accepted the statement and promised that Ayoub would not be physically attacked or threatened because of this. The group approved and sent the agreement to a court office to be officially recorded. Ayoub's supporters considered it a victory. The Cultural Center director felt good about the results of this democratic Kurdish-style mediation.

We also recorded the story of Rowan, an independent journalist from Kirkuk. "After publishing articles criticizing an extremist Islamic group in Iraq and violent practices toward women, I received death threats and then was shot and injured in front of my home. In 2006, I published an article asking the KRG to stop cooperating with the U.S. because the U.S. didn't do anything to help the poor and was killing innocent people. My article also referred to a local anti-terror force that the U.S. established and supplied with

> As Christmas was coming, we read scriptures about the light shining in the darkness and the darkness not overcoming it (John 1:3). I write from a place in the world so tangled in violence that people talk as though there is no really good solution. Each year in Iraq, it seems like the hopelessness and darkness increases.
>
> So what is the good news of Advent for the Kurdish or Arab Iraqi people? How does the light break into the darkness here? Has God forgotten them, or is God entering into their world?
>
> We don't see corrupt and violent institutions or international powers dramatically turning around. What we see are people willing to speak out, people giving themselves to help others in need. We see the light breaking in where we find institutions being transformed or people with a vision of another way to stop the cycles of violence. This way involves revealing the truth, working for reconciliation, and using the power of love and nonviolent confrontation.
>
> We hold on to the belief that the power of this light is stronger than the darkness. Wherever people are open to God's Spirit of love and truth, God will enter and work among and through them to break down the walls of hostility.

weapons, intelligence, and financial support and coordinated jointly with the KRG. It abducted and imprisoned many innocent people. After this article was published, American soldiers surrounded and then entered the newspaper office where I worked. They searched the offices and warned the staff in a threatening way not to write things like that. American Embassy personnel also questioned us in order to stop us. After this, I hid for a time."

Stories of cruelty and suffering are not easy to hear, but the truth must be told for there to be healing and change.

17

Anfal and Halubja Testimonies

ALI HAD BEEN A child during the Anfal when his family was taken and kept in a prison. Many of his family died or were killed and only he and an aunt survived. Sara told us about working in a hospital near Halubja during the March 16, 1988 chemical bombing and seeing the dead, burned bodies, crusted black, brought there. The Ba'athist government ordered them not to treat the burned and gassed victims, but to let them die, and then not to talk about it. She spoke about it with little emotion, but I sensed a lot of pain deep inside. This explained the distant, traumatized look I had noticed in her eyes when I first met her. Almost everyone here has a story connected with the Anfal, Saddam's genocide against the Kurds in Iraq between 1986 and 1989, resulting in approximately 182,000 killed.

The peacefulness and beauty of the drive through mountains for our initial visit, December 2007, to the city of Halubja, hid the stark horror of its past. People there now live ordinary daily lives, but believe it's important for them and the world to never forget what happened there. As Mohammed drove, he and Shad explained that "Anfal" literally means "spoils of war." It is the name of the eighth sura, or chapter, of the Qur'an, which tells of people taking the spoils of war. Saddam took it as a code for the genocidal campaign against the Kurdish people in Iraq, and by referring to the Qur'an, attempted to justify this genocidal campaign or make it sound holy.

Part Two: Summer 2006—Fall 2011

We first went to the damaged memorial on the outskirts of the city. Several residents told us that a mob of angry citizens burned it almost two years earlier because money given by other countries to improve the life of the survivors, many still suffering from medical problems, did not reach the people. Instead, they said, it went to building the monuments, to politicians' pockets, and to support the political party. Inside the charred and broken structure (repaired by the fall of 2009) we could still see the panels of names of the victims.

At the memorial cemetery, a span of white tombstones symbolized the death of 5,000 in the attacks. Soberly, I looked closely at the face of the large white stone statue of a woman in the cemetery and noticed that her eyes were hollow and her mouth was smoothed over. In another part of the cemetery, large marble slab memorials had been placed over mass burial sites. The most important part of this and other visits to Halubja, however, was listening to those who experienced and survived the horror and effects of the chemical attacks.

Arras Abad Akram, director of the Kurdistan Save the Children in Halubja and the Kurdistan Martyrs of Halubja, spoke to us about the Halubja "holocaust," as Kurds call it. His eyes welled up in tears as he said, "In the chemical bombing, I lost seven sisters, three brothers, my father and mother, uncles and grandparents." Shad, having experienced frightening times in her past, gracefully helped us navigate this and other testimonies, at times gently helping us reword a question.

Arras gave some historical background. In May 1987, during the later stages of the Iran-Iraq war, Saddam attempted to move the residents of Halubja into a collective town further from the Iranian border, to make it easier to fight Kurds who opposed his regime and prevent them from cooperating with Iranian troups. After a large number of residents resisted this move, the regime responded by a round of bombing that destroyed 512 houses and killed residents. In early 1988, there was sporadic fighting between Iraqi troops and Kurdish Peshmerga in the area, and people from nearby villages flocked to Halubja. From March 13–15, Iraqi planes periodically bombed the city.

On the morning of March 16, Iraqi military planes dropped plain white papers, Arras thought, to test the direction and force of the wind. At 11:35, Iraqi planes bombed the edges of the city with cluster bombs, killing many. Other planes flew low over the buildings dropping 500-pound bombs, destroying houses and killing people huddled in their underground shelters. Then planes dropped napalm bombs.

Anfal and Halubja Testimonies

Around 2:00, people smelled something strange. A soldier said he saw birds dying, so believed it to be poisonous chemicals. Chemicals used included phosphorus, cyanide, mustard gas, VX, and Tabin ingredients, which the U.S. and European and Asian countries sold to Iraq. The poison gas bombing continued until 8:00 p.m. and started again the next morning at 4:00, killing about 5,000.

Hundreds fleeing to Iran died on their way from cold or in the fighting between Iraqi and Iranian troops. Another 7,000 in the area were injured or died later from the long-term effects of the gas. "Those who survived suffered many health problems, such as cancers, miscarriages, deformed babies, eye and respiratory problems," Arras said. "By our most recent counting, nearly 440 chemical and napalm bombs were used in Halubja from March 16 until April 1." Every year, on March 16, all Kurdistan commemorates that day.

Then Arras's story became more personal. Just before the bombing started that morning, Arras went out with his friends looking for food. He saw a plane diving low and dropping something, and the air around him became very hot. He was injured from pieces of shrapnel and became unconscious. "Others took me to our neighbor's basement, where about eighty people crowded around. You could feel the houses shake."

"At 2:30 all of us in the basement started coughing. We had headaches, burning and itching skin, and difficulty breathing. A man with us, who had been in the army and had a gas mask, went outside and brought us water. He put water on blankets to put over us and covered the door with a blanket to reduce the effects of the gas." Arras lay there, disoriented and drifting in and out of consciousness. After 8:00 p.m., when the bombing stopped, the others helped him walk to the edge of the city. His heart was beating rapidly; his head hurt, and he couldn't see well. "You can't imagine how horrible it was, bodies all over the streets, many blackened, others alive, pleading for help," he said. "All I could think of was getting out of there."

On their way to the Iranian border, Peshmerga soldiers gave them a shot of atropine to counter the gas. Workers at the Iranian hospital washed his face, put ointment on his eyes, and changed his clothes. For four days he was in shock and didn't know what happened or how he got there. Then he became frantic and felt driven to find his family. Arras went back to Halubja, but was horrified to see bodies all over the ground. All the windows of his home had been blown out, and no one was around.

He saw Peshmerga soldiers loading swollen bodies onto a wagon. In the pile, he spotted his sister's sweater, and then his mother's arm hanging

PART TWO: Summer 2006—Fall 2011

out. He begged the men to let him bury them individually instead of dumping them into a mass grave. But then an airplane started bombing, so he fled. The chemicals were affecting him, so Arras returned to Iran.

When he later returned to Iraq, he was forced to join the Iraqi Army in what Saddam called a "reconciliation program," to repatriate the Kurds. He was sent to other parts of Iraq and to Kuwait. On a base in central Iraq he saw the chemicals stored that were used in the gassing. After 1991, he and other Kurds returned to Halubja, and he rebuilt his family home.

"We heal from this tragedy by helping each other, the victims of the violence," Arras shared. "When new children are born, they bring us healing, but most important for healing is that we not have more wars and more genocide. We must not let what happened to Halubja, to Hiroshima and Nagasaki, and with the Holocaust against the Jews, ever happen again! Now it's time to stop making chemical bombs everywhere. We need to talk about these things and see that the next generation knows what war really is and doesn't use their knowledge and technology for war, but for serving humanity. War never brings peace to anyone. But the question now is, 'How we can create a culture of peace?'"

> Near a house in Halubja we walked among a grove of trees. Waves of pain swept through me—a pain accumulating from listening to accounts of unspeakable horror. *Once more, I knew why I was here.* "We must find another way to live together in this world," I silently declared. "If we do not witness and tell the truth about the horror and futility of war, the rocks will cry out. God, turn our weak timidity into unstoppable strength! Transform this pain into countless actions for reconciliation, courageous works of love, out of which healing will flow."

"For years, the U.S. government claimed that Iran was responsible for the chemical attacks. It was only in the time leading up to the 2003 invasion that it dropped this claim as it built its case against Saddam. In 2003, U.S. Secretary of State General Colin Powell came to the graves at Halubja and made a speech blaming Iraq solely for the chemical attack."

"Saddam Hussein's execution in 2006, before the genocide trial against him for the Anfal Campaign was completed, frustrated the Kurds' search for justice. As a member of the Kurdistan Martyrs of Halubja, I will go to Baghdad with other survivors and testify at hearings to sentence

Anfal and Halubja Testimonies

'Chemical Ali' who was just convicted of atrocities of the Anfal and chemical attacks.[1] We don't want revenge, only justice. It's important that the chemical attacks and the Anfal be seen as genocide. "

Mamosta (in Kurdish, "teacher") also told us his story: "I had been a teacher in an Iraqi village close to the Iranian border. The Ba'ath government destroyed our home, orchards, and gardens in 1974. I was told to join the Iraqi army or be shot, so moved to Halubja to escape."

"During the bombing of Halubja on March 16, the gas initially blinded and stunned me." When Mamosta woke up in the night, everything looked green to him. In the morning, his daughter was dead and his son had trouble breathing. He buried those who died. Family members still alive escaped over the mountains to Iran. He and his wife lost five children—only two daughters survived. They now have many health problems.

"The world should have cried out, 'Why are you killing these people?' How are terrorists created? By humiliating and treating people badly. I tell my story in hope that the people of the U.S. could understand what horrible things the Kurds experienced and make sure it doesn't happen again to my grandson," who was sitting at his knees. "I'm afraid this could happen again if the status of Kirkuk isn't settled soon."

As we were leaving, I said to his wife, "I'm sorry that telling the story brings up the pain for you. She answered warmly, "Don't feel bad. We remember our children and live with the pain all the time. We don't want to ever forget them. Talking about them is healing."

"In 1958, Iraq changed from a kingdom to a republic," said Ali Khalifa, a mullah in Kirkuk and Shad's grandfather, as he told his story. From that time until the 1991 uprising, the Kurds helped different foreign powers (the British, Turks, the Shah of Iran, and the U.S.). Each group promised to give Kurds independence, but didn't follow through.

"During the Anfal campaign, starting in 1986, the Iraqi government destroyed mosques, churches, and houses, and forced us out. When the

---

1. On January 25, 2010, Ali Hassan al-Majid, the man called "Chemical Ali" was executed by hanging after the Halubja trial was completed.

army attacked my village, Khilabazani, they took livestock and everything valuable. They brought people to a large military prison, Topzawa, and separated out young and old, men and women. A soldier told me the teenage girls were given to Yemeni soldiers. They tortured or killed boys and men in front of their families. They took nursing babies from their mothers."

He and his wife were taken in buses with the older people to the Nogra Salman Prison in the desert between the Saudi Arabian and Iraqi borders. There, more than 10,000 men and women were crowded into huge buildings like cattle. They had not been given food or water since being detained. One guard told them, "This is your grave."

"About five to ten died every day. We got one piece of bread and a cup of water a day. People were starving. Twice, guards beat me with a cable." He and his wife were there seven months before guards started taking people away. His wife, however, died of starvation the day before he was released, August 8, 1988. When people were released, Iraqi officials threatened to harm them if they spoke publicly about their experience. They couldn't go back to their former homes, but were sent to government-built collective towns. He was in one near Erbil until he got his land back after the 2003 invasion.

"All this happened to us because of Kirkuk," he added. "After the Anfal, Saddam made the Kirkuk Province smaller by giving parts to other provinces. One of the first changes to be made now is to restore those parts to the Kirkuk Province. It would be fine for Iraqi Kurdistan to remain part of Iraq, as long as we have Kirkuk back and have our rights."

"I was taken through seven doors into the basement of the prison, and there I saw hell," Khalid Qadir Mohammed told us. In 1989, Khalid and a friend were arrested at gunpoint by Saddam Hussein's soldiers and taken to prisons in Kirkuk and Baghdad and then forced to join the Ba'athist army. Khalid escaped and hid in the mountains until the 1991 uprising. When the uprising failed, he fled to Iran. After the UN established the northern "no-fly" zone in northern Iraq on April 5, 1991, Khalid and his family returned to Rania.

"Because I was the oldest child in my family, and my father became ill while I was young, I was responsible for my brothers and sisters. I left school to make money by selling cigarettes. I loved to read, even though there were few books written in Kurdish. But I found books and newspapers written in Arabic and read as much as I could."

After returning to Rania in 1991, Khalid started the Rania Youth Center with the support of Kurdistan Save the Children. "We started out with one room and some broken-down furniture that the government donated to us," he said. "We offered one English language course and a course in tailoring. We had fifty students learning on one computer." The Rania Youth Center currently served 299 youth a day, offering classes in fine arts, computer programming, music, and sports. It had a library and put out a weekly newspaper. As Khalid spoke, his voice and eyes reflected his passion and love for his people.

Khalid and his wife, Nishtiman, an English teacher in a girls' high school, are partners and advisers to our team. They continue to connect people to the international community through a sister-city program between Rania and Duluth, Minnesota and are helping other Kurdish cities set up similar programs.[2]

Bullet holes and broken walls mark the battles during the 1991 uprising, when Kurds took control of "Amna Suraka" ("the Red Security Prison") in Suleimaniya from the Ba'ath Regime. Weathered Iraqi military tanks line one wall of the courtyard. The buildings have not been restored, but remain as a museum memorializing the cruelty of Saddam's regime. Rooms of pictures depict the atrocities of the Anfal genocide and chemical attacks. Shad explains things as she walked around with us on our tour. At the "secret" prison, where Kurdish prisoners had been tortured and killed, we walk through rooms where women had been tortured and raped. In other rooms, scenes of torture are staged, using realistic looking statues. I worked to hold back the grief welling up in me and managed to restrain it to minimal tears. Later, back in my room, I would let my tears flow more freely to release what I could.

The tour ends in a room where the walls are covered with 182,000 broken pieces of mirror, the official number of people killed, and the ceiling with 5,000 tiny lights, one for each of the Kurdish villages destroyed in the Anfal. They are not to be forgotten. *My government is right in being horrified by the atrocities of Saddam's regime, but in turn has also killed, tortured, and terrorized civilians here and around the world in the name*

2. See CPT Iraq Team Videos, "Khalid Qadir Mohammed's Interview."

of democracy or the war on terror. If it looks, it will see its own reflection in these tiny mirrors.

The lights and pieces of mirror also represent thousands of eyes and voices, seeing and speaking the truth about the futility of violence and the cruelty institutions of power use to hold onto power and wealth. *Each light demands that such atrocities never happen again.*

I remember my son, Dale, telling me, "When you write, include stories of hope." At times like this, however, such cruelty seems overwhelming. It's hard to feel hope or see God.

Walking out into the sunshine, I look for hope in the roses in bloom and fresh grass sprung up from winter rains. I resist getting caught in feelings of powerlessness when facing such fierce cruelty. My emotions are reeling, *but I affirm the power of life-giving realities that are more powerful than any evil memorialized here. I reclaim the realm of God that is received in the gentleness and openness of a little child, but also compels us to resist evil and make room for ways of living together that are healing and just. I struggle, but hold onto faith that this reality can break in and transform seemingly hopeless situations.*

Leaving the museum, I sense Shad's pain. As a child, she had arrived at a public square in Kirkuk just after Kurdish teenage boys were shot there by Saddam's forces and saw the pile of their shoes, many of which were from smaller children. Her family was forced out of their home and some family members killed during the Anfal. During the Kurdish uprising, her family went into hiding and then fled to Iran as refugees. Her spirit bears scars of this violence. We put our arms around each other's shoulders as we walk away.

Violent attacks on Kurdish villages, however, were still happening.

18

"Bombing Hurts, Please Stop"

Figure 9: Prde Hazwa IDPs and CPTers hold up
"Bombing Hurts! Please Stop" banner, August 9, 2008

"It was 2:00 in the morning on December 16, [2007] when Turkish planes started bombing our village [Leozha, an Iraqi village close to the border with Iran]," Musheer Jalal recounted, as we sat on mats in a house his family now rents in an Iraqi town farther from the Iranian border. By the time the fourth bomb hit their home, his family had fled to a nearby ditch. "Everything was on fire. I was running from the house when I heard Susan, my twenty-seven-year-old daughter, scream. She lost the lower part of her left leg from pieces of the bomb. Planes continually flew overhead, so it was several hours before we could carry her to a car that could take her to a hospital. She's still in the hospital, and is depressed. The most painful thing she's experienced," Musheer said, "is believing her life is over."

That night, Turkish jets bombed 34 villages in eastern Iraqi Kurdistan, close to the Iranian border. In Steroka, shrapnel struck Aisha Ibrahim in the head and killed her. The blasts destroyed her extended family's three homes and killed 480 sheep and goats. "She didn't do anything to deserve this," Aisha's daughter said, her voice wavering. Her brother added, "Turkey is targeting civilians, not the PKK (Kurdistan Workers' Party). We're surprised and disappointed that the U.S. is assisting Turkey. We used to support the U.S." The attacks that night displaced 350–400 families, destroyed a school, and damaged several village mosques. *Turkish planes flew fifty-plus miles south of the Turkish border—across Iraqi airspace—to bomb these villages.*

On our second visit with her family, Susan sat on her bed looking frightened and sad. "I have no hope for my life now," she told us. "I am not good physically or psychologically. I cry all day long." Mohammed, our driver, interpreted for Cliff and me as we sat with the family. He sensitively communicated our comments and questions to Susan and her family and helped us know how much to ask and when to leave. A few months later, with ICRC's help, Susan was able to enter a rehabilitation program in which she was fitted with an artificial leg, though she still struggled with depression.

We began visiting other areas along the border, meeting *mukhtars* (leaders) in the villages, discussing the issues with local residents, and getting clearance for this work from KRG officials. A local official told us, "Every day, Turkish planes fly over this area for surveillance or bombing, terrifying the people. We have a different opinion than the Iraqi government and Turkey on what is happening and what should be done. The issues behind the attacks are political. Finally the Kurds have their own government and the Turkish government sees this as a threat. The attacks are also meant to divert attention from the Article 140 referendum concerning Kirkuk and other disputed areas." He showed us bomb fragments found at the sites, pictures of damaged schools, and two videos of bombed areas.

Each government had ways of justifying its actions, pointing to treaties and historical circumstances. For decades, Turkey had repressed its Kurdish minority population. In 1984, the Kurdish liberation movement—the PKK—started attacking and killing Turkish soldiers. Turkey and Iraq made agreements between 1978 and 1987 allowing both to enter each other's borders to apprehend attackers.[1]

Around 1996, Iran began shelling Iraqi border villages more frequently, often during planting, harvest, or when their animals gave birth. Bombardments burned crops and destroyed fruit and nut trees. Attacks usually lasted a short time, so people retreated to caves or left their villages and returned when attacks subsided. Iran claimed that the villages were harboring members of the Iranian Kurdish opposition party, Kemolah, and then after 2004, the Party of Free Life of Kurdistan (PJAK), a sister organization of the PKK, largely based and operating in western Iran. Turkey claimed villagers were aiding and harboring members of the PKK. The people claimed these fighters were not in their villages.

Villagers adjusted to the pattern of sporadic bombing, but this changed with Iraq and Turkey's August 7, 2007 memorandum of understanding to cooperatively root out the PKK, labeling it a terrorist organization. Then on November 5, 2007, U.S., Turkey, and Iraq ratified the Trilateral Military Commission agreement to share military intelligence to help Turkey locate and fly over Iraqi airspace to attack the PKK. An offer to lay down their arms and negotiate, made by a major faction of the PKK in November 2007, was not taken seriously.

In late December 2007, Kurdish leaders publicly condemned the Turkish bombings, but the U.S. government denied that the bombings caused much damage. Here, as elsewhere, the general assumption of governments was that anything, even displacement or killing of your own people, is justified when it is said to be "for security." The common people, the victims, had little power over what was happening. As we studied this situation, our team refused to be subverted into justifying offensive military attacks in the name of defense and security. We chose to focus on compassion for human suffering and the basic rights of local civilians to live in their homes and carry out their work in safety.

As we documented the consequences of the attacks, it became clear to us that whatever violence had been perpetrated by all sides, resources from the U.S. should be put toward helping different parties address the problems and human rights violations at the heart of the conflict, and negotiate a resolution and end to the violent activity. U.S. assistance to Turkey to make the attacks did not decrease terrorism, but only perpetuated this violent conflict, caused more suffering, and increased the anger in the region toward the U.S.

---

1. See CPT Iraq Team Reports, "Where There Is a Promise, There Is a Tragedy."

Part Two: Summer 2006—Fall 2011

A controversial issue arose when residents in the bombed areas reported eye, nose, and throat inflammations, vomiting, breathing difficulties, itching, and other skin irritations. They suspected that Turkey used chemicals in the December bombings. A shepherd from the village of Levce reported that on the second day of bombing, livestock with no visible injuries began to die and their milk changed to a gray color and had a sour taste. A month later, 170 newborn goats from his herd died. When he took samples of animal meat and milk to a health center in Erbil for testing, the official told him his goats were grazing in a "dirty environment and the milk was poisoned." His veterinarian told us that three months before the bombings, the shepherd's animals had been vaccinated for POX disease and seemed healthy.

Susan Musheer, also from Levce village, told us that after their home had been bombed, many members of her family had trouble breathing, eye pain, and red spots on their faces. Family members began complaining of kidney and bronchial problems that remain with them, and other people from the village experienced similar symptoms.

The KRG Minister of Health and the Ministry of Environment (MOE) told us that they investigated this claim and didn't find anything abnormal. Soil samples showed only heavy metals. We didn't know to what extent the health problems were from general toxic residues from the explosive materials. Other officials told us, however, that the MOE and the other agencies in the KRG didn't have the proper equipment to test for added chemicals. The only way to get accurate information was to get the UN to have the testing done in Vienna. Kurdish aid workers also expressed skepticism about the objectivity of the local agencies responsible for testing the samples, or that they would take a stand publicly if they found chemicals involved, since these agencies depend on the government for operational funds or permission to work here. Because no agency seen as neutral and credible to the public followed through on this, there was no conclusive finding. As we continued reporting the effects of the attacks over the next three years, however, we continued to hear claims of mass deaths of livestock and toxic contamination in bombed areas.[2]

2. See CPT Iraq Team Reports, "Disrupted Lives."

"Bombing Hurts, Please Stop"

On an icy January day (2008), twelve human rights workers and journalists, gathered with us in Suleimaniya to think about possibilities for accompanying displaced villagers back to their homes and to help us shape our response to the cross-border attacks. Namo, of the Civil Society Initiatives (CSI) facilitated the discussion. One after another, people shared opinions that ranged from excitement and hope to serious doubts: "I don't think authorities will give you permission to stay in the restricted border villages, because of the danger." "It's a bold and exciting plan." "I don't think it would stop Turkey's bombing." "Let's demonstrate with the displaced in Erbil and launch an e-mail and fax campaign with the Bush Administration." "We could form a mock 'village' of IDPs at the U.S. consulate in Erbil."

Those meeting that day did not stay involved as a group, but several individuals, such as Venus, of the Kurdistan Human Rights Watch (KHRW), Parween Aziz, an independent human rights worker, Namo and Schorsh of CSI, and Aram of Kurdish Institute for Elections, continued to advise and work with us.

On February 22, Iraqi Kurds were alarmed when Turkey started a new air and ground offensive into a wide area of the Iraqi side of the Iraq-Turkey border, sending about 10,000 soldiers six miles inland. Many Kurds said that Turkey's bombing of six bridges farther inside the borders was evidence that it was not just targeting the PKK, but trying to undermine the stability and semi-autonomy of the KRG region. The KDP retaliated by destroying a number of Turkish intelligence bases inside Iraq.

People feared that Turkey was planning an expanded incursion deeper into Iraq and talked about the possibility of an all-out war. KRG news sources reported fierce clashes between Turkish forces and the Peshmerga. We heard that 5,000 Kurdish civilians went to areas in the Dohuk and Erbil Governorates, preparing to fight Turkish soldiers. On February 29, however, Turkey announced that it accomplished its mission, and its troops started withdrawing from Iraqi territory.

It was early June 2008. After Peshmerga guards examined our identification papers at the checkpoint, we drove up windy mountain roads. We passed flocks of sheep and goats, small towns and villages nestled on dry and rocky mountainsides in the foothills of the Qandil slopes. We were in the Pshdar district in northwestern Suleimaniya Governorate, between the final two checkpoints before the Iranian border. In order to visit the Prde Hazwa IDP camp, we got permission from the local mayor of the near-by town of Zharawa and the Asaish.

Around a sharp curve in the narrow road, we saw the first section of the camp, about fifty tents clustered in a dry, barren-looking area of the valley. We drove on to the second, where about eighty tents stretched out along the shallow river in a narrow valley between the mountains. Here, a few trees gave shelter from the intense heat of the mid-summer sun. Labels of UNHCR on tents and ICRC on water tanks told us that these and other international aid agencies supplied aid. About 600 persons lived here—132 families from nine villages displaced since March by Turkish military attacks and more recent attacks from Iran.

Residents seemed eager to talk about their situation. "Life is hard," one woman said grimly as we sat in her family's tent. Others complained that the water was not clean, that there was no privacy, and they couldn't plant crops or take care of their livestock. They described the time in early March when the bombing and shelling around their villages got heavier. It was terrifying for the children to go down into dark underground shelters. There they heard the bombs explode, and felt the ground shake all around them, not knowing if their homes would still be standing when they came back out. Many villagers stayed in caves for days. People were injured or killed. "Our village was in total confusion," one man said. "Many of our buildings and gardens were destroyed."

Sargul, from Lower Razga, whose wife gave birth to their daughter in a cave during the bombing, said, "We once lived in paradise and had everything we needed in our villages—grain, orchards, vegetables, and animals. Our water came down from the mountains and was clean and cold. During the economic sanctions, we grew food for ourselves and for people in the cities. We never had to ask for anything from the government. Here there's no work. Ask your government to make this stop so it's safe for us to go home. They can make camps for us, but it's better for us to be able to go back to our villages in safety."

Taban, a young nurse living in the camp after being displaced from the Arkesaru village, operated a medical clinic out of her tent. She recalled returning to her village in 1991, after her graduation, out of her love for the mountains and her people. "I walked with others half a day and reached our homes, destroyed by Saddam in the 1980s. There was no water, no electricity, and no roofs. We rebuilt them with our hands, tears, and joy. Now the bombing around the village has destroyed our houses and plows, and burned food for the animals. We're living off money from selling our animals, so I am afraid we won't have enough money to rebuild in the future."

On another visit three weeks later, about twenty villagers gathered outside one family's tent. While Joe and Chihchun met with the adults, twelve children gathered around Angela and me on a sandy area nearby. They told us about life in their villages and made drawings of what they saw during the attacks. Seven-year-old Ghazan pointed to images drawn on his paper. "This is the bomb next to our house, and this is me. I'm running away." Pointing at her drawing, Banaz said, "This is fire coming down from the bomb. These are cars taking us away." "Turkey attacks by plane, and Iran by mortars," an older boy informed us.

Figure 10: IDP camp child's drawing of bombing of his village home

The children said their families left their villages by foot (about an hour's walk), car, or tractor to get to this camp. Even at this time, from the camp, they were able to hear the bombing continuing in the areas of their villages. "When that happens we get so scared, we get sick," one boy admitted soberly. "Last week our families left this camp for a time when we heard the bombs, because we were afraid the planes would also bomb us here."

After spending time with some of the children in the camp, my teammate, Hilary Scarsella, wrote, "It does not matter if not one person is killed. It does not matter if not one home is destroyed. This child should not have to hide from bombs. The world must learn to care about more than statistics and death tolls. What about broken spirits? Traumatized hearts? Stolen dreams? Derailed lives? There are no flashy numbers. There is not a great enough amount of destruction at one time and in one place to attract the attention of the international media. Amidst all of the (popular) world tragedies that demand our emotional energy, the situation of the Kurds simply does not compete."

Later, a humanitarian aid worker told us his organization would provide alternative housing for the displaced families if they were still there when the weather turned cold. The organization only provides temporary housing and didn't want to do it too soon so the people wouldn't feel too comfortable and decide not to go back to their villages. We agreed that returning home was a priority over "resettlement," but understood that it was the villagers' realistic fear of physical harm that kept them from returning, not comfort in their new surroundings, and in the meantime, they needed a place where life was not so harsh and miserable.

On another visit to the camp, about fifty adults and children milled around as we laid out two large cloth banners on a sandy bank of the river. Written boldly on one was, "Bombing Hurts. Please Stop!" With paint, villagers put handprints and small drawings on this banner. Several children proudly held up their paint-colored hands for us to see. They filled the other banner with messages to governments and people of the world. "We don't want war." "Stop the bombing." "We want to live in peace." Others drew pictures of airplanes flying over houses, or of people running away.

Five days later, we went with two leaders of the camp to Erbil and met with a U.S. Embassy representative. "Thank you for getting rid of Saddam and shedding your blood for our people," Bapir, one of the leaders began. Then the leaders spoke about the border bombing. "Villages and villagers, not the rebel groups living in the higher Qandil Mountains, are the targets of the bombing by Turkey or Iran and are hurt by them."

"Bombing Hurts, Please Stop"

The Kurdish leaders described the difficult life they have living in the tents, and their need for alternative housing by winter if it's still too dangerous for them to return to their villages. When we mentioned the anger expressed toward the American government for giving Turkey military intelligence information and clearance to fly over Iraqi airspace to bomb along the Iraq-Iran border, the representative said, "We've also heard this." She agreed to consult with Kurdish officials about the IDP's material needs, as well as send a report of what was said at this meeting to the Embassy in Baghdad and the U.S.

A KRG Parliamentarian we talked with that day said, "I agree that the border conflicts need to be settled through dialogue and not violence. The U.S. has had a negative influence in this region. Now I hope America will put diplomatic pressure on Turkey and Iran to stop the attacks on border villages." After seeing the pictures we brought of the children at the tent camp, she said, "We need to see these children and not categorize them as terrorists."

By the end of October, fifty families were at the camp—about 200 people, including about twenty small children. Some of the men went back to their villages to care for their animals, feeling they had no choice economically. Older children lived with families in town so they could finish school. Many who stayed expressed grief over their loss of their traditional Kurdish way of life. One woman told us, "In the village, I would go out to the orchards early in the morning and pick fruits and vegetables. Then the family gathered to eat and talk. We were happy and grateful to God. Now, we're separated. What kind of life is this?" she asked with tears streaming down her face. An older woman said she felt shame because she could not offer tea and prepare a feast for her guests as she had been able to do in her own home. Her dignity had been taken away.

In later December, local officials gave camp residents approval to buy a small piece of land. The UNHCR authorized a contractor to build a new camp for 45 of the 120 families from the camp. Accomodations would still be temporary, so would consist of sturdier tents built on top of concrete foundations. The most desperate forty-two families, who could find no other housing, would be chosen to live there.

It was a rainy day in Suleimaniya with no letup, and it was my day to get bottled water for our team. I went out with our small pull-cart to get two three-gallon bottles in one trip. But I hadn't mastered the technique of strapping two bottles onto the cart. When I went over a bump while crossing the street, one of the bottles got loose and started rolling down the incline. It was a busy time of the day when children were leaving school, and men were going to the mosque for noon prayers. Suddenly, I became the object of their attention. Here was this international woman, running after a bottle of water rolling down the street. All I could do was to laugh with the people around me at the spectacle I was making. I caught up with the bottle, and strapped it on again, smiling at the people around me, my dignity replaced by camaraderie.

We saw beauty in the spirit of men and women working nonviolently for justice and healing.

19

Choosing Paths of Healing

It was the third day of our nonviolence training in Suleimaniya in early June 2008. Gathered were fifteen Kurdish women and men, members of grassroots organizations already working on issues such as combating violence against women, abuse of prisoners, and government corruption. All were working independently of the two main political parties. It was highly participatory, so we were *all* teachers *and* learners. Today's focus was on reconciliation between ethnic groups.

The scenario for our group role-play was the dilemma of Kirkuk, a city rich in oil that had been a pivotal center for Saddam's oppression of the Kurdish people. Over 300,000 Kurdish residents had been killed or forced to leave their homes and relocate to other parts of Iraq. Saddam's government moved Arab Iraqi families in to replace them.

We divided participants into three groups, each taking the role of one of the three major ethnicities in that city—Kurd, Arab, or Turkmen—who want different outcomes for the future of the city and governorate. Each group framed their point of view on the major issues, and articulated what their group needed from the others to solve their volatile problems.

"Any voting about the status of Kirkuk should be done in a way to give the three major ethnic groups equal footing—each getting 33 percent of the vote," maintained those representing Turkmen. Those representing the Arabs stated, "These have been our homes for two decades. We should be allowed to keep our property in Kirkuk and not be forced out." Those representing the Kurds insisted, "Not only must we proceed with the article 140 Referendum, so we can vote to be part of the KRG, but it must be a one person, one vote. The land of our families, who were brutally killed and forced out, must be returned to us."

Part Two: Summer 2006—Fall 2011

The next step was the hardest—trying to come to a joint solution acceptable to all three groups. After lively, emotional debate, we decided it would take longer than we had in our session to come to agreement on something so controversial and complicated. But the group worked at a process to try to meet needs of all parties involved.

No quick or easy solutions came out of this and other workshops sessions that summer, during which participants applied tools of nonviolence to some of the problems in their society. These human rights workers already knew what it was like to be oppressed and persecuted as a people. They knew that standing with those hurt and marginalized in society and working for change and healing was difficult, and that it was risky to openly oppose oppression. Yet they were developing tools for doing that work. We considered them more in tune than we to the needs of their people and the lies being told to keep oppression in place. They were more prepared to find creative actions that would expose those lies, take away their support of corrupt structures, and encourage their own people to develop more just relationships and structures in society.

Our interpreter, Shad, was a member of the training teams, helping to communicate nonviolence theory and facilitate the group activities in Kurdish or Arabic. We hoped these sessions would assist experienced workers to train others. One participant, however, told me that people here would take more seriously what an international trainer said than what an Iraqi said, and was willing to put up with the extra time for interpreting. That might be true, but we believed that the sense of superiority of and deference to internationals was a byproduct of Western colonialism that we didn't want to perpetuate.

As an organization and a team, we were trying to be more aware of oppressions operating in ourselves and in society. We asked ourselves, "How do we as a team either contribute to oppressions or model undoing them?" Many of us struggled with the privileges given to us as "whites" or as Americans. As a team, we discussed different forms of oppressions, including racism, classism, and consumerism. Where did we shop, locally owned neighborhood stores or large new supermarkets? Did we try to take buses instead of taxis? With whom did we associate? Did we try to speak Kurdish or rely on English? Did we listen mostly to the men in local situations, or did we also seek out the voice of the women? Did we unconsciously marginalize team members whose native language was not English?

Choosing Paths of Healing

Even though our intentions have been good, we realized that our team has at times seen ourselves at the center stage of our work instead of following the lead and supporting the leadership of local leaders. (As I write this now, our translator-advisor and other local partners have become more an integral part of our team's decision-making and work.) We agreed that when writing for our team we wanted to focus primarily on the accomplishments and struggles of local people rather than on ours. As an organization and team, we sought to understand ways oppression was entrenched in our lives and our organization, and worked to eliminate racist or paternalistic attitudes and methods in our operation. We wanted to make our team a "safer" place for people of all backgrounds to work.

One woman, who took part in the trainings and later became a partner and adviser for our team, was Parween Aziz, currently working for Help Age International, and as a volunteer with WAFDI and KHRW. Having seen the suffering caused by injustice and corruption, she had been involved, since 1991, in various organizations for social change and as a community health worker. Initially she worked with government-related organizations, but when leaders of these organizations persecuted and slandered many activists and she saw the corruption among those leaders, she joined non-governmental organizations, or took independent action for human rights. "Working as an independent person is interesting but not easy," she said. "I moved from group to group finding different ways to serve people. They couldn't control me. If I felt I could not make changes through them, I moved on."

Parween was one of five persons in Suleimaniya to start up Masella, a nonviolence organization that publishes booklets, newspapers on nonviolence and organizes actions. This local group is connected with a nationwide internet-based association promoting nonviolence, called *La'onf* (in Arabic, "no violence"), with a goal of stopping violence in all parts of Iraq.

"Nonviolence is new for us," Parween told us. "We only knew fighting. Now we can work together and dialogue—like Gandhi. Nonviolence is a stronger way. It's slow and it takes time, but it's a safer road. I have benefited personally by using nonviolence to solve family conflicts."

Aram Jamal, director of the Kurdish Institute for Elections and member of Masella, was, like Parween, part of the committee that planned our June workshop. "I can't tell you exactly when I started to believe in nonviolence—sometime during all the wars and violence here," he said. "While at the university I felt that violence could be used against the enemy. People try to fix political problems through violence, but with time I saw that violence doesn't change the situation. It just produces death and more violence." A change in his thinking came in 2004, when he saw Arabic versions of documentary films about nonviolence such as *A Force More Powerful*[1] and *Gandhi*.[2] Since then, he had been showing these films around Iraqi Kurdistan, followed by a discussion on the values of nonviolence.

At the annual day of awareness of violence against women, Aram and other human rights activists covered their mouths with tape and stood at a busy street corner, because Kurdish leaders were touting great accomplishments in stopping such violence. "Women's voices are still silenced in society and there's still too much violence against them, so it's not time to celebrate or speak of accomplishments," he said. "There is, however, an increasing awareness of nonviolence in our society." To foster this, he suggests integrating nonviolence programs into the school system in ways "that bring it into children's lives." His dream is that people in authority learn nonviolent ways of using power.

Figure 11: Aram Jamal (center) and other Kurdish human rights workers vigil, with tape over their mouths, symbolizing the silencing of women

A number of one-day nonviolence and reconciliation workshops involved Iraqis of various ethnic backgrounds from four northern governorates outside the KRG region—Diyala (Baqubah), Taanimm (Kirkuk), Ninewa (Mosul), and Salahadeen (Tikrit). When participants met in subgroupings of the same background, many resisted listing positive things

1. *A Force More Powerful*, directed by Steve York.
2. *Gandhi*, directed by Sir Richard Attenborough.

about the other ethnic groups with which they had tensions. When they came back to the larger circle, however, and listened to those from other backgrounds share their pain, they expressed more empathy with them. Many commented on how similar the suffering of each ethnic group was.

On one of those days, two men, one Shia Muslim, and the other Sunni Muslim, both leaders in their communities, disagreed openly and repeatedly countered the other's comments. Then at the end of the session on reconciliation, the group took part in the "heart" exercise, in which participants voluntarily held the paper heart, and shared how a particular time of violence they experienced affected them. Then they tore off a piece of the heart to symbolize the way violence wounded their spirit.

Many shed tears when those of other backgrounds told their stories. The Shia leader recounted the tragic killing of several of his family members. Immediately, the Sunni leader, who had been in conflict with him that day, stood up and walked over to his antagonist. We watched, spellbound, as he hugged and kissed him on the cheeks and called him brother! Everyone applauded.

In early December, at another one-day training with fifteen young adult leaders from the conservative Muslim city of Halubja, we introduced ourselves as members of Christian Peacemaker Teams. One man asked, "What are you doing here as Christians?" In response, we explained that our purpose was not to push our faith on them. We generally don't initiate speaking to Muslims here about Christianity. Our work is to reduce violence, support local people using nonviolent ways of dealing with problems, and be of help to victims of violence.

"But why does your organization put 'Christian' in your name?" another asked, implying that it was offensive to Iraqi Muslims. "This is our identity," we answered. "We do this work because of our faith and out of our faith. You get strength to do your work out of your Muslim faith." I said we were sorry for the harm Christians have done to Muslims over the years and the U.S., to Islamic societies. We couldn't undo it but we wanted to work together for ending hostilities between people of our two faiths.

Then questions shifted to those of us who were American. "Why are you working here, when there's a lot of violence in your country?" one pushed. "Yes, there's a lot of violence in America, and when we're there, we're among those working to stop it," we answered. "One reason we're here is because our country initiated the war in Iraq and has caused a lot of damage to your society. We want to be a different kind of presence, a healing one."

Part Two: Summer 2006—Fall 2011

"While the Kurdish people were being gassed by Saddam, the U.S. did nothing to help us," one came back. "They've treated our people badly in occupying our country. It's only when they wanted to justify starting a war here that they spoke about our suffering." "Yes," we responded, "our nation did fail you and cause you much suffering. That's one reason we're here. Most Americans don't know what you've experienced. When we're home, we tell our people what's happening here, which helps them speak out and try to change our government's policies."

> "So who are *we*, to speak to the people here about healing?" I continually ask myself. I am a Christian, yet when I am among Muslims I see things with new eyes and begin to understand how they see Christianity. These experiences make me think about what is essential in faith, and defuse "all good-all bad" or demonizing thinking.
>
> The people of Iraq have experienced the hypocrisy of western leaders and nations or heard a distorted version of Christianity that justified military and economic aggression in their country and around the world. Christian groups have put too much emphasis on saying the "right" words about God or equating witnessing for one's faith with using words. A more powerful witness is when the "word becomes flesh"—that is, when God's Spirit becomes visible in our actions and lives.

About thirty—students, local political leaders, journalists, a UN worker, and a local physician—gathered in early December 2007, at a public forum in Suleimaniya. Three members of the Muslim Peacemaker Team (MPT) had come north from Najaf and were eager to meet Kurds working on human rights issues and see how they might collaborate. But this afternoon two of the men gave a report on the problems Iraqi people have suffered because of U.S.'s use of weaponry containing more than 500 tons of depleted uranium (DU).

Dr. Najim Askouri was a nuclear physicist, trained in Britain and one of the leading nuclear researchers in Iraq until his departure in 1998. He returned to Iraq after the fall of Saddam. Dr. Assad Al-Janabi was the director of the Pathology Department at the public hospital in Najaf. The focus area of the two men's study was Najaf, a city of over one million people, and the wider Najaf governorate, an area where DU was used. Theirs was not an exhaustive study because of the limits of personnel, resources, and equipment, but it was based on substantial public data, and thorough research.

In 2004, in the aftermath of the 2003 U.S. invasion, there were 251 reported cases of cancer. By 2006, that figure rose to 688. By 2007, it was 801. This showed an incidence rate of 28.21 by 2006, in contrast with the normal rate of eight to twelve cases of cancer per 100,000 people. Significant is the fact that the dramatic increases are in the cancers related to radiation exposure—especially the rare soft tissue sarcoma and leukemia—and that the age at which cancer begins is dropping rapidly, with incidents of breast cancer at sixteen, colon cancer at eight, and liposarcoma at one and a half years. Dr. Assad noted that 24 percent of the cancers reported occurred in the eleven to thirty age-range.

Dr. Najim described what happens when DU in weapons hits a target. It aerosolizes and oxidizes forming two oxides. The first oxide is water-soluble and enters the aquifers and food chain. The second is insoluble and settles as dust that's carried by the winds. If this dust enters the lungs, it can cause problems as it penetrates cell walls and impacts the genetic system. In 1991, the U.S. military used 350 tons of DU, and 150 tons during the 2003 bombing of Baghdad.

Dr. Najim shared that his grandson was born with heart problems, Down Syndrome, an under-developed liver, and leukemia. He believes these were caused by the parents' exposure to DU. "Cancer in the conflict area is a health epidemic and will only get worse," he said. "In sixteen years, the cancer rate in Najaf has more than tripled, as it has done in Basra, Kuwait, and Saudi Arabia." Using a Geiger counter, their research team discovered radiation levels of thirty to forty counts per minute in the Najaf area, compared to ten to fifteen counts per minute at the Tawaitha nuclear research reactor site outside Baghdad.

He concluded his talk by asking, "Wouldn't it be *just*, to ask for equipment to continue the testing, to locate contaminated sites, for a hospital to care for children born with genetic systems impacted with DU, a center for study and decontamination of affected areas, and support for a special environmental department at the local university?" He didn't think the U.S. would grant total compensation, but believed it was appropriate to make requests for cleaning the environment and caring for those exposed to DU.

Dr. Fuad Baban, a prominent Kurdish physician attending the forum, pointed out that even though "DU was not used by Saddam, the body's immune system does not distinguish between chemicals or radiological materials from weapons. Both destroy cells, and cause cancer and birth defects." He had written a report of studies of chemical weapons used by Saddam's forces during the Anfal campaigns. He believed DU dust from the 1991 and 2003 U.S. attacks in central and southern Iraq has spread up north through winds and dust storms.

"As of 2003, depending on the year and season, about 40 to 60 percent of the marshlands in southern Iraq has been re-flooded," Arab, Kurdish, and American co-workers at Nature Iraq (NI), an Iraqi nonprofit organization working to protect and restore the country's environment, briefed us as we met with them in Suleimaniya. "That's compared to their extent in the 1970s, before Saddam Hussein drained them in the 1990s in order to control rebels there. He had reduced the reeds to less than 10 percent of their previous size."

According to NI conservation staff, water systems within Iraq have not been managed well. Dams provide tap water for large cities, but also cause destruction to the rivers and submerge quality agricultural lands. Water purification throughout Iraq still has many problems, and the water is highly contaminated by a "cocktail of toxins." Besides military-related toxins, massive amounts of dioxins from landfill dumps are washed by rainwater into the water systems. Fish harvested from the waterways are contaminated. According to Anna Bachman, an American member of their team, "It is most likely true that more people in Iraq die of environment degradation than from all the violence that the country is dealing with."

In their advocacy work, NI tries to convince the government to protect the biodiversity of species and to see the health of birds, mammals, and plants as linked to the good health of the people and the nation as a whole. "As Iraq rushes to re-develop," she said, "we need to apply the precautionary principle that if we don't know whether the things we are doing or using harm us, we should take precautions and rebuild Iraq in a way that is environmentally sustainable."

About 200 independent journalists and human rights workers gathered somberly in a park in Suleimaniya in late July 2008 to mourn the death of Soran Hama. This twenty-three-year-old independent journalist from Kirkuk had just been shot and killed in front of his home on July 22. He had received death threats after publishing an article exposing corruption among Kurdish officials involved in a local prostitution ring.

Choosing Paths of Healing

Speakers spoke about Soran and his work. "We must continue to tell the truth about the problems in our society," said a journalist. "But if we do, we know we may also receive retaliation." Another speaker called on the U.S. and Central Iraqi Government to help investigate such attacks, since the KRG would not. We stood among people who knew they could also be persecuted for speaking out and working for truth and justice. They were not alone, however, but part of a community of support made up of others with the same commitment.

A week later, we interviewed Salah, another journalist from Kirkuk, who told us, "In Kirkuk, people of the free pen [independent journalists] fear they will be killed like Soran. After his death, a list was circulated of twenty journalists in Kirkuk that had been threatened. I was on that list, since I have criticized the Kurdish government." He was also critical of the U.S. for not taking a strong enough stand against the killing of dissenters.

There comes a time in late June, when the heat becomes intense—when it gets over 115 degrees Fahrenheit. We find ourselves gulping down more water and resting in the mid-afternoon. Even here in the north, where it's usually ten degrees cooler than in Baghdad, it can get up to 125 degrees in mid-July through August. One answer to the heat is a picnic in the cooler mountains.

One hot July day, several of our team went with a group of young adults to a picnic area called Sergalul. We climbed into a bus stuffed with picnic gear and lots of food. On the bus, the group sang and clapped. Some even stood up in the aisles and danced in Kurdish style. We found a picnic spot nestled under the trees along the branches of a rocky stream flowing down the mountainside.

Several of us walked uphill to giant boulders and then walked along the lower stream. When the women waded in a pool under a short waterfall, one started splashing everyone else, and soon we were all happily soaked. In between meals, we sat on a rug on the ground, eating sunflower seeds and joking. One young woman started throwing the shells at the men. Soon, the men threw handfuls on us until it became an all-out shell-fight. It was 9:00 that evening when we got home, tired but happy.

20

"Kurds and Turks Are Brothers"

MACHMOUD SHOWED US A spring flowing out of the snow-capped mountains to a meadow below, where the village of Kani Spi (in Kurdish, "White Spring") was established. Our team visited this fertile mountainous area in northern Erbil Governorate near the Iraqi-Iranian border in October 2008, as monitoring and reporting the effects of border bombings became a primary focus of our work. Battles were fought there during the Iran-Iraq war, leaving its fields full of landmines. After the 1991 uprising against Saddam, Machmoud returned to Kani Spi, but lost his lower leg to a landmine. After the Mines Action Group (MAG) and the UN carried out a de-mining operation around a number of villages in the area, families moved back to rebuild Kani Spi.

During the summers of 2007 and 2008, Iran fired rockets at the village, killing livestock, setting fire to crops, destroying homes, terrifying and displacing the people. The families retreated to the town of Choman, fourteen kilometers away. Since then, they spend their summers in Kani Spi, farming and caring for their sheep, and move back to Choman for the winter. Though Iran said it was targeting PJAK, Machmoud claimed that no members of that group were around their village.

On another visit to that area, in the nearby-city of Soran, Chihchun and I entered a colorfully painted room where children and adults were receiving physical therapy. The mayor of Choman showed us around the Soran Association Care for Handicaps (SACH). He introduced us to the staff, all handicapped in some way. According to SACH, there have been six million landmines in Iraq, affecting 19,290 villages, with 9,000 victims.

In his district alone, there were 3,500 handicapped victims of landmines and bombings.

"They want to empty this corner of the country, where Turkey, Iran, and Iraq meet," the mayor said. "Turkish and Iranian military do joint operations, and sometimes their officers come together here to assess the situation. Bombing the border weakens Kurdish society and the KRG. When people had to leave their villages, they left agricultural land, bees, orchards, nuts, and vegetables—all good quality products. So our society has to import more of these goods, hurting the economy. If villagers have to move into town, they often can't find work and need aid from the government. The average displaced family loses $15–20,000 a year. Kurds have lost a trillion dollars from cross-border attacks."

Yellow and orange leaves hung on the trees that fall as our car drove through the mountains of northern Iraq into the Dohuk Governorate. Around each bend of the windy road we saw new colors and contours of rocks and soil. Higher mountains in the distance already had a dusting of snow. Outside Bamarne, a town of about 300 families, eighteen miles south of the Turkish border, we passed a Turkish base on the edge of the town.

The Mukhtar of Bamarne told us, "These bases were established in 1996, during the PUK—KDP civil war after KDP leaders made an agreement with Turkey that it could come up to twenty kilometers inside the border. At the same time the PUK asked Iran to help them. The agreement has expired, but the Turkish military refuses to leave, and Kurdish officials feel helpless to make them. Turkey keeps them here to cause instability in this region." From his back door, the Mukhtar pointed to a mountain to the north and said, "Soldiers attack whenever they see anyone on the mountain, because the PKK occasionally travels through here."

When we returned to Bamarne a year later, the Mukhtar showed us an orchard close to the Turkish Military base. We saw about a hundred charred apple and almond trees. "The third week of October, just before harvest," he explained, "Turkish soldiers used the muffler of a tank to set them on fire. When villagers complain about destruction of property, Turkish officials say that it won't happen again or that it's for security."

The head of the Asaish in the town of Kani Masi, an Assyrian Christian, said that in 1996 Turkey also established a small base at the edge of his town. He added, "The people in town are mostly Christians, but the area is half Christian, half Muslim who have lived together peacefully. When an organization offers aid to either Christians or Muslims, the people insist it gives aid to the other group as well." His guards took us to visit some of the attacked villages. One was Merkajiya, about twelve kilometers inland from the border.

"Heavy Turkish bombing here between 1994 to 1996, resulted in destroyed homes, farmland, livestock, crops and displacement of hundreds of families," said the Mukhtar of Merkajiya. "Much of our land was burned, and a lot of animals killed. The Turkish army took and tortured my brother, broke his arm, and put a plastic bag over his head to suffocate him, but he survived." When Turkish soldiers left, many families returned and the KRG finance minister gave them resources to rebuild a destroyed church. Now the Turkish military in the nearby base launches rockets periodically at Merkajiya and twenty other nearby villages, usually during the spring or summer harvests. "Why do they do this? We are not military people. This is our weapon," he said, holding up a pair of pruning clippers.

"In January, when snow closes our road, I'll stay here even if they bomb. I love this place and want to stay where my family has lived for generations. In the past, we lacked nothing. We don't want aid. Just get rid of this threat from Turkey so we can live in peace."

As we traveled farther west and reached a higher elevation, snow had transformed the hills and mountains around us into a stunningly beautiful white wonderland. Thick snow clumps clung to the branches of the trees and shrubs. The road had been plowed, so we had no difficulty driving. Our driver initiated a stop to make snowballs and play in the snow. On the edge of Zakho, we used the last hour of daylight to look at an ancient stone bridge. Built before modern equipment was available, it impressively arched up and over the Khabour River.

The next day we found the village of Grebye, nestled in a valley southwest of Kani Masi. A Turkish military base stood on a small hill thirty meters from the elementary school, on land that Turkish forces confiscated from the village Mukhtar in 1996. We sat around a small cylindrical wood stove in the Mukhtar's home. He told us, "The soldiers do not attack our people, but no one can go close to the base." While serving us tea, his wife said anxiously, "The tank guns are pointed at the town. The children are terrified when planes fly overhead."

"Kurds and Turks Are Brothers"

Figure 12: Turkish base on hill, school below, in village of Grebye, January 1, 2009

On December 12, 2008, we sent an open letter to President-elect Obama. After describing the situation along Iraq's northern borders and the results of Turkey's cross-border attacks, we concluded with the following:

> As we talk to Kurdish people, we hear a call for the United States to abide by international law and the Fourth Geneva Agreements, standards to which it holds other countries: not to kill or injure civilians, and the responsibility of an occupying power to protect and care for the civilians under its control. Therefore, we urge you to:
>
> 1. Reverse U.S. policies that assist Turkey's attacking Kurdish Iraqi civilian populations, and put diplomatic pressure on Turkey to pursue diplomatic and peaceful solutions to the PKK-Turkey disputes.
>
> 2. Refuse to support new agreements that would expand the rights of Turkey's military to send more troops or establish more bases in northern Iraq and put pressure on Turkey to remove existing bases.

3. We also invite you to come here and visit some of these villages and IDP camps and talk with the people. They are very welcoming and hospitable. We would be glad to introduce you to them and be of what assistance we can.

We got no response.

The issue of Kirkuk was an important and hot one for Kurds, so in between travels in the border areas, our team visited that city. Our hosts, the head of the PUK and the Mayor, both Kurds, said the population consisted of about 52 percent Kurds, 35 percent Arabs, 12 percent Turkmen, and about 12,000 Christians. They spoke of the importance of implementing article 140 of the Iraqi Constitution, which mandated a referendum by the end of 2007 to allow people there and in other historically Kurdish areas to vote whether to become part of the KRG or stay under the main control of the Iraqi Central Government. It was to be carried out in three steps: (1) Displaced people return to their place of origin. (2) Through a census, produce an up-to-date electoral register. (3) Hold a referendum on incorporating Kirkuk into the KRG. "Unfortunately, they're still in the first step, which is very difficult. Kurds, Turkmen, and Arabs get financial compensation for relocating," one official said. "About 70 percent of this is done. We want one Iraq, but restore Kirkuk to the Kurds. The U.S. has brought in some positive civilian projects, but, unfortunately, has been against the referendum."

"The struggle for the control of Kirkuk is an old one and not just about oil," the leaders explained. "Over the centuries, it had been a strategic place for trade. Then the discovery of oil in the 1920s complicated it more. In 1968 the Ba'ath Party deported Kurds from Kirkuk and brought in Arab families, part of the 'Arabization.'" Once again they see the head of Iraq, now Prime Minister Nouri al-Maliki, as trying to control Kirkuk, by financially supporting local Arab militias there, replacing Kurdish Peshmerga with Iraqi soldiers, and changing their elected council system.

Members of the Assyrian and Evangelical Churches in Kirkuk voiced their concerns to us about security there. One said, "Because America is perceived as Christian, Islamist radicals who resent U.S. presence take their anger out on local Christians." Many of the Christians live in Kurdish neighborhoods, considered safer for them, and avoid going into "Arab" areas in southern Kirkuk where they fear being killed. A week before our visit, the Armenian Church and a car owned by a Christian were attacked.

After a number of Christians were killed in Mosul a month earlier, about 2,000 families—almost half of Mosul's Christian population—fled that city. Many came to Kirkuk, where the presence of nine Christian churches dates back to the first century. In all Iraq there had been two million Christians, but two-thirds (about 600,000) of the Iraqi Christians have moved to the KRG or outside the country. Despite this tension, we were glad to see bundles of goods collected by women in the Evangelical Church ready to be distributed to Muslim prisoners in a Kirkuk prison for the upcoming Islamic feast of Eid Al-Fitr.

On another trip out of the KRG region we went to the Makhmour Refugee Camp in a flat, desert-like area, similar to other parts of central, southern, and northwestern Iraq. Once inside the camp gates, the traditional stone with mud-mortar-built homes and stone fences made it seem like an old, traditional Iraqi village. Along the narrow streets, mothers were hanging up laundry, and older children were walking home from school or playing soccer. Inside the office, one of the leaders gave us a brief history of the camp.

"Sixteen years ago our families left our homes in southeastern Anatolia, Turkey because the government imprisoned and tortured Kurds who spoke and taught the Kurdish language and observed our cultural practices. At first we lived as displaced persons in Turkey, but in 1993 and 1994 we moved into a UN camp set up just inside the Iraqi border. Turkey continued to bomb and raid along the border, so the camp moved south." Since most of these 12,000 refugees—63 percent women and children—had relatives in the PKK, Turkey periodically raided the camp, accusing residents of participating in terrorist activities.

"We want to go back to our homes in Turkey," another explained, "but to do that, we need the Turkish government to give amnesty to us and the thousands of Kurds in Turkish prisons and guarantee our safety as we return. The U.S., however, has supported Turkish suppression of Kurds. We need international groups to put pressure on the U.S. and Turkey to change their repressive policies and to see us not as 'terrorists,' but as people longing for respect as a people and culture."

Our hosts invited us to the hall of the "Association of Families of Martyrs" where over fifty men and women stood in a line and greeted us warmly. On the walls were hundreds of pictures of their fathers, sons, or husbands—family members killed by Turkish forces.

Part Two: Summer 2006—Fall 2011

"The women here are part of a nonviolent civil movement called, "Mothers for Peace," also known as "Peace Mothers," started in 1999, with over 1,000 Kurdish mothers in Syria, Iran, Iraq, and Turkey," a woman explained. "We make banners, join marches, and participate in demonstrations, calling on everyone fighting in the Turkish-Iraqi border conflict to lay down their arms and use political and diplomatic means, and respect the Kurds' basic human rights. We also speak out against other forms of injustice, like poverty and hunger. One of the messages on our banners is 'Kurds and Turks are Brothers: We Want Peace.' We invited non-Kurdish Turkish mothers to join us, but they haven't come. Neither Turkish nor Kurdish mothers should have to cry again or see our children tortured and killed. It's time for forgiveness and reconciliation."

The following year, eight women, fourteen men, and four children from the camp were arrested for being part of an October 2009 peace march in Turkey, calling for a peaceful, negotiated resolution to the Turkey-PKK conflicts. They were charged with spreading PKK propaganda, promoting separation politics, and associating with a terrorist organization.

Today, I went down the line of women and greeted each one. Their faces showed deep pain and suffering. In their eyes I saw anguish, but also much strength. They were beautiful because they communicated openness and love. In that brief time, God's presence among us seemed very real. The love I was given for these Turkish women, who had endured so much, strengthened *me*.

We left, awed also by their expectations of us—so much greater than what we could give. We didn't have great influence on our government and weren't able to focus on the wider issues of Kurdish rights. We could, however, affirm the beauty and humanity of these people and their work for peace, and repudiate, in our writing and speaking, the blanket-label of "terrorist."

> Just before Christmas, I wrote: "It was into a world such as this that Jesus was born. He knew about the seemingly insurmountable power of world empires and how helpless the poor felt to change things. And yet he chose not to be consumed by hate or take the role of a helpless victim. He chose a different way. He reached out in healing to the victims of pain and violence while confronting, with the power of love and truth, the corrupt and oppressive power structures of his day."
>
> "Working here is not a sacrifice, because I experience a joy that comes when we open our lives more deeply to embrace the peoples of the world—the displaced, the broken, as well as those caught in the webs of wealth and power, and allow God to use us in the work of reconciliation."

"Kurds and Turks Are Brothers"

Ceremonies in Baghdad on January 1, 2009, officially opened the huge U.S. Embassy and turned the Green Zone over to the Iraqi government. More than 4,000 U.S. State Department staff and military officials, however, would continue to live and work in the Green Zone. A U.S. Embassy representative in Erbil explained a chain of steps proscribed in the Security of Forces Agreement (SOFA), in which the current 120,000 U.S. soldiers leave the country, and Iraqi forces assume full responsibility for security and control of it's airspace by June 30, 2010. U.S. soldiers were currently conducting military patrols, but were forbidden from carrying out operations without prior Iraqi approval and detaining any Iraqis without an Iraqi order. By 2011, U.S. troops should be gone, except for what was deemed necessary in the Green Zone to protect U.S. diplomatic personnel. As to bases remaining in Iraq, he said, "that's up to the Iraqi government to decide."

By early 2010, the U.S. was to turn over its detention system to the Iraqi government. Iraqi officials would review the cases of the 13,000 security detainees still in U.S. custody, and decide to free them or press charges. By mid-March, we heard that 1,991 detainees had been freed since the first of the year.

A Kurdish friend told us, "Even if they want the U.S. to leave, Kurds are afraid it will strengthen the power of Prime Minister Nouri al-Maliki and the Iraqi Central Government, which won't be kind to the Kurds or follow through on Article 140." Tensions between Maliki and the KRG had been increasing in the fall, when Maliki said the 2005 constitution gave too much power to the governorates. Maliki called for amending the constitution and other steps to weaken the power of the KRG in the disputed areas. He said that only the Central Government and not the KRG was allowed to grant visas and residency cards to internationals.

Several news sources, early this year, reported less violence in Iraq during the last six months. Instead of the previous 50–250 Iraqis killed daily, the new average is 1–24. One of our friends came north from Baghdad, saying that even though there's less crime, kidnappings, or bombings in the city, there's a heavy sense of despair. "They're not sure if the reduced violence is temporary, or stable," he said.

Part Two: Summer 2006—Fall 2011

We also talked to a Kurdish friend, who grew up in Baghdad, but moved to Suleimaniya two years ago. His family just returned from a trip to Baghdad to sell their house. He described their old, "ethnically cleansed" neighborhood as tight and unfree, almost like a prison, with neighborhood militia checkpoints everywhere. He said, "People don't go out on the streets at night as they used to and have become more hardened and suspicious."

Times with children helped me see more than just the discouraging realities of the situation in Iraq. One afternoon when I went grocery shopping, a boy about twelve, returning from school, started walking next to me. I enjoyed talking back and forth with him in simple English before he turned off on a side street. Another day, on the street, a girl of about eight held out a piece of round flat bread to me. I took it and thanked her. Then she held out another. It seemed important to take both. "Zor 'spas!" ("Thank you," in Kurdish), I responded. This was the week-long Muslim celebration of Eid Al Adha, a time of generosity. We felt welcomed by the people around us as we visited neighbors and friends. I felt most touched, however, by this girl's spontaneous act of giving.

But violence also came in institutional forms that minimized people's voice or ability to better their lives.

21

"We Do This Work Because We Must"

By March 2009, we had visited ten village areas and seen eleven Turkish military bases or outposts sprinkled along the northern Iraqi border. We now hoped to do more to stand with and support those affected by the attacks. In a series of meetings over several months with leaders from the villagers of the Chumjee area, we listened, learned, and cultivated trusting relationships. We jointly developed a plan of accompanying them home for shorter or longer periods so that they could care for their fruit and nut trees and other property. "We want you to raise the voice of our people," one told us. "No other international groups have been here to help us." "It's a good plan," said another, "if we can do it, but there's no guarantee of our safety if you go back with us."

After visiting the UN and other agencies, however, the village leaders decided they wanted more support from these organizations to advocate for their safety and help them rebuild their homes before returning. Kurdish authorities also made it clear that they wouldn't allow us to accompany villagers into this more "restricted" area since they did not want to take responsibility if something happened to us.

Although these plans didn't work out, we continued to visit other border areas and found other ways to accompany villagers as they tried to stay on their land or as they told their truth and pleaded for basic human rights. Doors opened for us to visit villages recently attacked. We documented the consequences of the cross-border bombings on the villagers and put our findings into a more comprehensive report, published a year later, in March 2010, called "Where There Is a Promise, There Is Tragedy." We distributed it to Kurdish, U.S., and international agencies and government offices.

Our car drove down the dusty gravel road, in late April 2009, between the towns of Zharawa and Sangasar to the new tent camp for the IDPs from the Prde Hazwa camp. It was a cluster of 3.4 by 3.8 meter tents set up on cinder blocks and crowded on the flat, treeless land. Each of the forty-five families had two tents, a washroom and a squat toilet, connected to a common cesspool. We called this the "Basteson Camp," since it was next to the village of Basteson. Water was provided by the UNHCR. Families received their monthly government food distribution and some food from the ICRC.

Musa and his wife, Fatima, residents of the camp, told us their tragic story. "On February 14, the KRG reported on TV and radio an agreement between Iran and the KRG that Iran would stop shelling civilian populated villages. As soon as we heard this we went back with others to our village, Razga. For two weeks, we lived there in peace, but then Iran started shelling again. At 9 p.m. on March 10, while we were sleeping, an Iranian mortar came through our roof and burned the inside of our house. I had burns on my head, back, and leg, and injuries from the shrapnel, crippling me. Fatima was injured and burned too, but one and a half year-old Mohammed, our only son, was killed," he said as the tears welled up in his eyes. We could only listen and care for them in their pain.

Over the next months, our team, with Shad, Mohammed, or Parween, continued to visit this camp, writing and sending the residents' stories out over international media. Team members produced and submitted the video "Zharawa Tent Children: Joy" to YouTube.[1]

In mid-summer, with temperatures between 100–120 Fahrenheit in the overcrowded camp, no electricity to refrigerate food, and a scarcity of water, many worried about the spread of disease and felt conditions in the camp were unbearable. They risked taking their children back to the villages, leaving a few adults in the camp.

By October, area government officials had provided a generator, but the families didn't have the money to buy fuel to run it. A water system being built by the U.S. military was not finished, so the Zharawa municipality trucked in water. Three months later, six families remained in the camp. The well was finished, but the pump hadn't been installed.

---

1. CPT Iraq Team Videos, "Zharawa Tent Children."

"We Do This Work Because We Must"

On narrow, windy roads, between snow-capped mountains and past flowing creeks, we drove into the Sitakan district, in the northeast corner of Iraq, near the borders of Turkey and Iran, an area of recent attacks. Nestled in those mountains was the village of Daraw. At the school, the teacher talked about past attacks on the village, resulting in injuries and deaths. He spoke of the children and village with tenderness and concern. "Turkish planes flew over the school for up to an hour at a time. The children were terrified, not knowing if they would be bombed. I tried to keep the children calm, but sometimes a few would run to their homes as soon as they heard the planes, without considering the dangers."

In the village of Zhelea, we sat around a cylindrical wood stove in a simple stone dwelling. Twenty-year old Ru'been had undergone two surgeries for multiple wounds from an Iranian shelling attack four months earlier, on July 18, 2009. While he grazed their sheep, goats, and cows in the mountain area of Megamier, about eighteen Iranian rockets hit, killing twenty of his family's sheep and twenty-seven cows. One rocket exploded just in front of their tent, tearing into Ru'been's neck, shoulder and armpit. He lost consciousness. Family members drove him to Erbil for surgery.

"Sometimes I can hardly move my neck and shoulder, and sometimes I have no feeling in that area," he said. Because of the pain, he hasn't been able to study or work. He stopped attending his seventh-grade class in school since the pain was greater in the cold schoolroom.

Due to the attacks, his family had lost about fifty animals and $8,000 a year, about half of their previous annual income. "We no longer go to certain mountains to graze our animals, get firewood or gather mushrooms and herbs in the springtime, but we don't want to leave our ancestral home and give up our traditional way of life."

Two weeks later, I met with a U.S. State Department representative, as part of our team's monitoring U.S. troop reduction and tensions along the "Arab-Kurd ceasefire line," or "corridor" areas—the borders between predominantly Arab areas controlled by Arab Iraqi forces, and predominantly Kurdish areas controlled by Kurdish military units. He affirmed the importance of dealing with Article 140, and of reconciliation between Arabs and Kurds.

I spoke about the consequences of Turkish and Iranian bombing for the people along the border, explaining that these attacks mainly target the villages farther inland from the border and have little strategic effect on

Part Two: Summer 2006—Fall 2011

PKK Military camps. I added that the Kurdish people believe the real purposes are to destabilize and weaken Kurdistan's limited autonomy and clear the border areas. I told him about Ru'been's injuries and the school children terrorized by Turkish planes circling over their school and voiced our objections to the U.S. assisting Turkey's military with intelligence information.

He listened respectfully and then stated calmly that it is important that U.S. collaborate with our ally, Turkey, to fight the PKK, a U.S. labeled "terrorist" organization. He believed this effort would make those areas safe for the displaced people to return. "We cannot expect Turkey to negotiate with terrorists," he said. I responded that villagers do not see the attacks as making it safer for them, but as tearing their lives apart.

I wrote to friends back home, "This official justification for military agreements and actions, frames our country's thinking and numbs our natural outrage. It makes it harder to keep in focus the humanity and basic right of the people caught in the crossfire to live peacefully in their homes, as well as the futility of violence to solve conflicts or bring peace. Labeling people 'terrorists' and then refusing to negotiate with them locks governments into military solutions. This excuses them from taking seriously and addressing the long-time injustices at the root of the conflict. It has become increasingly clear that diplomatic negotiations and addressing these root causes are the only ways to resolve this and many other conflicts in the world. Meanwhile, we see what our country's anti-terrorism really means for the people here on the ground."

> This pre-Christmas time reminds me of the words of Isaiah, (Isa 42:1–6) about the one God was sending to bring a new way of life. He would be filled with God's Spirit. "A bruised reed he will not break, and a dimly burning wick he will not quench; he will faithfully bring forth justice in the earth." Here in Iraq, we believe God cares for those bruised by violence or whose wicks are dim as they cry out for justice. It has been a privilege to walk with them as they seek healing, and at the same time experience God's healing care for the bruised and weak parts of our own lives.

"We Do This Work Because We Must"

"This is how the oil is benefiting us and our city," Hawar said, referring to the many potholes in the streets on our way to a women's center in Kirkuk in late December 2009. We were visiting Hawar and three other women, each belonging to a different organization there and involved in peace and reconciliation projects. They invited us to come, learn about their work, and think about possibilities of working together.

"I had been an English teacher and a principal in a girls' school," said Rana, a Shia Muslim Arab woman of about forty. "Then three years ago my husband [a Shia Arab newspaper editor] was killed, and I decided to take up the work he was doing. I now direct a foundation and am the editor of a newspaper with staff from different ethnic backgrounds. I advocate for journalists' rights, create TV programs, write about environmental issues, and devote a newspaper page to peace themes. I also train youth media workers through 'Writers Without Borders' in Kirkuk."

Serwa, a Turkmen, enthusiastically described her "arts-for-peace" program. "We have them now in twenty-five schools, in Kirkuk and other northern Iraqi areas, for children from Turkmen, Kurdish, Arab, and Christian families aged eight to sixteen. In a project where they depicted other ethnic groups in their drawings, a Muslim child drew churches, a Christian child drew mosques, and Kurdish and Arab children drew pictures of Kurds dancing."

"Families here encourage ethnic divisions," said Amina, a high school teacher and a Christian, "but so do the schools when they have separate lines for Kurdish, Arab, and Christian students. In our program with 128 Turkmen, Kurdish, Arab, and Christian girls, we counter these divisions. Girls from sixteen high schools come together to play volleyball and build friendships. For half an hour before each game, they discuss how to work for peace."

"Before 2003, I was just a housewife," Hawar, a young Sunni Muslim woman about thirty years old, said with a grin. "Then I decided to serve others beyond my own family. Helping others solve their problems and developing a more stable society also strengthens *me*." Working at a women's shelter is one way she combatted violence against women. She wrote poems and then started working through the media, "because it can reach more people."

"Since the downfall of Saddam, there are more organizations working for women's rights, but there has also been more honor killing. There's a law against it, but the men are rarely prosecuted. Modern communication technology, available in Iraq after 2003, has also had its negative side. Those wanting to control women spread pornography with it to incite violence against them or put women's pictures on the Internet, who are then targeted."

Hawar currently trains twenty women from different ethnic backgrounds to write about ethnic and peacemaking issues. "My two-year-old project called, 'Together for Peace,' brings religious leaders together to build relationships of trust and encourages them to work together on service projects to help the people of Kirkuk."

At the same time, Hawar was realistic about the dangers of her work. "I've received two death threats in the last two years," she said soberly, "so my family worries about me. Two years ago, when many Christians were killed in Kirkuk, my husband and I helped organize public protests against the killings. A year later, party leaders threatened my husband's life after he wrote about the corruption of political parties, so he left Iraq."

Then, with a sense of determination, she said, "We do this work because we *must*! The power of deadly force leads to more death, poverty, and suppression of the human spirit. *Survival* in our community means learning to live together peacefully. *We* might not see peace in our lifetime, but *we must choose a way that can stop the cycles of violence and bring life for future generations.*"

"Corrupt government leaders are our main problem in Kirkuk," stated Rana. "Most work only for their interests or their ethnic group and stir up mistrust toward the others to maintain their power. We adults grew up in multi-ethnic communities, but now some leaders have started private single-ethnic schools that try to shape the children's minds and separate them from children of other groups. I'm afraid this will increase mistrust and hate in them."

The women spoke about how they would like to improve their community. Hawar said, "I would form a process for people to raise their concerns and demands to the government and educate the government about human rights, how to serve their people, and to be ecologically responsible. Under previous regimes, people learned to solve problems by 'the way of two bullets.' We need to learn and teach the government to solve problems in peaceful ways." Amina said she would "find where political leaders agree and where they are far apart, and then take those points on which they agree and organize to achieve them."

"We Do This Work Because We Must"

We left, encouraged by the vision of these women for grassroots movements and curbing the cycles of violence. This conversation led to a joint project with Hawar the following summer—a six-month peacebuilding program with a small group of young Kurdish, Turkmen, Arab, and Christian women from Kirkuk. It involved monthly workshops on peace themes, and the women launched a "zine," a small magazine, about their lives, tolerance, and nonviolence, with articles, photographs, drawings, and stories, in Arabic, Kurdish, and Turkmen. They distributed it in Suleimaniya and Kirkuk.

It was February 2010. Suddenly, shots rang out eight blocks from our house in Suleimaniya, on an otherwise quiet evening. Our neighbors told us, "Men in black cars opened fire on a crowd in front of the PUK headquarters. It's probably connected with the elections." As the March 7 Iraqi parliamentary elections campaign season got underway, there was the predicted increase of car bombs, IEDs, and assassinations of candidates in central or southern Iraq. Not as expected, however, was the violence in the Kurdish region.

I remembered the povinicial elections, a year earlier, January 31, 2009, when members of our team were international election observers in Khanaqin, in northern Diyala Governorate. Government agencies' mishanding of pre-election registration for Kurds in the northern Iraqi governorates resulted in approximately 16,000 Kurds being unable to vote. We saw this as a form of institutional violence and knew that this could end up fueling more anger and future inter-ethnic violence in Iraq.[2]

This year, tensions in Suleimaniya were mostly between the Kurdistani List—a joint ticket of the two main parties, the PUK and the KDP—and the almost one-year-old Gorran Movement (or "Change Party"), which advocated geting rid of corruption and changing the KRG's political systems. In the July 2009 KRG Parliamentary Election, Gorran and the two other opposition parties, the Kurdistan Islamic Union and Kurdistan Islamic Group, won 35 of the 111 seats in the KRG Parliament. This happened in spite of opposition leaders' claims that the PUK and KDP threatened and used violence against opposition supporters and systematically falsified and rigged the election process and results. We heard that since last summer, 1,566 soldiers and policemen had lost their jobs or been

---

2. See CPT Iraq Team Reports, "Khanaqin Election Observation 2009 Report."

demoted because they voted for Gorran. This spring, many teachers, mullahs, and other citizens, openly aligning themselves with the Gorran Party, were harassed, beaten, disappeared, or tortured by anti-terrorism groups.

After being threatened with arrest, since publicly saying they voted for Gorran, eleven men took refuge in the guarded Gorran headquarters. One was a former officer in the Ministry of Peshmerga, who told us, "My commander told me to say I couldn't read or write, even though I can, and someone would help me vote. Instead, I voted by myself, and got fired from my job. I was told I could have my job back if I got a paper saying that I'm a member of the PUK, but I refused. Now, I'm afraid for my life. Several other men who spoke openly about their vote have been arrested by intelligence or anti-terrorism units."

Twenty-one-year old Dana was one of those abducted by armed men and tortured last summer for campaigning for Gorran. "During the campaign this spring," he said, "the PUK made false charges against me. Every day they called my cell phone, saying, 'When we arrest you, we will kill you.'" Dana had difficulty sleeping and smoked a lot to deal with the stress. We contacted a member of UNHCR, who called Kurdish security officials to question them about Dana's case and let them know others were watching what happened.

Another Peshmerga officer, who took refuge at the headquarters, reported that while he was gone, a black car circled around his family's house between 2–5 a.m. Men dressed in black, with black masks, broke through the gate and entered their garden. His son called the police, who came with sirens and lights flashing, causing the men in black to leave. His family was traumatized, and his wife became ill.

These eleven asked our team go with them to their court hearings. We explained that there was no guarantee that internationals could protect them, but organizations such as CPT, UNAMI, ICRC and Amnesty International (AI) could bring public attention to the violence perpetrated against them and encourage all sides to solve this situation legally and without violence. In response, our team made two videos of the men telling their story and posted them on CPT's website and You Tube, with subtitles.[3] We contacted AI and a local journalist for international press services about publishing a story about the situation. A protection officer

---

3. For a video interview with Dana and other men taking refuge at the Gorran headquarters, see CPT Iraq Team Videos, "Persecution of Goran Supporters Continues in Iraqi Kurdistan."

at ICRC agreed to work with the families of the jailed men. UN human rights workers would contact the KRG Minister of the Interior.

By early May, most of the eleven had left the compound and gone home, yet had cases pending in court. In late May, Dana asked us to meet him at the courthouse. We didn't get permission to go into the courtroom with him, but the judge was aware that internationals were outside. The judge told him there were currently no formal charges against him. He returned home, but still got threatening phone calls. Eight months later, Dana safely left the country with the help of UN officials, and was in Turkey trying to get political asylum in another country. We heard that most of the other men had been reinstated in their jobs.

Along the borders we found people caught between their need for security and their determination to remain in their villages.

22

What Does One Say to the Parents of a Fourteen-Year-Old Girl Who Was Killed?

A LULL IN THE cross-border bombardments that winter (2009–2010) was broken in April when waves of attacks, mostly from Iran, struck along the Iraq-Iran border. Villagers and local officials told us that just before attacks they saw Turkish surveillance planes flying overhead. During four days of continuous Iranian shelling of the Pshdar area, many villagers stayed underground in dugout shelters and some of the children took their final exams. Others fled. The attacks killed or injured livestock and destroyed much of the spring planting. Some villagers thought it was connected to nonviolent demonstrations and strikes by Kurds in Iran close to the Iraqi border, protesting Iran's execution of Kurdish political prisoners.

On May 15, shrapnel struck fifty-three-year-old Amira in her left arm and leg, breaking both limbs. In the midst of shelling, her family carried her, wrapped in a blanket, for the two-hour walk over rough terrain from her village of Maradu, to the Qaladza Hospital. From there, she was transported to a hospital in Suleimaniya, an additional three-hour ride, where she underwent surgery to remove shrapnel and reconstruct her arm and leg.

The Doli Shahidan camp in a treeless flood plane was now the temporary home for 408 families from twelve villages north of Sangasar. One Sarosh Village family told us, during our visit, that they fled June 8, after

What Does One Say to the Parents of a 14-Year-Old Girl Who Was Killed?

four hours of heavy Iranian shelling inside their village. About a hundred animals were killed or injured, and trees and crops were ruined.

We heard many complaints in the camp: "It's extremely hot." "There's no electricity." "We have no family toilets or washrooms." "At home we had our work. Here there's no way to earn money." Thirteen-year-old Hamdi said, "Back in the village we played together. Here, there is nothing to do but to look for shade." "In our villages we had more water and food and cool places to rest during the day," said ninety-one-year-old Ashia from Ash Qulka village. "I am afraid people will die here during the Ramadan fast in August. It's hard for me, an old woman."

Fourteen-year-old Basoz, from the city of Rania, had been visiting her grandparents in the village of Weza, in the Choman district. On May 29, she and her sister were preparing tea for relatives working in their fields when an Iranian rocket exploded close by and killed her. Three weeks later, Chihchun and I, and a reporter for Human Rights Watch sat outside Basoz' uncle's home in Weza, looking downhill at the newly planted fields. The uncle told us that Basoz's mother was in shock when she found out about her daughter's death and said, "It's horrible to send your daughter off, and her body is brought back to you."

"Over the last ten days, more than 200 rockets have exploded around our village," he said. "People here are terrified and many have left. Our plants will die if we don't water them every two or three days." He explained that farmers in this mountain area must plant within a fifteen-day period in late May and early June to get a harvest. "Farmers who had planted, but left because of the shelling and weren't able to water their crops, have lost about $7,000 in income. These have been our farms for generations, and we're determined to stay."

What does one say to the parents of a fourteen-year-old girl who was killed in a border attack? Chihchun and I faced this one month later, as we sat in Basoz's family's home in Rania to express our sadness for their loss. We mostly listened. Family members showed us pictures, and we felt drawn together as they shared sadly but lovingly about her. "Thank God our other daughter went to call the others in for tea before the rocket killed Basoz," said her father.

Two days later, we attended a public memorial for Basoz in Rania, sponsored by a local civic organization. The family greeted us warmly and insisted that I sit next to Basoz's mother. The program included the showing of a local TV reporter's documentary film about the bombing, Basoz's death, and the short video Chihchun made about the Choman farmers.[1]

---

1. CPT Iraq Team Videos, Yuan, "Voices—Life under Military Threats."

Part Two: Summer 2006—Fall 2011

One leader of the Basteson IDP camp spoke briefly about displacement from their villages. Our team's statement called for a peaceful settlement of the border conflicts.

At the Rania Youth Club in mid-June, a youth guitar band with singers performed several Kurdish songs to about a hundred people. This was one of several rallies organized that month by Kurdish organizations calling for an end to the bombings through diplomacy. The eighteen-year-old emcee of this event told the story of Basoz and of Susan. She said, "The Kurdish people are like a human body. When one organ has pain, the whole body cries."[2]

On a hot July evening, we sat on an open cement slab next to a weatherworn tent in the Basteson IDP camp. A family served us rice, bread, vegetables, and yogurt drink, a luxurious meal in these surroundings. After supper, others from the camp gathered, and we spent the evening hearing about their families, looking at pictures, and having fun with the children. That night, we slept on mats in a family's thatched-roof shelter next to their tent.

I thought about these gracious, hard-working people who have been the backbone of Kurdish Iraq's agricultural economy, but are now seen as dispensable as the border violence continues. To some, they are just numbers of displaced people, but to us, they are mothers with babies giggling on their laps, young children who want a more stable life, and old men and women whose loving eyes sparkle when they reminisce about their lives in their villages.

As the morning of July 23 progressed, laughter and animated sharing rippled among the thirty-nine people coming to visit the residents of the Basteson camp. We sat around a large tent as the women passed heaping platters of the traditional Middle Eastern food, dolma. Chihchun and Mohammed, our interpreter, driver, and friend, who had now become a team partner, planned this giant picnic, called "Dolma Day," as a way to raise awareness of the displaced families' situations and build relationships between them and people from neighboring cities. Human rights workers from Suleimaniya and Rania helped organize the event and provide food.

2. CPT Iraq Team Videos, Yuan, "Rania Rally."

What Does One Say to the Parents of a 14-Year-Old Girl Who Was Killed?

Figure 13: Women and children eating in tent at Basteson IDP Camp on "Dolma Day," July 23, 2010

After the meal, children gathered in circles to draw, while adults sat in smaller groups, taking pictures together and talking about their families. Local reporters milled about, videotaping and interviewing. Some visitors walked through the rest of the camp, getting a better sense of what it might be like to be forced from home and live in such conditions. Amira, who had recent surgeries on an arm and leg from her May 15 injuries, sat among the crowd with a radiant smile. With her left arm still in a sling, she was a visible reminder of the reason for the camp's existence—continued attacks, making it dangerous for them to return home.

Azad, currently living in the camp, commented, "Although the dolma was great, it was the people coming to be with us that was most important." The visitors seemed moved personally by this event. As we were leaving the camp, the director of a Kurdish NGO said with emotion, "Thank you. This has opened our eyes to what's happening here."

Part Two: Summer 2006—Fall 2011

Leaders of the nine villages represented in the Basteson Camp had been meeting over the past months with all levels of government officials, requesting help to build a *new* village. In one meeting an official told them, "Why don't you just go back and stay in *your* villages? When the bombs come, you can run." At that, Michele, who was there, responded quickly, "There have been enough deaths. Have you forgotten the baby boy who was killed last year? How many more lives must be lost?"

Through the summer, none of the local officials took steps to help with a new village project. During Ramadan, many families returned to their villages where it was more tolerable to fast than in the hot tents. We appealed to UN agencies and local authorities to help the people find substantial housing. NGO workers told us that local officials prevented them from assisting Basteson Camp residents because they were "long-term IDPs."

> It's December 15, 2011, and a voice on the radio grabs my attention as I compile this book. "Today, the U.S. military mission in Iraq has formally ended," the news reporter said. "Defense Secretary Leon Panetta and other U.S. officials paid tribute to the sacrifices of U.S. troops." "To be sure," Panetta was quoted as saying, "the cost was high—in blood and treasure for the United States and for the Iraqi people, but those lives were not lost in vain—they gave birth to an independent, free and sovereign Iraq." In the next three days, it was reported that the last U.S. convoy rumbled out of Iraq, but that there will still be U.S. forces there as "advisers" and "trainers" for Iraqi security forces and about 200 military personnel in the "Green Zone" (and who knows how many contractors) with the U.S. diplomatic mission. (*cont.*)

The KRG Prime Minister had just given permission for people in the Dorishahidan IDP Camp to build homes for the winter, but not the Basteson families. Those in the other IDP camps received 1,000,000 ID (about $847) from the government, yet the Basteson IDPs only received 450,000 ID since their displacement in 2008. One village leader said, "The problem is not the political parties. A mayor helps only people of his own tribe." We never fully unraveled this disparity, but now we understood that getting help depended on one's party, tribal affiliation, and relationship with officials. In October, human rights worker, Parween, found funding for building small homes for the two remaining families at the camp.

What Does One Say to the Parents of a 14-Year-Old Girl Who Was Killed?

"I feel more secure now than I did in 2006," a respondent from Baghdad said in answer to our team's survey of Iraqis of different backgrounds and affiliations from around the country in July 2010. Based on that survey, Marius van Hoogstraten, with the help of others on the team, compiled a report titled, "Iraq After Occupation—Iraqis Speak about the State of Their Country as the US military Withdraws," released in August, 2010.[3] "I lived in a 'hot' insurgent Sunni neighborhood," commented another Baghdad resident. "There's less tension now." All those surveyed reported an increased sense of security, except for those in Iraqi Kurdistan, which has had a higher level of security since 1991.

A significant number of respondents, however, did not attribute the improvements to the "surge," the increased deployment of U.S. soldiers to Baghdad and the Anbar Governorate in 2007. They saw the presence of U.S. forces attracting the violence of the insurgents—the main source of insecurity—and U.S. withdrawal from cities as a key factor in the improved security. Other factors mentioned were the retreat of Muqtada as-Sadr's militia, and the establishment of the "Sons of Iraq" or the "Awakening Movement"—former Sunni insurgents who the U.S. military paid to fight Al Qaida and maintain order.

Many respondents said the Iraqi security forces had made positive advances, though a majority had concerns about their trustworthiness, independence, and lack of knowledge about human rights. They had serious concerns about the credibility of Iraqi politicians, the "abominable state of public services," the economy,

> (*cont.*)
> Whether you believe the sacrifices were not in vain, depends on where you stand. Are you a governmental or military official who needs to justify the obscene costs? Did your corporation make billions in contracts throughout this war? Are you an Iraqi whose society has been broken, who's had family members killed, or who's been forced out of his house by another ethnic group? Are you a soldier who has lost his limbs and has brain damage, or the wife of a fallen soldier?
> Fairly representative of Iraqi people is the one who said, "We were waiting for Panetta to apologize to the Iraqi people for the mistakes and crimes committed by the U.S. soldiers during the occupation time.... He praised the sacrifices of the U.S. soldiers and forgot about the Iraqis killed because of his government's mistakes in Iraq" (Sameer N. Yacoub and Sinan Salaheddin [Associated Press], "Iraqis glad to see U.S. depart, but fearful for future," *San Francisco Chronicle*, December 16, 2011.)

---

3. CPT Iraq Team Reports, "Iraq After Occupation."

and corruption. Ethnic and religious tensions and possible interference by neighboring states still threatened the country's stability.

Some who were interviewed suggested creating a united supreme court, amending the constitution and electoral laws, and defining the powers of local governments and federal institutions. One mentioned the importance of establishing "the rights of the family, women, children, and people with special needs," as well as "equality of opportunity" and equitable distribution of wealth. Many mentioned the need for reviving the economy and improving public services. Most agreed that the U.S. and its allies bear considerable responsibility for the current state of Iraq, but also that Iraqis must take initiative to attain these goals.

In the report's conclusion, the CPT Iraq team recommended that as it reduces troops in Iraq, the U.S. strengthen Iraqi society by supporing "the revitalization of Iraqi economy, the reconstruction of public services, reconciliation efforts, and a culture of accountability and human rights in Iraqi security forces," while respecting Iraqi sovereignty.

> I am told that in any tragedy, one is also given gifts. This was true now in the love our family shared as we gathered to remember and celebrate Art's passionate life. But just before the memorial service, I received one of the best gifts I could in such circumstances, when, *my son Dan walked in!* We were able to reunite and share together our grief for Art's death. For me, Dan had just been "restored to life." He was restored to our family circle. And in the coming year we began rebuilding our relationship, with respect for our various differences of outlook—something for which I am deeply grateful, as I could not know then that it would also be the last year of *his* life.

It was in the middle of all this, on July 28, 2010, that I got the call from my son, Dale, about Art's death. It shook my life. I had to look again at who I was and where my life was going. It abruptly halted my work in Iraq, but others on the team continued on as I went home and needed time to face the loss and pain and begin a journey of healing and acceptance. My love for the people of this land, though, didn't end. It stayed with me and helped me deal with my grief. In time, I made the decision to continue the journey with my sisters and brothers peacefully seeking justice and renewal.

I returned the following spring in the midst of a local uprising!

23

Kurdish Spring

THE WORLD TOOK NOTICE this winter as people poured into the streets of Tunisia, then Egypt and other Middle Eastern countries, in what was called the "Arab Spring." Masses of people were emboldened to work to dismantle corrupt and dictatorial regimes. In February 2011, Iraqis also began protests that did not manage to change the government and might *appear* crushed, but have set in motion powerful currents that could be unstoppable.

Before I returned in March 2011, our team was reporting about the uprising underway in Suleimaniya. Three thousand people amassed in the city center on February 17, 2011 for the first demonstration. It ended peacefully, but after it was over, about 200 men marched to protest at the KDP party headquarters. After a stone-throwing battle, members of the KDP forces shot into the crowd, killing a fourteen-year-old boy and injuring forty others. In the days that followed, thousands flooded the square to condemn the shooting.

KDP officials sent anti-terrorism units and thousands of additional Asaish, Peshmerga, and Civil Activity Police into the city. On February 19, about fifty masked men, with suspected ties to the PUK burned the station of independent NRT TV and Nalia Radio, which had been covering the demonstrations. Protests about corruption, unemployment, and lack of democracy were also springing up in other parts of Iraq.

According to Nawshirwan Mustafa, former high-ranking member of the PUK and now leader of the Gorran movement, the crisis had long existed. The system gave political, financial, and economic benefits to the inner circle of the party leadership, but not to the rest of the population.

Part Two: Summer 2006—Fall 2011

Now, after deep frustration and lack of trust in their leaders and governing institutions, the population was rising up to demand their rights. Instead of addressing these concerns, the ruling leaders labeled it a security threat and used state terrorism to suppress it.[1]

After February 17, demonstrations continued in the square daily, often ending in violent confrontations with security forces. Protesters demanded that Kurdish authorities arrest and convict those who killed and wounded the protesters, and that all military forces be withdrawn from the city. Kurdish President, Massoud Barzani, responded to this demand, saying that all *demonstrators and organizers of demonstrations* should be prosecuted. On February 21, members of a federation of local NGOs formed what they called the "White Group" (white symbolizing, in this culture, peace), or what we called the "Wall of Peace" (WOP) to keep the demonstrators from throwing stones at the police, and the police from beating demonstrators.

Figure 14: Wall of Peace standing between crowd and security forces in Azadi Square, Suleimaniya, February 22, 2011

On February 22, about 4,000 to 5,000 artists, students, journalists, religious clerics, women, laborers, and the unemployed, crowded in the

1. Mustafa, "About the Crisis in Iraqi Kurdistan."

city center of Suleimaniya, now called, "Freedom Square" or in Kurdish, "Maidani Azadi." Music and poetry interspersed the speeches. Then the leaders released two doves, saying, "These birds represent peace and hope to us." The birds circled above the cheering crowd. Our team was there at the invitation of protesters to document the event and stand with the WOP. Wearing white vests and holding a wide white ribbon, about eighty people formed a semicircle around the square. Behind them stood over a thousand armed security forces, and in front, about 5,000 demonstrators.

At least three times that day, angry demonstrators from the square charged toward the line of security troops, but the WOP stepped between the two groups and calmed things down. Then members of the WOP handed out plastic flowers to the forces. Some of the soldiers held the flowers in their hand; others put them in the barrels of their rifles. Many made eye contact with the people, and the tension level dropped. Another day, a crowd of people began taunting the soldiers. The WOP intervened and someone from the stage began the chant, "These Peshmerga are our brothers." Soon everyone in the crowd joined in.

Figure 15: Soldiers with flowers in their gun barrels, in Azadi Square, Suleimaniya, February 22, 2011

The protest on February 26 started out peacefully, until a sound bomb went off behind the stage. People ran, and security forces fired on the crowd, leaving two dead and eleven wounded. After that, however, protesters and security forces publicly reconciled, with many soldiers putting down their weapons, saying they wouldn't shoot their brothers. Another day, the soldiers mixed in with the demonstrators, who welcomed them by clapping.

After this, the WOP decided their presence wasn't necessary, but they formed the "Ad-Hoc Committee of Azadi Square," which gave leadership to the protests. Pro bono lawyers from the Independent Group of Lawyers visited jails, defended those arrested, and gave documentation to Amnesty International (AI), which called on the KRG to rein in their forces. It was in the midst of this that I returned in March. At that time, members of our team were present at the protests daily, and consulted regularly with leaders.

Falah Muradkhan explained in an article that after the civil war between the KDP and PUK from 1992 to 1996, the people accepted the misconduct of the two parties out of fear of the return of the Ba'ath regime rule. The threat of interference by neighboring countries and the new threat of terrorism thwarted their hopes for economic and democratic development. The ruling parties used the people's resources for upgrading the military and their parties' militias and amassing huge personal wealth. The first KRG elections in 1991 resulted in the PUK and the KDP each getting about 50 percent of the vote. Since then, the Barzani and Talabani families have had a "strategic agreement" that maintained a fifty-fifty division in power, no matter what the vote was. Together they silenced any voice of dissent. The ruling families were above the laws and controlled the resources, lawmaking, parliament, and courts for their own interests.[2]

Throughout weeks of relative peace at the square, there were sporadic acts of violence against protesters, usually after the protests dispersed. There was also violence against protesters in other KRG cities, such as Qaladze, Halubja, Rania, Kalar, and Chamchamal.

On many occasions, individuals at the demonstrations suddenly did things to incite violence, such as provoking fights or throwing stones. Organizers later found that these were provocateurs sent in by the KDP or PUK parties to discredit the protests. Most of those times, the demonstrators understood what was happening and responded quickly to prevent fights or violence. One day, Michele and I saw a man run up with a knife and slash the large pictures on the walls. Immediately a group of men surrounded him and carried him out of the square.

One of those arrested for speaking out at the demonstrations, was Mullah Kameron Ali Khwarham (known as "Mamosta"). He called for a

---

2. Muradkhan, "The Middle East Uprisings and the Specificities of the Events in Iraqi Kurdistan."

revolution without violence—a "jihad." He urged the armed forces to put down their guns and appealed to the demonstrators to see the soldiers as their brothers and not throw rocks or hurt them. "The jihad I am speaking about is not a violent struggle or a struggle of believers against non-believers, but the nonviolent struggle of truth and justice against corruption and injustice."

Weeks later, we spoke to Mullah Kameron in his home. As we sat together on the floor of his sitting room, he took time to respond to his four children and held them affectionately on his lap. He helped his wife serve food and included her in the discussion. He said, "I felt responsible to go to the demonstrations after the violent response of the authorities. I wanted to let the protesters know that some religious leaders are with them. There's a passage in the Holy Qur'an that says if you see those in power oppress the poor, but you remain silent and do nothing about it, you are standing with the powerful."

"But authorities twisted my words to use against me," he explained. "Picking out the word, 'jihad,' they accused me of advocating violence. Government leaders threatened me. Anti-terrorist forces came to my house, put a mask on my head, took me to jail, and tortured me." When he was charged under the anti-terrorism law, which could mean the death penalty, pro bono lawyers, protest leaders, and members of CPT and AI put pressure on authorities for his release. After listening to his whole speech recorded by KNN-TV, in which it was clear he was calling for a peaceful struggle, the judge reduced his case to a civil charge.

Other leaders spoke about the presence of the anti-terrorism unit at the demonstrations—forces trained and supplied by the U.S. One said, "The unit, run by Jalal Talabani's nephew, Lahore Talabani, was originally set up to fight outside terrorists. Now the parties are using it to terrorize their own people and whoever criticizes Jalal Talabani and the PUK party. Because of U.S. backing, the U.S. has a responsibility to hold them accountable."

In a few weeks, the demonstrators added other requests: (1) End political inheritance and family rule, and develop a democratic system in which parliament, government, and legal authorities are independent. (2) Fight corruption and convict offenders. (3) Dismantle the ruling parties' control over police and security forces and end their violence and extrajudicial detentions. (4) Draft a constitution and laws to serve the people. (5) Respect freedoms of speech, media, association and assembly.

On April 11, the crowd in the square voted to accept the "Maidani Azadi's (Freedom Square's) Road Map" for a peaceful transition of power.

PART TWO: Summer 2006—Fall 2011

It called for the resignation of the ruling political parties, the head of the KRG and his cabinet, and the Kurdish Parliament. Around that time, the three opposition parties, not directly aligned with the protests, also called on the government to resign and an interim government to prepare for early elections.

After attempts to demonstrate in Erbil were repeatedly met with violent repression, a coalition of professionals and mullahs decided to protest again on April 18. Organizers invited our team to be present as observers. But when we heard that security forces would be sent into Freedom Square in Suleimaniya for a confrontation that same day, we decided to stay here.

On that sixty-first day of the demonstrations, protesters gathered apprehensively, as soldiers, police, and anti-terrorism units positioned themselves on streets close to the square. With one of the protest organizers, Michele and I walked over to about twenty young men who were talking about confronting the soldiers and throwing rocks. The organizer skillfully listened to them and then spoke firmly about refraining from violence. Some of them decided to stay in the square and respond nonviolently. Members of our team mingled among circles of protesters and dialogued about the importance of nonviolence.

The crowd cheered when a speaker announced that a thousand people were protesting in Erbil, then again when it one announced that Suleimaniya University students were sitting in the street when soldiers prevented them from reaching the square. Then security forces launched tear gas into a crowd along the street. People ran back towards the square grasping for water for their eyes and faces. Some had trouble breathing. (Later tests made on the gas showed that stronger chemicals were added to the normal tear gas.) Some protesters burned tires in order to keep the soldiers from reaching the square. After half an hour, however, people ran towards the square as the sound of gunfire got closer. Michele stayed on the phone with a U.S. Consulate representative, feeding her information about what was happening and countering false reports from government officials that there was no shooting.

Most of the protesters followed the organizers' urging to remain nonviolent and in the square. All of a sudden, shooting began from snipers on surrounding roofs. Many people ran. With others, we moved behind stone pillars. The U.S. representative could hear the shooting over the phone and said she was appealing to high-level KRG authorities to order it to stop. Organizers called for the demonstration to end and people to leave. We couldn't see any other way we could be helpful there, so between rounds of shooting our team left with the others.

Kurdish Spring

Later that evening we heard that hundreds of protesters had twice gone back into the square and that both times soldiers attacked them with guns, batons, and tear gas. The soldiers burned down the stage and destroyed the banners. A spokesperson for the emergency hospital later reported that ninety-nine people were admitted, sixteen from gunshot wounds. We also heard that in Erbil, ten journalists and many protesters were attacked and at least twenty-four arrested.

That night and the next day, up to 10,000 new security forces came in and lined city streets. Backup soldiers positioned themselves around the outskirts of the city. Authorities banned all demonstrations, with a "shoot to kill" order that was changed a few days later to "shoot the legs" of anyone who disobeyed. The streets were open to traffic, but if anyone appeared to group together or approach the square, they risked being arrested and beaten. The cities of Halubja, Rania, Koya, Qaludze, Kalar, and Chamchamal were also under military occupation. The U.S. maintained its policy of verbally supporting the right of the people to demonstrate nonviolently and denounced the KRG's forces' use of violence against unarmed demonstrators. But this rang hollow to many protesters, considering what was happening.

"Now our leaders are killing their own people," a university student told us the day after the crackdown, her eyes full of disgust. She, too, was walking around the city center. Another student said, "In the brutal attacks on the demonstrators, we see the face of Saddam."

We asked a soldier from another Kurdish city what he thought about the protests. "These are people trying to cause problems," he said. "We're here to keep the peace." Protest leaders explained to us that the government learned its lesson from the early protest days when the security forces were won over by the kindness of the demonstrators. Now it brought in forces from outside the area, soldiers who wouldn't know or be as sympathetic with people here.

On our way home, my teammate, Lukasz Firla, and I stopped when we saw a crowd of students milling around peacefully in front of the University. A young woman told me, "Sixteen buses with over 300 students and teachers were kidnapped when they drove to the courthouse this morning to protest. We're going to stay here until they're released."

Soon security police arrived and stood in a line along the street. I greeted them in Kurdish, with no response. My attempt to find and talk to their commander was interrupted when, without provocation, police sprayed red-dyed water over everyone with firetruck hoses and then charged into the crowd hitting students with batons, electric cattle prods, and marbles shot from slingshots. A policeman beat Lukasz on the leg before we followed students who dispersed. A block away we heard shooting. Later, we heard that a hundred students were injured and seventy-five arrested.

The following day a student who had been on one of the buses told us, "The Asaish took our buses to a deserted area, and forced us to stay on them for eight hours in the hot sun, with the windows and doors closed. They threatened to beat us if we phoned anyone. They pulled out, and sometimes beat or threatened student organizers, teachers, members of opposition parties, women with head coverings, or men with beards." Finally, security forces let them go in twos to walk back to the edge of the city. When we asked him how this would affect the student protesters, he said. "It's like putting kerosene on a wound."

A few days later, students from Suleimaniya University and the university in Koya went on strike. Our interpreter, Mohammed, helped organize a strike among public school teachers and some students, demanding that security forces leave the city. Religious leaders called on political parties to resolve this situation immediately. Though protests had been banned, many told us the determination of the people for change had not been crushed.

On April 27, Michele accompanied several protest leaders meeting in Suleimaniya with U.S. Embassy representatives to give an account of the demonstrations. "We were not demanding an overthrow of the government or endorsing any party," one of the leaders told them. "Our main concern was restructuring the government so that it would be accountable under the rule of law and deal with the corruption and party domination of the government."

"The demonstrations were nonviolent and set up democratically," our Kurdish colleague explained. "Neither Iran nor the Islamic movement were running or influencing them." While admitting that some of demonstrators threw stones, she gave specific examples of how provocateurs sent in by the KDP or PUK parties were often responsible for starting and escalating the violence in order to discredit the protests and justify a large security presence. "The authorities used their party-run media to slant the news in a way that made it look as though the demonstrators were initiating the violence and destabilizing security in the city, necessitating their bringing in massive amounts of troops."

Upon leaving the meeting, one of the protest organizers found several messages on her cell phone warning her not to go outside because Asaish vehicles were circling the building looking for the organizers. She knew this could mean being abducted, beaten, and charged with organizing illegal demonstrations. A guard at the building drove them to a safe location where they stayed for three hours before going to their homes. Michele experienced, more personally, a little of the threat leaders have lived with the past two months.

After two weeks, Kurdish authorities began to withdraw forces from the city centers. Protest leaders pulled back to gather strength and strategize, but were still being harassed, beaten, and detained. "We don't feel safe," one told us in late May. "They're still watching us and can pick us up at any time and beat us." We heard that during the past three months, 500 protesters in Suleimaniya had been abducted, kidnapped, or tortured, and sixty in Erbil.

One evening in May, Ismail, a regular speaker during the protests, was driving with friends. Two cars pulled in front and stopped their car. Eight men in ski masks jumped out, forced him into their car, and put a mask over his head. They drove outside the city and beat him with cables and the butt of a gun, breaking his nose in three places. They cut his arms and back with knives, and threatened to kill him if he ever took part in protests again. When he said he'd do it again, they broke his finger. He was recovering from surgery on his nose when our team visited him a month later. During the protests, he had received threats, the government cut his salary, and a high government official offered him a new apartment if he stopped speaking from the stage. He refused, saying he would not sell out himself or his beliefs.

Idris Omar and Dana Jamil formed the "Cultural Café," a place to gather for frequent political forums and discussions, keeping the spirit alive among protesters. The government threatened to shut it down. Team members had a regular presence there in support.

On June 26, Karwan, a protest leader and lawyer, who had represented protesters, was shot. When we visited him in the hospital the next day, he told us, "When I was paying at a car parking lot, I suddenly felt pain in my leg. I fell and saw a man, dressed in a traditional Kurdish Peshnmerga uniform, aiming at my head with a handgun. I managed to roll over a low wall just in time. The shooter fired four more shots at me as I hid behind the wall. It was clearly an assassination attempt. I had been threatened by the PUK ten days earlier." Three weeks later, investigators found that the bullets shot at him were the kind that only security forces use. In mid-July, Karwan held a seminar at the Cultural Café describing how the KDP and PUK abused the court system. Three days later, three gunmen came to his house and one told him, "Next time I will shoot your head, so keep quiet and don't appear again."

PART TWO: Summer 2006—Fall 2011

Parween marched with a group of women decrying the terrorizing of the demonstrators. She and other members of NGOs went to meet with Prime Minister Barham Salah, asking, "Why aren't you arresting the killers of the protesters?" She referred to a "hit-list" of people involved in the protests, and said, "If you want to arrest them, arrest all of us." Barham Salah said he wouldn't arrest her or the others with her.

On July 14, student organizers called for another round of protests. As soon as people approached Azadi Square, however, security forces blocked them and began to beat and arrest people. It resulted in over fifty arrests.

After the closing down of Azadi Square, the people of Kani Spi asked our team to stay in their village, near the Iraq-Iranian border, for their planting and harvest season. So, in the middle of June, as summer temperatures topped 100 degrees Fahrenheit, Lukasz and I moved there, each in a small tent among the villagers' Bedouin-style tents or tiny block and adobe, dirt-floor houses. While in lower altitudes things were a dry sandy color, it was still green in the mountains.

In the cool early mornings, I stepped out of my tent to the splendor of the mountains around the village. I greeted families and walked with them to the freshly plowed fields to plant tomato plants or okra, bean, and sunflower seeds. After the men opened up the water flow from an uphill spring so it would fill and soak the soil in the hoed furrows, we placed the seeds on a side of the furrows. Then the men hoed dirt over them. In the afternoons, I helped women of the village with other tasks or played games with the children. One afternoon, I sat on a rug in one of the tent homes while the women rolled out the thin, nanny tiri bread, and baked it on a curved metal plate on top of live wood coals.

> I found myself being folded into their lives, and some of the reserve, protecting my heart from pain and loss, was coming down. I came to give, but their openness and love allowed me to receive from them. They understand what it's like to have pieces of their life that give them security and stability ripped away, and feel they have no choice but to keep walking ahead.

We were thankful there was no shelling near the village, though on two different mornings we heard shelling in the distance. After eight days, however, when Lukasz and I left Kani Spi for a break, authorities would not allow other team members to take our place in the village, because there was more Iranian military activity in other places along the border.

I left Iraq in late June, just before Iran intensified rocket and helicopter attacks along the Iraqi side of the border, killing four civilians, injuring twelve, and tearing up newly planted fields. More than 800 families fled their village homes, and a hundred families formed a tent camp in the Pshdr Valley. Then on July 16, Iran invaded inside Iraq with 16,000 soldiers and 200 Turkish "advisers." They established outposts and moved tanks within striking range of villages. The shelling and invasion had not reached Kani Spi, but people there worried and had trouble sleeping. They evacuated one night when the shelling got close.

My departure from Iraq, once again, was sudden. It was in the midst of this work when I got word that *my son Dan died* after a struggle with a painful physical ailment.

In the coming months, our team collaborated with Kurdish partners in a series of protests. In front of the Iranian Consulate in Erbil on August 11, the team displayed a simulated scene of the aftermath of a village attack using a child-size mannequin covered in a white sheet, dried plants, and rocket fragments, along with pictures of tent camps. Printed on their banner in Persian, Kurdish, Arabic, and English was, "Iranian shelling destroys village life." They read and handed a statement to the representative of the consulate. On August 18, Bapir, who had been a leader in the former Basteson IDP camp, joined our team in a vigil in front of the KRG Parliament building in Erbil. He spoke with media and three members of Parliament. At a similar demonstration in front of the U.S. Consulate, the consul refused to speak with them and demanded that they leave.

> *Another death ... less than a year later. I don't want to face this! Yet, when death comes, it gives you no choice. I knew many Iraqi mothers who faced one tragedy after another, but felt helpless to change their situation. What about Basoz's parents, and the parents of 1½-year-old Mohammed? Somehow they found the strength. By this time I could trust that I would be given that same strength to walk through this, I just didn't want to have to, and have to deal with the pain.*
>
> *As I walk through this new grief, I am haunted by those years of Dan's withdrawal from the rest of the family ... I was deeply grateful for the last year of reuniting with him and rediscovering who he was. There was no doubt about the love between us.*
>
> *(cont.)*

PART TWO: Summer 2006—Fall 2011

On August 21, Turkey bombed and killed seven members of a family as they traveled in a pickup truck on a frequently used road in the Pshdr District. Three weeks later, Mohammed decorated his pickup truck with banners and Kurdish flags, put a mannequin with blood-stained clothes on the roof along with pictures of the victims and drove his truck slowly around the city.

As I think over the past nine years of working in Iraq, one important story that I haven't told stands out in my mind. For this, we move back in time to January 2010.

> (cont.)
> I knew that his death was not related to my being in Iraq. And he did not tell family members, before his death, what he was going through. But many painful thoughts plagued me. *I was out of the country and not there for him. Could I have helped him get more medical help? I knew my working in Iraq was a source of conflict and pain for him through those years. Was I wrong to keep going back?* My head and reason told me one thing, but my emotions were conflicted. *How could I know what would happen to others in my family when I made my decisions—decisions based also on my heart—on what I felt compelled to do?*

24

Returning to Rutba

"They want to meet, people to people, and try to repair the hurt between Americans and Iraqis," said Sami Rasouli, our guide, longtime Iraqi friend, and one of the founders of Muslim Peacemaker Teams (MPT), as we met with the Iraqi Ambassador in Amman, Jordan on January 14, 2010. "They want to diffuse prejudices so Americans can see Iraqis as people, not terrorists, and Iraqis see Americans as people, not infidels." Sami showed the Ambassador our letter of invitation from MPT and urged him to give us visas to enter Iraq by land.

We had applied for visas through the Iraqi Embassy in the U.S. months before, without any definitive answer, and had been in Amman five days, trying from here. I had left our team in northern Iraq and joined this small group in Amman, not knowing if my residency card from the KRG would be enough for me to enter Iraq from the Western border.

We had just told the Ambassador the dramatic story of our caravan of three cars traveling very fast along the highway from Baghdad to Jordan seven years earlier, on March 29, 2003, after an Iraqi official forced us to leave the country during the U.S. invasion.[1] While our first two cars sped ahead, the third car hit shrapnel on the road, blew a tire, and flipped over. In spite of U.S. bomber planes overhead and knowing there had been bombing in the area earlier that day, Iraqi men driving by risked their lives to stop and transport our injured men about five miles away to the only hospital in that area, in the town of ar-Rutba.

When we saw their car was no longer behind us, we had to argue with our drivers to get them to turn around and go back into the war

---

1. For more details, see Gish, *Iraq*, chapter 8.

zone to look for them. We found the empty wrecked car at the side of the road. Other travelers directed us to the hospital, but there we found the crumbled building with its roof caved in—bombed by U.S. forces three days earlier.

"So where are they?" we asked anxiously, trying not to think of the worst possibilities. We finally found them receiving medical care in a tiny, unequipped, makeshift clinic nearby. Large white bandages covered Cliff Kindy's stitched head. Weldon Nisly had a cracked rib and broken sternum and thumb. Shane Claiborne's shoulder was dislocated. Their driver had cuts and a leg injury. Sang Hyun had bruises and facial cuts. Weldon and Cliff might have died had they not received immediate care.

When getting ready to leave, I thanked the doctor in charge, who vented his anger and grief about the Iraqi men, women, and children dying and being terrorized by the bombs. Then he looked at my grief-stricken face and tears and stopped. "But you are all good people," he said gently. When I and others offered to pay, he refused and told us, *"Christian, Muslim, Jew, Americans, Iraqis, whoever you are, we will take care of you."* After saying goodbye, we were all able to crowd in the remaining two cars and continue the trip to the Jordanian border and then Amman.

We dreamed of returning some day to find the medical workers and thank them. Now, eight of us were attempting to do that. *But would we get in?*

Sami told the Ambassador that seven years ago we had experienced a *unique* event, but the Ambassador answered, "No, no, no, this is the *normal* way for Iraqis to react." Then he added, "Iraq is now chaotic and broken, but before Americans came to Iraq, there were two things Iraq didn't have: terrorists and sectarian fighting." Then he authorized us to be given special three-month visas. The following morning, we were on our way to the border.

We were an interesting group. Greg Barrett, an independent journalist and writer, did the major organizing work for the trip.[2] Sami Rasuli, a U.S. and Iraqi citizen, had set up the Iraqi side of the trip and was going as guide, representative of MPT, and interpreter. He went to Rutba in July and again a couple days before our trip, to check out the security situation and prepare the way. Medical workers and public officials he talked to there thought the area was currently stable enough for us to come.

Jamie Moffett, went as a filmmaker. Four of us had been on the original trip in 2003—Cliff, Shane, Weldon, and me. Cliff, a longtime member

---

2. For his account of the 2010 trip, see Barrett, *The Gospel of Rutba*.

of CPT, spoke of how special the initial Rutba experience had been for his life. He saw this trip as peace-building between Iraq and the U.S. people. Weldon, a Mennonite pastor, told us, "It's like coming around full circle—coming back to the place where my life was saved. It was one of the most significant events of my life."

Also with us was Logan Mehl-Laituri, who had been in Iraq as a U.S. soldier for over a year. There, he came to see that as a Christian he couldn't kill, and applied for conscientious objector status. Now he wanted to return to Iraq and meet Iraqis in a non-military role, understand from the other side, and seek healing from his earlier experiences.[3]

At the border, Jordanian officials were surprised to see a group of Americans coming to cross by land and tried to discourage us. They called a U.S. military captain, on the Iraqi side, who met us with two Humvees at the crossing.

"It's highly dangerous for you to go into western Anbar Province," the captain, accompanied by a large, burly contracted soldier, told us sternly. He went on to describe particular atrocities we could experience. When they questioned us about our "security," we said we were *safer* without guards with guns and if they *didn't* accompany us. We persisted. They finally gave up and said, "We can't keep you out of Iraq. We just needed to *warn* you." We assured them, "You did your job." Later, on the Iraqi side, we asked an Iraqi policeman if it was safe for us to drive to Rutba, and he said, "Yes."

Tired, but with some excitement, we finally left the border, met the two drivers sent to meet us by Sami's contact in Rutba, and traveled on the four-lane highway through the mostly flat, open desert land. I felt grateful for the way the door opened at each step of our trip. The road was in good condition, but we saw occasional rusted vehicles along the sides. To our left, just before the turnoff to Rutba, was a U.S. military base. At least three places along the way there were blue Iraqi police trucks parked along the road, so I concluded the road was well guarded. Or were they there because two cars with Americans were driving in?

Just outside of Rutba, we were stopped for another thirty minutes at an Iraqi military checkpoint. Guards summoned an Iraqi police commander to come and question us. He called the hospital to verify our story, and finally let us pass. On the edge of town, we saw new homes, but still many damaged buildings, piles of rubble, and an Iraqi military base on our left. About 4:15 p.m., we arrived at the rebuilt Rutba hospital.

---

3. For more about his journey, see Mehl-Laituri, *Reborn on the Fourth of July*.

Part Two: Summer 2006—Fall 2011

A group of hospital administrators, security personnel, and local citizens welcomed us. As we sat in a crowded circle around a large office, Cliff spoke about the accident and how medical workers here helped him even though the hospital had been bombed. Shane told about the center for reconciliation in Durham, North Carolina, named Rutba House, and Weldon spoke about his dream of returning and thanking those who saved his life.

The officials of Rutba hosted us in a building used for staff and guard housing. There were extra guards posted around the building for the first night and day because of our presence. The mayor said it was actually safe for us in Rutba, a town of about 30,000, but they had us stay there "so people inclined to make trouble, for their advantage, can't."

The next morning, the mayor welcomed us in his office. "No other American *civilians* have come here in the last years, only Americans in Humvees," he told us. "We hope to have more international civilians come to Western Iraq. A few years ago, there was more violence here. In the past three years the U.S. military raided the clinic and hospital several times. The violence decreased in the last year and half, because the U.S. military mostly retreated to their bases. But there are elements in Iraq trying to take advantage of this, those wanting to create terrorism and instability, and exhaust American forces and the Iraqi people."

"We have seen two kinds of U.S. forces here," he continued. "Those here from 2003 to 2006 caused more destruction and killing. Since 2007, American soldiers have been less aggressive in the way they treat Iraqis. With the absence of U.S. troops in population areas, it allows for reconciliation among the sectors of civilians."

Shane showed him the button he had before the 2003 invasion, on which was written, "I have family in Iraq." He said, "Now I truly have family here." He and others on our team talked about the possibility of a sister city relationship between Rutba, Iraq, and Durham, North Carolina.

Dr. Rasul, medical director of the hospital, grew up in Baghdad, and had worked in Baghdad and ar-Ramadi. He came to Rutba in 2004 because it was safer even though, in the following years, there was Al Qaida and counterinsurgency violence here. Currently there were ten doctors, and thirty nurses, but they needed to send more complicated cases to hospitals in Ramadi, a three-hour drive away. "The government doesn't give all the money allotted for running the hospital," he said. "We need a generator so we can have constant electricity and be able to provide the services of a full hospital. Before the bombing in 2003, it was fully functioning. Then, until it was rebuilt in 2007, we operated out of the clinic. Treatment here is free, but three doctors on duty see 600 patients each day, so can't give them much time. If people want more attention, they come to our private clinics and pay a small fee."

"There's a shortage of doctors in Iraq," he continued. "Only about 20,000, because 2,000 have been killed and others have left the country since the invasion. There's a significant increase of cancers and birth defects here due to the use of DU during the 2003 bombing. Fallujah, however, has a larger increase because of additional toxic materials from the November 2004 bombing of the city."

That afternoon, we met with a prominent religious leader who told us, "In the past, religious groups in Iraq lived together peacefully. With the 2003 invasion and occupation, sectarian tensions surfaced and are perpetuated by political parties. U.S. forces bombed homes, shot people when they got too close to convoys or didn't see and stop at the checkpoints, raided homes, terrorized the families, threw men on the ground and handcuffed and kicked them in front of their children. Soldiers randomly detained youth on the streets, who had nothing to do with violence. They did it with the attitude, 'I can do whatever I want.'"

When Weldon asked about the role of nonviolence in rebuilding Iraq, the religious leader turned it around, saying, "The U.S. is the most violent country and won't let other countries get nuclear weapons, while supporting Israel with many nuclear weapons. The war on terror is directed toward Muslims, supposing that Muslims are violent savages."

I asked his opinion about how quickly U.S. forces should leave Iraq. He responded, "What would you answer if the Iraqi army occupied you? The U.S. never did protect Iraqis anyway. Sectarian forces might fight if the U.S. leaves, but the U.S. leaving will be good."

At a boy's elementary school, the principal gathered about forty boys to greet us in the schoolyard. He told us, "U.S. forces raided the school several times, storming the door to the main office, even though we offered them the key." Cliff told the boys the story of our first visit to Rutba. The principal responded, "We are joining you to strive for peace." Then Shane said, "We will continue to work for the same human rights you're working for, so no more fathers and sons are killed. This confirms that compassion is more powerful than war."

Back at the hospital, a businessman spoke to us, saying, "Saddam was powerful and cruel, but in spite of this, we were safe and generally happy. There was little crime. We could leave our homes unlocked and walk around anywhere. We didn't have a problem with drugs or strife between religious and ethnic groups. If you ask anyone which time was better, they would say, 'Under Saddam.'"

Most moving to us in Rutba were the times we spent with medical workers who had treated our injured, and an ambulance driver who carried Weldon from the car into the makeshift clinic seven years ago. When the driver walked into the room, his eyes lit up, and he excitedly walked over to Weldon and hugged him. He recalled that the staff had been really busy that day, because there were lots of injured people, and said, "The man who had brought your injured men to the clinic told us, 'I found them hurt on the road. They need help.' I was feeling sick myself with asthma, but when I saw Weldon, so tired and weak, I carried him into the clinic myself."

"We've been traumatized by the invasion," he said soberly. "We saw homes destroyed and children killed. One thing very painful for me was the time soldiers stormed into my house and pulled down and destroyed a cabinet with nice china I had bought on my travels in the army—for no other reason than to humiliate or be cruel. I kept silent, afraid of being handcuffed and tortured if I spoke."

"One day, I was driving a woman, who was in labor and needed a cesarean, to the hospital in Ramadi," he added with a pained expression. "She was bleeding and in agony. American soldiers stopped us and put me face down on the ground for three hours while they searched the ambulance, even though they heard the woman moaning and pleading for help. But they didn't care. We've only seen the violent side of the U.S. in 1991 and 2003. Your visit gives us the other side of the American people."

The next morning two men, a medical assistant and a nurse, who had helped to treat our men in 2003, walked into the room and greeted us warmly. Soon we were animatedly recalling what had happened. The nurse was the one who put a sling around Shane's shoulder and arm. Both helped to stitch Cliff's scalp. The nurse told us, "They were treated in a place with no electricity, little equipment or medicines."

We thanked them again, but the men insisted that their ability to see us as brothers and sisters and not their enemy was not an exception. As one said, "It is the nature of Iraqi people. What we did, came from what we were taught and believe. It is what Islam is *really* about. Thank God we could do the job!"

"I can hardly believe you came this far to thank us," another exclaimed. "We pray that others of your people could act out of the same humanity. This moment makes me very happy. It's my reward for all of my thirty years of medical service."

Weldon responded, "We have not forgotten and we will never forget." Shane added, "Though what happened is not an exception for Iraqi people, this story has been transformative to many in the U.S. who've heard it." Our Iraqi friends answered, "Just as you are committed to telling about what you experienced, we are also committed to sharing it."

After three amazing days in Rutba, we left, reminded of the suffering caused by the war, but also grateful for the way we were received. Once again we experienced the power of love in the midst of war to break down the barriers between those who were considered enemies.

AFTERWORD

Walking Through Fire

THE PEOPLE OF IRAQ have been walking through fire as they've dealt with the horror and the terrible costs of war on their nation. All involved in the fight have been victims of the system of war and power-seeking policies. It's been a hard journey, and likely to be a long one. Their ordeal urgently compels us to do what we can to prevent such a tragedy being thrust on any other country where our nation seeks to justify violent intervention.

The lives of the Iraqi people reveal strength and courage, and reflect a beauty of culture and spirit. Many tap into the resources of their faith as they say "no" to continuing the violence and revenge, and give themselves to finding strong, nonviolent ways of working for justice and reconciliation. It's been a privilege to walk alongside them.

My journey with them has involved some of the most difficult but also most rewarding times of my life. The Iraqi people have given and taught me so much. In the same way that walking through fire has burned, but also strengthened the Iraqi people, it has done that for me. I am not the same person who first came to Baghdad in October of 2002. I have experienced brokenness and have had my life restored. I've been seasoned and weathered in the violent storms of this devastated country.

My heart has learned to deeply love and also to deeply break as I carried the pain of the Iraqi people and faced my own. I have been finding my way through this pain, just as they have been forced to. I have struggled to accept a world that is full of undeserved suffering and loss caused by the callousness and cruelty of others. At the same time I never want to lose sight of beauty and kindness and of the redemptive power of love. I have chosen to keep on walking forward, to keep working with others around the world who have caught a vision of the power of truth and love to confront and transform evil—the power-seeking violence and greed that exploit and crush a people for an institution's, government's, or individual's gain.

My simplistic optimism has fallen by the wayside, but not my faith or my hope.

It is one thing to talk about love, but another thing to really experience its power to break down fear and the barriers of hostility. At such times I have been given the gift to know that this power is real—*so real that I have been willing to give my life for it.*

Glossary

Definitions

abaya—black robe that conservative Muslim women wear that fits on their heads and flows around them to their ankles, but not covering their faces.

dolma—Iraqi Arabic name for festive Middle Eastern food of vegetables stuffed with a rice and meat mixture. In Kurdish, "yaprakh."

gray areas—contested areas outside the KRG controlled region where the population is mostly Kurdish and is eligible for the referendum under Constitution, Article 140. Such areas include Khanaqin, Makhmour, and Sinjar.

hijab—a scarf tied or pinned under the chin, worn by Muslim women usually fully covering their hair.

juba'a—a long, lightweight coat worn by Muslim women, which goes down to their ankles.

keffiyeh—red and white, or black and white, Middle Eastern scarf worn around the neck or as a male headdress.

mukhtar—leader of a Kurdish village.

Glossary

ACRONYMS AND NAMES OF ORGANIZATIONS, GROUPS, AND AGENCIES IN IRAQ

Ba'ath Party—The Iraqi political party of the former regime of Saddam Hussein.

BIAP—Baghdad International Airport Prison, a U.S. detention center at the International Baghdad Airport.

CARE International—An international relief and development agency.

CPT—Christian Peacemaker Teams—A Chicago/Toronto-based nonprofit organization that sends violence-reduction teams into international places of conflict.

CMOC—Civilian Military Operations Center, regional coalition military offices in Iraq where Iraqis could register complaints or ask for information or help. In 2004 the name was changed to General Information Centers (GIC).

CPA—Coalition Provisional Authority, the post-invasion international civilian administration in Iraq, overseeing the governing and rebuilding of Iraq.

CSI—Civil Society Initiative, an independent Kurdish organization in Suleimanya that organizes grassroots groups to monitor human rights violations of the government and advocates for prisoner rights.

CPJ—Committee for the Protection of Journalists, an international organization based in New York.

Dar al Muhabha Orphanage—An orphanage for severely handicapped children in Baghdad, run by the Sisters of Charity of Mother Teresa.

Darstan Group for Children Media Organization—An organization in Sulaimani with a project for building relationships between local Kurds and Arab IDPs, through media programs with children.

Dinga Neue Radio Station—The first women's independent station in the KRG, started by WADI and located in Halubja.

Glossary

DU—Depleted Uranium, Uranium 238, a highly radioactive and toxic by-product of enriching uranium, with a half-life of 4.5 billion years, used by the U.S. and UK in the 1991 and 2003 wars against Iraq in bullets and bombs and to line military tanks.

GIC—General Information Center—Regional coalition military offices in Iraq where Iraqis could register complaints or ask for information or help. Formerly called CMOC.

Green Zone—The "International Zone," the heavily fortified area in central Baghdad, in what was the former grounds of Saddam Hussein's Republican Palace, that became the headquarters for the CPA and the U.S., UK, and Canadian embassies in Iraq.

Help Age International—An international organization assisting senior citizens, with a branch in the KRG controlled region.

IAC—Iraqi Assistance Center—An agency based in the "Green Zone" that acted as the CPA's liaison to Iraqis for seeking information or help.

ICRC—International Committee of the Red Cross.

IDP—Internally displaced person.

IGC—Interim Governing Council, made up of Iraqis picked by L. Paul Bremer, and governing from July 13, 2003 to June 1, 2004, when it became the Interim Government of Iraq (IGI).

IHEC—Independent High Electoral Commission—The Iraqi commission that oversees national elections.

ING—Iraqi National Guard, the new, post-invasion, Iraqi military.

IPT—Iraq Peace Team—An organization of international peace activists formed by VITW in October 2002, opposed to the war in Iraq, living in Iraq and documenting conditions before and during the invasion. CPT was a part of this group at that time.

KHRW—Kurdistan Human Rights Watch—An independent Kurdish human rights organization working for democracy building, preventing violence against women, and offering health, economic, and legal assistance to displaced persons.

Glossary

MAG—Mines Action Group, an international organization that removes landmines and unexploded ordnances, with a branch in the KRG controlled region.

MHR—(Iraqi) Ministry of Human Rights established by the CPA after the invasion.

MNF and *MNF-I*—Multinational Forces/Multinational Forces of Iraq—Coalition of international military forces that carried out the invasion of Iraq, then in May 2004 became known at MNF-I.

MOE—(Iraqi) Ministry of Environment.

MOI—(Iraqi) Ministry of Interior.

MOD—(Iraqi) Ministry of Defense.

MOJ—(Iraqi) Ministry of Justice.

MPs—Members of Parliament.

OWFI—Organization of Women's Freedom in Iraq—An Iraqi women's organization, based in Baghdad, working for full rights for women in Iraqi society and against abuse of women.

Peshmerga—Literally in Kurdish, "those who face death," former Kurdish Iraqi guerrillas who fought against the Ba'ath Regime and led a campaign for autonomy for the Iraqi Kurds in northern Iraq—currently Kurdish members of the Iraqi military, based in the KRG controlled region.

PJAK—Party of Free Life of Kurdistan, a sister organization of the PKK, started in 2004, largely based and operating in western Iran.

PKK—[Partiya Karkeren Kurdistan] Kurdistan Worker's Party, the armed Kurdish liberation movement, based in southeastern Turkey and along the Turkey-Iraqi border. It has fought for an independent Kurdish state, but also for full political freedom, the right to speak the Kurdish language and observe Kurdish cultural practices in Turkey.

Sadrists—Supporters of Muqtada as-Sadr.

Shia Muslims—One branch of Islam, with its most holy shrines located in Najaf and Karbela, Iraq. Sixty percent of Iraqis are Shia.

SOFA—Security of Forces Agreement—U.S. Agreement made with Iraq on January 1, 2009 for Iraqi forces to assume full responsibility for Iraq's security by June 30, 2010.

Sunni Muslims—The largest branch of Islam worldwide, but about 40 percent of the Muslims in Iraq.

UNAMI—United Nations Assistance Mission for Iraq.

UNHCR—United Nations High Commissioner for Refugees.

UNICEF—United Nations International Children's Emergency Fund.

VITW—Voices in the Wilderness—Chicago-based non-profit organization working since 1996 to end economics sanctions on Iraq, established IPT in October 2002, and after the invasion reincorporated as Voices for Creative Nonviolence (VFCN).

WADI—Association for Crisis Assistance and Development Cooperation—A Kurdish organization that works for the democratic reconstruction of Iraq and to combat violence against women and other marginalized groups in Iraq.

WAFDI—Women's Alliance for a Democratic Iraq, an organization working for equal rights for women in Iraq, with its international headquarters in Arlington, Virginia.

Bibliography

Abu-Nimer, Mohammed. *Nonviolence and Peace Building in Islam: Theory and Practice.* Gainesville: University Press of Florida, 2003.
Attenborough, Sir Richard, film director. *Gandhi* (Culver City, CA: Sony Picture's Columbia Tristar Motion Picture Group, 1982).
Barrett, Greg. *The Gospel of Rutba: War, Peace, and the Good Samaritan Story in Iraq.* Maryknoll, NY: Orbis, 2012.
Brown, Tricia Gates, ed. *118 Days: Christian Peacemaker Teams Held Hostage in Iraq.* Chicago: Christian Peacemaker Teams, 2008.
CPT Iraq Team Reports. "Disrupted Lives: The Effects of Cross-border Attacks by Turkey and Iran on Kurdish villages." June 2012. http://www.cpt.org/work/iraq.
———. "Iraq After Occupation—Iraqis Speak about the State of Their Country as the US Military Withdraws." August, 2010. http://www.cpt.org/files/CPT_Report_Iraq_after_Occupation.pdf.
———. "Khanaqin Election Observation 2009 Report." February 2009. http://www.cpt.org/files/Khanaqin-Election-Observation-2009-CPT-Report.pdf.
———. "Where There Is a Promise, There Is a Tragedy: Cross-border Bombings and Shelling of Villages in the Kurdish Region of Iraq by the Nations of Turkey and Iran." March 2010. http://cpt.org/cptnet/2010/04/05/iraq-update-march-2010.
CPT Iraq Team Videos. "Khalid Qadir Mohammed's Interview." CPT Video 8:24. Posted June 22, 2010. http://cptiraq.blogspot.com/2010/05/khalid-qadir-mohammed-rania.html.
———. "Persecution of Goran Supporters Continues in Iraqi Kurdistan." CPT Video 7:11. Posted April 2, 2010. http://www.youtube.com/watch?v=BpCb1ngkhpE%20%20.
———. Yuan, Chihchun. "Rania Rally." CPT Video 7:12. Posted June 24, 2010. http://www.youtube.com/watch?v=oXajYJ3tj24).
———.Yuan, Chihchun. "Voices—Life under Military Threats." CPT Video 3:23. Posted July 13, 2010. http://www.youtube.com/watch?v=Bmz6Bi6ojGw.
———."Zharawa Tent Children: Joy." CPT Video 5:07. Posted June 27, 2009. http://www.youtube.com/watch?v=IGskmxUmsXI.
Easwaran, Eknath. *Nonviolent Soldier of Islam: Badsha Khan, A Man to Match His Mountains.* Tomales, CA: Nilgiri, 1999.
Fuller, Max. "Crying Wolf: Media Disinformation and Death Squads in Occupied Iraq." Center for Research on Globalization. November 10, 2005. http://www.globalresearch.ca/crying-wolf-media-disinformation-and-death-squads-in-occupied-iraq/1230.
———. "For Iraq, 'The Salvador Option' Becomes Reality." Center for Research on Globalization. June 2, 2005. http://globalresearch.ca/articles/FUL506A.html.

Bibliography

Gish, Arthur. *Muslim, Christian, Jew: The Oneness of God and the Unity of Our Faith.* Eugene, OR: Cascade, 2012.

Gish, Peggy. *Iraq: A Journey of Hope and Peace.* Scottdale, PA: Herald, 2004.

Hirsh, Michael, and John Barry. "The Salvador Option." *Newsweek*, January 9, 2005. http://www.thedailybeast.com/newsweek/2005/01/07/the-salvador-option.html.

Fourth International Geneva Conventions. Part II, Article 18 and 20. August 12, 1949. Published by International Committee of the Red Cross. http://www.icrc.org/ihl.nsf/full/380.

Kember, Norman. *Hostage in Iraq.* London: Darton, Longman and Todd, 2007.

Khan, Maulana Wahiduddin. *The True Jihad: The Concepts of Peace, Tolerance and Non-Violence in Islam.* New Delhi: Goodword, 2002.

Klein, Naomi. "Baghdad Year Zero: Pillaging Iraq in Pursuit of a Neocon Utopia." *Harper's Magazine*, September 2004, 43–53.

———. *Shock Doctrine: The Rise of Disaster Capitalism.* New York: Holt, 2007.

Loney, Jim. *Captivity: 118 Days in Iraq and the Struggle for a World without War.* Toronto: Knopf, 2011.

Mehl-Laituri, Logan. *Reborn on the Fourth of July: The Challenge of Patriotism and Conscience.* Downers Grove, IL: InterVarsity, 2012.

Muradkhan, Falah. "The Middle East Uprising and the Specificities of the Events in Iraqi Kurdistan." April 18, 2011. http://www.ekurd.net/mismas/articles/misc2011/4/state4991.htm.

Mustafa, Nawshirwan. "About the Crisis in Iraqi Kurdistan." *Kurd Net*, May 21, 2011. http://www.ekurd.net/mismas/articles/misc2011/5/state5112.htm.

Porter, Henry. "Tom Fox, Death Squads, and the Dogs of War." Political Cortex Website, March 13, 2006. http://www.politicalcortex.com/story /2006/3/12/1947/73089.

———. "Wikileaks Documents Confirm Tom Fox Died For Our Sins." *Op Ed News*, October 23, 2010. http://www.opednews.com/articles/Wikileaks-document-confirm-by-Henry-Porter-101022-915.html.

Shirazi, Iman Muhammad. *War, Peace and Nonviolence: An Islamic Perspective.* Elmhurst, NY: Tarsile Qur'an, Inc., 2001.

Talabany, Nouri. "Iraq's Policy of Ethnic Cleansing: Onslaught to Change National Demographic Characteristics of the Kirkuk Region." London: PDF Report, 1999.

York, Steve, film director. *A Force More Powerful.* Washington DC: York Zimmerman, 2000.

www.ingramcontent.com/pod-product-compliance
Lightning Source LLC
Chambersburg PA
CBHW031807220426
43662CB00007B/554